# THE THIRTIES

ALAN JENKINS

# THE THIRTIES

STEIN AND DAY/Publishers/New York

First published in the United States of America
by Stein and Day/*Publishers* 1976

Copyright © 1976 by Alan Jenkins

This book was designed and produced by George Rainbird Ltd,
Marble Arch House, 44 Edgware Road, London W2 2EH

Picture research: Mary Anne Norbury
Design: Trevor Vincent
Index: Ellen Crampton
The text was Filmset by BAS Printers Limited, Wallop,
Hampshire
The colour plates and jacket were originated by Amilcare Pizzi
s.p.a., Italy who also printed and bound the book

Stein and Day/*Publishers*
Scarborough House, Briarcliff Manor, N.Y. 10510

**Library of Congress Cataloging in Publication Data**

Jenkins, Alan, 1914–
    The thirties.

    1.   United States—Civilization—1918–1945.   2.   United
States—Social life and customs—1918–1945.
3.   Great Britain—Civilization—20th century.   4.   Great
Britain—Social life and customs—20th century.   I.   Title.
E169.1.J45          941          75-45511
ISBN 0-8128-1829-6

*Frontispiece:*
Girl on a caterpillar roundabout at Southend.
Photo by Bert Hardy which when first reproduced
had to undergo minor alterations
before it was considered decent
*Title page:*
Design adapted from a Golders Green Hippodrome programme
of 1937

# CONTENTS

# ACKNOWLEDGEMENTS

A large number of friends on both sides of the Atlantic have contributed you-absolutely-must-mention ideas and facts to this book. Memory being a subtle liar, I have checked their and my own recollections with published sources wherever possible. I would like to thank in particular John St. John of Heinemann and John Hadfield of Rainbird for help and suggestions, my wife for her knowledge of Thirties fiction and song-lyrics and Georgie Wood for his personal memoir of Ruth Etting; also Alan Wykes, Paul Scott, Edward Ardizzone, Joan and Lee Stock, Alan Martin, Barbara Campbell Golding, Bunny North of Atherton (California) and Jack Surdam of Buffalo (N.Y.) An exhibition, "Hampstead in the Thirties" (November 1974–January 1975) at the Camden Arts Centre, helped to recreate the political tension in art and design.

I must acknowledge a considerable debt to my habit of hoarding old magazines, such as the pre-War *London Mercury*, *Nash's*, *Night & Day*, and *Picture Post*, and the different views of the world presented by the *New Yorker*, the *Tatler* and the *Queen*, the *Isis* and *Granta*.

Once again, may I warmly thank Mary Anne Norbury for her imaginative picture research, and John Foster White for his sympathetic reading of the book in typescript. I am also grateful to Trevor Vincent for his brilliant design of the book, to Raymond Mander and Joe Mitchenson for checking all my references to the theatre, and to Maureen Nakhimoss of the Radio Times Hulton Picture Library for her interest and help.

*Among books consulted were:*

The Scientific Outlook (*Bertrand Russell*), ALLEN & UNWIN, 1931
A Letter to Oxford (*Tom Harrisson*), THE HATE PRESS, 1933
Music Ho! (*Constant Lambert*), FABER, 1934
Rich Land, Poor Land (*Stuart Chase*), WHITTLESEY HOUSE, 1936
The Private Life of London Films (*C. A. Lejeune*), NASH'S MAGAZINE, 1936
Present Indicative (*Noël Coward*), HEINEMANN, 1936
Middletown in Transition (*R. S. and H. M. Lynd*), HARCOURT BRACE, 1937
The Town that was Murdered (*Ellen Wilkinson*), GOLLANCZ, 1939
My America, 1928–38 (*Louis Adamic*), HAMISH HAMILTON, 1939
The Long Week-End (*Robert Graves and Alan Hodge*), FABER, 1940
Since Yesterday (*Frederick Lewis Allen*), HAMISH HAMILTON, 1940
The Thirties (*Malcolm Muggeridge*), HAMISH HAMILTON, 1940
Ego 4 (*James Agate*), HARRAP, 1940
The Isthmus Years (*Barbara Cartland*), HUTCHINSON, 1943
The Life Of Neville Chamberlain (*Keith Feiling*), MACMILLAN, 1946
Harry Price, Ghost Hunter (*Paul Tabori*), ATHENAEUM PRESS, 1950
Famous Trials (*ed. J. H. Hodge*), PENGUIN, 1950–56
The Aspirin Age (*ed. Isabel Leighton*), THE BODLEY HEAD, 1950
Homage to Catalonia (*George Orwell*), SECKER & WARBURG, 1951
A King's Story (*Duke of Windsor*), CASSELL, 1951
World Within World (*Stephen Spender*), HAMISH HAMILTON, 1951
The Trouble With Cinderella (*Artie Shaw*), FARRAR, STRAUS & YOUNG, 1952
Hatred, Ridicule and Contempt (*Joseph Dean*), CONSTABLE, 1953
A Book of Trials (*Sir Travers Humphreys*), HEINEMANN, 1953
Nine Troubled Years (*Viscount Templewood*), COLLINS, 1954
Mr. Cricket: autobiography of W. H. Ferguson, NICHOLAS KAYE, 1957
King George VI (*J. W. Wheeler-Bennett*), MACMILLAN, 1958
The Light of Common Day (*Diana Duff Cooper*), HART-DAVIS, 1959
The Road to Wigan Pier (*George Orwell*), SECKER & WARBURG, 1959
Vanity Fair (*ed. Cleveland Amory and Frederic Bradlee*), VIKING PRESS, 1960
They Saw It Happen (*Asa Briggs*), BASIL BLACKWELL, 1960
Hons and Rebels (*Jessica Mitford*) GOLLANCZ, 1960
Courtroom, U.S.A. (*Rupert Furneaux*), PENGUIN, 1962
The Group (*Mary McCarthy*), WEIDENFELD & NICOLSON, 1963
The Age of Illusion (*Ronald Blythe*), HAMISH HAMILTON, 1963
Glyndebourne (*Spike Hughes*), METHUEN, 1965
Harold Nicolson: Diaries and Letters 1930–39, COLLINS, 1966
As I Recall (*John Boyd Orr*), MACGIBBON & KEE, 1966
Exhumations (*Christopher Isherwood*), METHUEN, 1966
Chips: the Diary of Sir Henry Channon (*ed. R. R. James*), WEIDENFELD & NICOLSON, 1967
The Life that Late He Led: a biography of Cole Porter (*George Eells*), W. H. ALLEN, 1967
The Years of the Week (*Patricia Cockburn*), MACDONALD, 1968
The New Deal: a Documentary History (*ed. W. E. Leuchtenberg*), HARPER & ROW, 1968
Editor (*Kingsley Martin*), HUTCHINSON, 1968
Leslie Baily's BBC Scrapbooks, ALLEN & UNWIN, 1968

Musical Comedy (*Raymond Mander & Joe Mitchenson*), PETER DAVIES, 1969
The Literary Life (*Robert Phelps & Peter Deane*), CHATTO & WINDUS, 1969
Drinka Pinta (*Alan Jenkins*), HEINEMANN, 1970
Fifty Classic Motion Pictures (*David Zinman*), CROWN PUBLICATIONS INC., 1970
Prime Time: the Life of Edward R. Murrow (*Alexander Kendrick*), DENT, 1970
Hard Times: an Oral History of the Great Depression (*Studs Terkel*), ALLEN LANE, PENGUIN PRESS, 1970
Cars of the 1930s (*Michael Sedgwick*), BATSFORD, 1970
Britain in the 1930s (*Noreen Branson & Margaret Heinemann*), WEIDENFELD & NICOLSON, 1971
The Decorative Thirties (*Martin Battersby*), STUDIO VISTA, 1971
The World of Art Deco (*Bevis Hillier*), STUDIO VISTA, 1971
Darryl F. Zanuck (Don't Say Yes Until I Finish Talking), (*Mel Gussow*), W. H. ALLEN, 1971
Philip (*Basil Boothroyd*), LONGMANS, 1971
The Moon's A Balloon (*David Niven*), HAMISH HAMILTON, 1971
The Penguin Book of Comics (*Alan Aldridge & George Perry*), 1971
Jazz Masters of the Thirties (*Rex Stewart*), MACMILLAN, 1972
Between the Wars (*ed. Julian Symons*), BATSFORD, 1972
A Chapter of Accidents (*Goronwy Rees*), CHATTO & WINDUS, 1972
Handbook of English Costume 1900–1950 (*Alan Mansfield & Phillis Cunnington*), FABER, 1973
Picasso & Co. (*Brassaï*), THAMES & HUDSON, 1973
The Journals of Anaïs Nin (*ed. Gunther Stuhlmann*), QUARTET BOOKS, 1973
American Art of the 20th Century (*Sam Hunter*), THAMES & HUDSON, 1973
Semi-Detached London (*Alan A. Jackson*), ALLEN & UNWIN, 1973
The Infernal Grove (*Malcolm Muggeridge*), COLLINS, 1973
Glenn Miller and His Orchestra (*R. Simon*), W. H. ALLEN, 1973
Hitler (*Joachim Fest*), WEIDENFELD & NICOLSON, 1974
The Complete Hostess (*G. Quaglino*), HAMISH HAMILTON, 1974
The Seven Ages (*Christopher Hollis*), HEINEMANN, 1974
Crusade in Spain (*Jason Gurney*), FABER, 1974
Edward VIII (*Frances Donaldson*), WEIDENFELD & NICOLSON, 1974
O'Hara (*Finis Farr*), W. H. ALLEN, 1974

The lines on page 86 are taken from W. H. Auden's *Collected Shorter Poems* (Faber & Faber 1950); those on page 88 from Cecil Day Lewis's *Overtures to Death* (Cape 1938); those on page 93 from Robinson Jeffer's *Sinverguenza* and *Be Angry at the Sun* (Random House Inc.); and those on page 92) are from Stephen Vincent Benét's *Burning City* (Holt, Rinehart, and Winston, Inc. 1933). The lines from 'You're the Top', by Cole Porter, at the beginning of Chapter III, are reproduced by permission of Chappell & Co. Ltd. In Chapter VII, the lines from 'Falling in Love with Love' (lyric by Lorenz Hart) are reproduced by permission of Chappell & Co. Ltd., and the lines from 'Would You Like to Take a Walk?' (H. Warren, M. Dixon, B. Rose) are reproduced by permission of Francis Day & Hunter Ltd. The lines from 'Amy', by Horatio Nicholls in Chapter IX, are quoted by kind permission of Lawrence Wright (C) 1930.

FALLING IN LOVE AGAIN
V. Leach.
VALSE SONG
MUSIC BY
FRIEDRICH HOLLÄNDER
LYRICS BY
REG CONNELLY
&
SAM WINSTON
EMIL JANNINGS
WARDOUR
with
MARLENE DIETRICH
The BLUE ANGEL
1/-
COPYRIGHT
CAMPBELL, CONNELLY AND CO. LTD.
Music Publishers
10-11, DENMARK STREET, LONDON, W.C.2.

# BITTER-SWEET

August, 1930. I am fifteen. I am sitting, alone at a table, drinking tea and eating chocolate éclairs at Appenrodts', on the corner of Haymarket and Piccadilly Circus. A violin and piano play 'Lover, Come Back to Me' from *The New Moon*. Although it is the holidays, I am wearing my school blazer and grey flannel trousers, to save my mother buying any new clothes before the autumn term.

I have done a fearful thing. For the second time in my life, because I wanted something really badly, I have drawn out all my Post Office savings and brought them to London with the intention of going to a theatre, a cinema, or a concert, *every day* for a fortnight. This is the result of a plot between my parents and my grandparents, with whom I am staying at Clapham Common, to let the boy have his head for once; it also enables my parents to have a holiday on their own, the first for many years.

I had better explain about Appenrodts'— a curious and expensive choice for a boy who is just about to enter the Sixth form. This Edwardian venue, its cream-and-gilt wedding-cake décor crumbling and soon to be destroyed, once had a reputation. I have overheard my mother say (thinking of twenty years ago) that "undesirable women" frequent it. Ever since, the name of Appenrodts' has had for me the same wicked romance as that of Marlene Dietrich, whom I have just seen in *The Blue Angel* at the Regal, Marble Arch, climbing a spiral staircase and dropping her frilly knickers on the besotted head of Emil Jannings—probably the most traumatic experience of my adolescence.

The only other people in the café are two middle-aged ladies at a corner table, with parcels of shopping and turban-like hats. They are not exactly desirable; yet you couldn't call them undesirable. It slowly dawns on me that perhaps the undesirable women don't come here until later in the evening. I dare not

'Turban-like hats', detail from a
Marshall and Snelgrove advertisement of 1933

ask the waiter. As I leave, I hear one of the turbaned ladies say to the other: "Are you sure Winchester is *right* for Nigel?"

Outside, in Piccadilly Circus, there is still one hansom-cab, beloved of American tourists and roystering young men on Boat Race night. Some of the swirling buses still have open top decks. The London Pavilion, where I have just seen *Cochran's 1930 Revue* (upper circle: 3s. 6d.), has a sign proclaiming it "The Centre of the World": it will soon be a cinema. There are shoeblacks on the corners of Lower Regent Street and Shaftesbury Avenue. As the afternoon fades, and the Sandeman's Port electric sign lights up, flower girls gather round the statue of Eros, offering "lovely violets" to couples in full evening dress on their way to dinner and theatre. Underneath the Circus is the new circular Underground station, triumph of civil engineering, minor wonder of the world, equipped with Automaticket machines, and a chart called "See How They Run" recording every train that passes through. We have nothing like it in Birmingham. Some days I buy an all-day ticket and go to remote places like Dagenham and Hounslow.

(*above*) A shoeblack
(*right*) Sir Henry Segrave in his motor boat Miss England
(*below*) First night audience at the Phoenix Theatre, 1931

I am not well up in current affairs. Something called the London Naval Treaty has happened. Mr. Hatry has gone to prison for almost wrecking the Stock Exchange, whatever that is. Some people called Kulaks have been destroyed in Russia, and some other people called Nazis have just been elected to the Reichstag, which I know is the German Parliament.

Sir Henry Segrave has been killed in his speedboat at 100 m.p.h. on Lake Windermere. I know that a new planet called Pluto has recently been discovered, and that the Chrysler Building, just completed in New York, is 1,046 feet high.

These things are not yet important to me. What *is* important is a tune called 'With A Song In My Heart', sung plummily by a baritone named Eric Marshall in Mr. Cochran's Revue ("a very frank show"—*Punch*) and a tiny American girl called Ada-May in the same show who sang 'What Became of the Rest of Mary?' by Beverley Nichols, who has, with doubtful taste, made Mary's Little Lamb *eat* Mary, so that the last line of the refrain, having indicated, by nods and winks, certain unnameable portions of her anatomy, asks: "What became of the—er—*bits?*" Mr. Nichols has also had the bright idea of showing a film called *The Shaming of the True* in which comedienne Maisie Gay and other members of the cast walk up from the audience and, apparently, *into* the film. Miss Gay, in a sidesplitting sketch without dialogue called 'The Latecomer', gets her festoons of beads round the necks of a stage audience, throttling them as she tramples across them to reach her seat. There is a ballet, of all things, by Boris Kochno, with Lifar and Nikitina, and the show ends like a music-hall with an unforgettable drummer, Jack Powell, in "Jazz in the Kitchen", beating out intricate rhythms on saucepans and kettles and even on the bald pate of the double-bass player in the pit orchestra.

I have seen, too, Marie Tempest and Henry Ainley at the Haymarket Theatre in a sophisticated comedy, *The First Mrs. Fraser*: it must be sophisticated, because it is about divorce, a seldom-mentioned word in my youth. And Miss Tempest came within a hair's breadth of the censor when she uttered a line referring to a certain nightclub where "the women are half men, and the men are half—nothing!" And—supreme experience—at His Majesty's Theatre, on the opposite side of Haymarket, I have at last seen *Bitter-Sweet*, whose tunes I have been playing on the piano for months. I also am trying to write songs, and I realize that they are all imitation Noël Coward. In my private fantasy, I *am* Noël Coward: brilliant, witty, adored by women. I do not yet know that he is homosexual: when I find out, the shock lasts for two days.

The Chrysler Building

(left) Marie Tempest and Henry Ainley in *The First Mrs. Fraser*

(right) The first scene of *Bitter-Sweet* which opened in 1929

(below) Adrianne Allen, Noël Coward, Gertrude Lawrence and Laurence Olivier in *Private Lives*

(opposite below) Scene from the Busby Berkeley film musical *Golddiggers of 1933*

*Bitter-Sweet* feeds an appetite for Central European nostalgia which has been stirred in me by a student exchange with an Austrian boy. There is a number in it called 'Ladies of the Town': no doubt these are the "undesirable women" my mother meant: they have frivolous names like Mitzi and Fritzi. We are going to have a lot of Mitzis and Fritzis on the stage during the next few years, as Austro-Hungarian spectacular shows invade the West End, preceding and then accompanying the refugees from Hitler.

"... China?—Very big.—And Japan?—Very small." The love scene, Act I, *Private Lives* (to which I shall be taken for my sixteenth birthday treat), setting the tone of all love-dialogue, on stage and in middle-class life, for the decade, had been conceived by Noël Coward in Tokyo. He cannot know, any more than 99 per cent of the newspaper-reading public, that next year very small Japan will invade very big China and then leave the League of Nations. Could war come again? ... Shut the idea out of your mind: we shall have other things to worry about, the pound, the Loch Ness Monster, India, the state of British cricket, hunger-marchers, that trouble-maker Churchill who wants to re-arm. . . .

I know so few things. I know there are—one million?—two million?—unemployed, grey-faced men who hang about railway termini wanting to carry your bag and do the porter out of his tip; but I do not yet feel that there is anything I can do about them. The unemployed live mostly in the north, and in districts of Birmingham like Aston, where my school runs a "club for indigent boys": we refer to them jocularly as "the indignant boys".

I know that someday I will fall in love, and it will all happen against a background of Ambrose's Mayfair Hotel Band and dancing and champagne (which I have tasted only once, at a wedding). I know that if I want to go to a university I must win a scholarship: I cannot foresee that in three years' time I shall be helping to pass an Oxford Union motion "that this house will not fight for King and Country", or that seven years after that I shall be in the Army.

From Hollywood comes one of the great Thirties words, *glamour*; another is *sophistication*: both acquire new mass-culture meanings. Dreams, bread and circuses, masses of girls in Busby Berkeley musicals, a world of sheer fantasy in which all classes drown their insecurity. The highlife symbols of champagne (or sparkling Moussec if you can't afford it), top-hat, white tie and tails; the ability to lose yourself in that which you can never possess; people who have never eaten a restaurant or hotel meal can yet sing a song called 'Dinner At Eight' ("two gardenias by your plate"); and around 1935 I hear a phrase, "dancing on the edge of a volcano", and begin to understand that all our fun is a retreat from fear. Then, in a kind of sound-montage, Ellington's reed section, topped by Johnny Hodges' sugary soprano saxophone in 'Sophisticated Lady', merges into an air-raid siren, and Tauber's magnificent tenor and Rudy Vallee's croon slowly become the shriek of Hitler.

Billie Burke and Marie Dressler in the film *Dinner at Eight*

# HAPPY DAYS ARE HERE AGAIN

Rudy Vallee

"Life is just a bowl of cherries—don't make it serious," crooned Rudy Vallee in George White's *Scandals* of 1931. He was crooning it to a land where for many people life was a bowl of dust; where unemployment was heading towards thirteen million; where thousands of American families faced eviction for non-payment of rent; where no plume of smoke was to be seen coming out of factory chimney stacks; where reasonably well-dressed fnen went to the back doors of restaurants to salvage bits of food from garbage bins; where shop fronts, boarded up, could not find tenants; where almost everybody learnt the trick of lining their shoes with strips of cardboard to make them last longer; where meat, if you could afford it at all, was bought only once a week. New skyscrapers stood empty. Trains ran with half the usual number of passengers or freight cars, and hoboes sneaking free rides. The new car market collapsed; the used car market boomed. Wives of unemployed husbands took jobs as stenographers. To be a graduate meant to be without a job. In speakeasies men swapped hints on how to avoid income tax. If you had servants, you either fired them or persuaded them to stay on without pay, because if they didn't they would simply have to stand in breadlines or queue at soup kitchens.

This was Depression; the slump, deeper than anyone could have imagined, after the Twenties bull-market and the 1929 crash; the first middle-class poverty that America had ever known; the worst years America ever went through, not excluding two world wars.

Nobody knew what to do about it, because for several years nobody succeeded in diagnosing it. A public opinion poll on America's problems in 1930 put "administration of justice" first and Prohibition second; "collapse of public morals" followed as about the seventh priority, and "unemployment" was eighteenth. Legs Diamond and Dutch Schultz were

then more frightening than breadlines. President
Hoover still believed in self-help: to have unemployment relief on the lines of the British "dole" would be
"soul-destroying." The experts were no help: "I'm
afraid," said Charles M. Schwab, boss of Bethlehem
Steel, who had been one of the 'buy now!' optimists
of the bull-market. "Every man is afraid." Henry
Ford, by now gaga, said: "These really are good
times. There is plenty of work to do if people would do
it." President Hoover, baffled after his prophecies of
great leaps forward, said: "The march of prosperity
has been retarded." And in Britain Montagu Norman, Governor of the Bank of England, said: "I
approach this whole subject not only in ignorance but
in humility. It is too great for me."

The business magazine *Fortune* in 1932 found it
possible to print an article entitled "No One Has
Starved". Maybe they hadn't—yet. Nevertheless in
New York about a million of the city's 3,200,000
working population were out of work. It was better to
be on relief, when families whose earnings had
averaged 35 dollars a week were bringing in just over
8 dollars. Relief would at least bring in 40 or 50
dollars a month, which would keep you in groceries.
But you couldn't be on relief if you were just out of
college and had never worked. Like Henry Fonda
and James Stewart, who sang songs for dimes on the
sidewalk.

In Philadelphia it was reckoned that 27 per cent of
schoolchildren were undernourished. Chicago
teachers in May 1932 had been paid only five months'
salary in the past year. Thousands of them had lost an
average of 740 dollars each in bank failures, and
nearly as many had lost an average of 3,292 dollars in
lapsed assurance policies; 805 had borrowed from
loan sharks at rates of up to 42 per cent a year, and
759 had lost their homes because the city had defaulted
on wages and so none of these people could pay their
taxes. In St. Louis, it was reported, "large numbers of
the destitute have been living on refuse dumps along
the river where they build shacks and dig in the dump
for food."

Every big American city had its "Hooverville"
where unemployed men (without women) lived like
this. Charles R. Walker, writing in *Forum*, reported
that at Ambridge, Pennsylvania, he met a Slav who
had emigrated to the States in 1902: "If you had told
me, when I come to this country, that I now live here
like this, I shot you dead."

16

(*above*) President Hoover
(*opposite*) New Yorkers waiting for coal
(*below*) Placard carriers in the Bronx, 1932
(*bottom*) Children in the Bonus Marcher's camp, 1932

Men who were out of work, bankrupt, semi-starving, yet somehow drove around in ancient Buicks and Pontiacs looking for jobs. "We're the first nation," Will Rogers said, "ever to go to the poorhouse in an automobile."

Louis Adamic, the writer, kept a Depression diary. November 13, 1930: "I watched a bread-line on 3rd Avenue near 36th Street, conducted by some kind of gospel mission. In the line I saw a man wearing a topcoat that must have cost $70 or $80 when it was new." April, 1933: "The other night Stella's mother was afraid to open the door when a Western Union boy rang the bell about one o'clock. She thought revolution had broken out and there was a mob outside. . . . Last fall and winter numerous people everywhere had stocked up with food supplies to last them a year."

By the end of 1931 there were said to be 82 breadlines in New York alone. In Times Square and Columbus Circle they were run, from 8 till 12, by Hearst newspapers, paid for largely by readers, using Army trucks plastered with advertisements for the papers to distribute ham and cheese sandwiches. Well-dressed crooks collected breadline money and used it for their own families. More gentlemanly was the robber who held up the Sun Oil gas-station at 845, Copley Road, Akron, Ohio, stole $33, and said to the attendant: "I'm sorry to do this, but I have a wife and three children to support. I hope you're covered with insurance."

Unemployed miners exercised their "picking rights", helping themselves to coal and illegally selling it. They were defended by priests who said: "Coal bootlegging has no bad moral effect on honest working people. It keeps them from starving and turning into criminals."

Family life in the Depression is well-documented. Sometimes a family was driven into closer unity by adversity, usually held together by Mom. Other families were split, while being forced to occupy the same apartment. Divorce was more expensive than separation. Workless fathers felt themselves despised, and in the sweltering summer beat up nagging wives and crying children. There was a medical phenomenon known as "depression impotence". Children tended to ask teachers or policemen what they should do about new shoes: they were scared to ask their parents. Wedding rings were pawned to pay the rent.

Banks are not supposed to crash, but in September 1931 no less than 305 banks did crash, followed by 522 more in the next month. In February 1933 began the real "Bank Crisis": state after state closed its banks to prevent runs by panic-stricken depositors. On March 5 every bank in the country, by special proclamation, closed for four days. While they were shut, people lived on cheques and credit, and hoarded canned food. Another diarist of these times was Ruth McKenney, better known as the author of *My Sister Eileen*, then living in Akron, Ohio. "Sunday, February 26, 1933: Bank officials didn't show up at church services and weren't home at 1 o'clock to eat the usual big Sunday dinner with their families." On Monday morning Akron banks were operating "on a limited withdrawal basis", and tellers were desperately maintaining that "everything's all right—new accounts are growing."

The great cheer-up song of the Thirties was 'Happy Days Are Here Again' (we knew it in Britain on a top-selling record by the coloured duo, Layton and Johnstone). It had been copyrighted as long ago as November, 1929. Now it had a new lease of life as Franklin Delano Roosevelt's campaign song. It didn't quite have the emotional appeal of 'Singin' in the Rain', but with a drink or two inside you, you could shout it. Some time in 1930, after Roosevelt's re-election as Governor of New York State, his State Democratic chairman, James A. Farley, told the press: "I do not see how Mr. Roosevelt can escape being the next presidential nominee of his party." He had run for Vice-President as long ago as 1920, the year before polio struck at his leg-muscles and lower stomach. No press photographer ever showed him on crutches or in a wheel chair. He was the first President for years who *smiled* ("that Christian Science smile," sneered H. L. Mencken: "too eager to please," frowned Walter Lippmann).

"He exuded confidence," Roy Jenkins said in one of his Chichele Lectures at Oxford. "He knew every trick of communicating it to the public." Thus his drive to a Chicago meeting from the airport was as important as whatever he said at the meeting. "As he rode," a Chicago reporter wrote, "he grinned and waved his hands and tossed his great leonine head with laughter that was returned by the people on the sidewalks." Walter Lippmann said that he had "neither a firm grip on public affairs, nor very strong convictions." Oliver Wendell Holmes said: "A second-class intellect, but a first-class temperament."

Mrs. Franklin D. Roosevelt, 1936

However, the "second-class intellect" knew how to use other men's brains. He had revealed very little of what he intended to do as President; indeed his wife Eleanor had said far more, and of a very idealistic nature.

Roosevelt was already gathering round him a circle of advisers—the *New York Times* called them the Brains Trust—among them Sam Rosenman, who wrote many of his speeches; Doc O'Connor, his law partner; Raymond Moley; Rexford Tugwell; and Adolph Berle. All university professors; all from Columbia. Not the kind of men Hoover or Coolidge would have chosen to help them map out a national programme: not bankers, but theorists. To them were added, later, William C. Bullitt, Roosevelt's "scout in Europe", and James Warburg, who "mixes finance with the composition of revue lyrics set to music by his wife."

We now know, from Joseph Lash's *Eleanor and Franklin*, that Eleanor never really wanted her husband to be President, feared the idea of being First Lady in the White House. She had been horrified by the breadlines of the Depression, the use of "troops and tear gas to rout the jobless army veterans from their squatters' shacks in Washington." She used phrases like "reorganizing our economic structure"; she "ladled out soup on the breadlines, gave lifts to tramps, and sent hungry men to her house with instructions that they should be fed."

Franklin, too, had radical ideas; but the first task was to get elected. So Doc O'Connor said that the Democrats' first priority was to "get the pants off Eleanor and on to Franklin." Nevertheless Eleanor became the first First Lady who really entered into partnership with her husband when he became President. Wearing her famous velvet dress and coat of "Eleanor blue", she held press conferences, at which she served "7-cent luncheons" as an example of wholesome economy. She answered three hundred thousand letters in her first year; wrote a monthly syndicated "woman-to-woman" article for the North American Newspaper Alliance, and a regular column, "I Want You to Write Me", for *Woman's Home Companion.*

Less than a month before his inauguration, on Saturday, March 4, 1933, an assassin named Zangara shot at Roosevelt in Miami, missed him, and fatally wounded Mayor Cermak of Chicago instead. Five days before his inauguration, the "banking panic" had still further frightened the nation, which had the worst Treasury deficit ever recorded. So people were more than ready to listen to speeches containing Churchillian phrases such as "the only thing we have to fear is fear itself", and "private economic power is . . . a public trust." In election speeches he had criticized Hoover for "extravagance" and promised a balanced budget, drastic economies—and the repeal of Prohibition. People didn't quite know what he meant by "sound money" and "reflation" (a new word then). Now, in power, he said: "The money-changers have fled from the temple" (no more Wall Street?); "discipline and direction under leadership"; and, over and over again, the word "action". If necessary, he would ask Congress for powers "as great as the power that would be given to me if we were in fact invaded by a foreign foe."

It seems to have been Stuart Chase, author of a book called *A New Deal*, who supplied the package name for what followed. It was written into Roosevelt's 1932 nomination speech by Raymond Moley. ("New *Day*" had been the title of Hoover's programme). You could regard it as the "saviour of capitalism", the "beginning of socialism," or "a virtual dictatorship," or possibly all three. With

President Roosevelt about to deliver
one of his "fireside chats"

astonishing rapidity the centre of the United States moved from Wall Street to Washington, D.C. "We turned to an untried man, just as did the people when they turned to Abraham Lincoln in 1861," writes one historian. That untried man, within a few days of his inauguration, formed the unprecedented habit of *talking* to the nation several times a week on the radio in what he called "fireside chats".

He began with unemployment, went on to labour relations, agriculture and—a new phrase—Social Security. He achieved tremendous things, but it was a rough ride, and there were still ten million unemployed in the second year of his second term, the year of the Fair Labor Standards Act which aimed at "a floor under wages and a ceiling above prices." As Roosevelt himself admitted, it was not "Dr. New Deal" but "Dr. Win-the-War" who eventually cured unemployment. The Tennessee Valley Authority, the federal refinancing of farm and home mortgages, the reform of business, the National Industrial Recovery Act, were experiments watched by the whole world, especially by the Left, who saw in all this national planning something of the Russian Five-Year Plan.

The National Recovery Act (which Roosevelt called "the most important and far-reaching legislation ever enacted by the American Congress", but which was eventually declared unconstitutional)

contained a Section 7a which said: "employees shall have the right to organize and bargain collectively through representatives of their own choosing." Unfortunately it didn't say *how*, and employers, frightened, started their own management-dominated "company unions". The 1935 Wagner Act brought order a little nearer by defining "unfair practices".

A Civilian Conservation Corps found work for two million in reafforestation schemes. The Civil Works Administration provided four million jobs on public works projects; its critics said of it that some of the jobs it provided, by relief money, were useless, such as teaching tap dancing, Latin by correspondence course, and in one notorious case an activity, never defined, known as "boon doggling", which thereupon became a national joke. The Tennessee Valley Authority was set up to build dams and power-plants which would increase the wealth of a region that included pieces of seven states; the Works Progress Administration to coordinate many of these and other projects; there were even Federal arts projects. A Senate Committee on Banking and Currency investigated "public irresponsibility and private greed" in big business. A National Youth Administration provided "work scholarships" and aid. The 1935 Social Security Act, providing old age pensions, unemployment insurance and help for the disabled, was designed, Roosevelt said, to prevent "the recurrence of severe depressions in the future."

By 1934 there were already superficial signs of recovery—within reach of the employed only. To restore confidence, swashbuckling General Hugh Johnson, administrator of the National Industrial Recovery Act, urged people to stop saving against a rainy day and *buy*. People noted hopefully that the Boston Red Sox had attracted 145,000 more customers; that betting on horse-races had been legalized in New York; that "cocktail bars are blossoming in fantastic forms" since the repeal of Prohibition; "head waiters have stopped scowling"; "a lot of people are no longer hiding and hoarding"—they were buying new automobiles, new clothes.

Not in Oklahoma they weren't. The world suddenly learnt a new phrase: Dust Bowl. A Miss Caroline Henderson wrote an article in the June 1935 issue of *Atlantic Monthly* describing the failure of erosion control, and deaths from "dust pneumonia." "Our soil is excellent—we need only a little rain. . . .

An abandoned farm after the great dust bowl storm, Oklahoma, May 1937

The disastrous effect the Ohio River had on the city of Cincinnati, Ohio, in January, 1937

*(above)* 'The "Sharpville" of the 1930s'—police and strikers at Republic Steel, Chicago, 1937
*(opposite above left)* John L. Lewis, by Edmond X. Kapp

Wearing our shade hats, with handkerchiefs tied over our faces and vaseline in our nostrils, we have been trying to rescue our home from windblown dust.'' In South Dakota the first great dust bowl storm had broken on Armistice Day, 1933. On the 470-acre Karnstrum farm in Beadle County, the family "soaked sheets and towels and stuffed them around window ledges.'' Roofs of sheds "stuck out through drifts deeper than a man is tall.'' Roads just disappeared. "One coughed up black,'' said Mr. Karnstrum.

'Home on the Range'—"where seldom is heard a discouraging word,'' sang Bing Crosby. In the Great Plains, over-grazed then planted with wheat that wouldn't grow in the parched summers of 1934 and 1935, with a heat of 108°F., people "packed everything into old cars and drove West.'' We shall meet them again in Steinbeck's *The Grapes of Wrath*.

In Pittsburgh, how different: the city under 10 to 20 feet of water, and without light, electricity or transport. That was in 1936, when "the Merrimac, Connecticut, Hudson, Delaware, Susquehanna, Potomac, Allegheny and Ohio all went wild.'' Floods and erosion: at least they showed what the TVA was trying to prevent. In January 1937 the Ohio River had the worst flood in American history: 900 people died, and 500,000 families were homeless. There was martial law in Cincinnati as dead horses, cattle and people floated through the streets.

"I see one-third of a nation ill-housed, ill-clad, ill-nourished,'' said Roosevelt in his 1937 inaugural address. He was speaking in the middle of the General Motors sit-down strike against low wages, irregular employment, the speed of the assembly line and the

recording everything. Howard Fast tells us that both the Chicago *Tribune* and Paramount News suppressed the story. This was the "Memorial Day Massacre" which *New Masses* called a "publicity pogrom."

The New Deal had plenty of critics. Adolph Berle, one of the Brains Trust, saw it as a conscious working-out of which political system to adopt: "in a world in which revolutions just now are coming easily, the New Deal chose the most difficult course of moderation and rebuilding." The Marxists, of course, thought that the whole thing was impossible within a capitalist framework. Ben Stolberg and Warren Jay Vinton, in *The Economic Consequences of the New Deal* (1935), said the New Deal had no policy, it had "reestablished scarcity" and "put all the survivors to work for the greater glory of Big Business. . . . there is nothing the New Deal has so far done that could not have been done better by an earthquake." Lincoln Steffens, who had been to Russia (but not recently) said: "Communism can solve our problem. That's any muckraker's proclamation."

William Randolph Hearst thought it "absolute state socialism." Henry Ford refused to cooperate. "Dr. Roosevelt is a Quack" was H. L. Mencken's headline in the *American Mercury*; and the people around him were "the sorriest mob of mountebanks . . . professional do-gooders . . . vapid young pedagogues." To ex-President Hoover the New Deal was "an attack upon free institutions", "coercion and compulsory organization of men", the sort of thing martyrs in Nazi concentration camps were dying for having opposed.

And Frank Sullivan, "the cliché expert", amused himself and *New Yorker* readers by collecting examples of how to hate Roosevelt. FDR was an idealist, a Communist, a Fascist, "trying to start a dynasty with James Roosevelt as Clown Prince"; taxpayers were paying for his fishing trips. You must hiss his name or picture. You must refer to him as "that madman in the White House", "that fellow down in Washington", or (to someone you really disliked) "Your *friend* Franklin D." "Half these people on relief are really foreigners, anyhow—taking the bread out of our own people's mouths." Roosevelt was "destroying the American way of life" with "an orgy of spending". And a riddle: "Why has Snow White only six dwarfs now?—Because Dopey's in the White House."

dismissal of Union men. It was technically illegal, and the police were called in: they used buckshot and tear-gas. The strikers fought back with pipes, bits of metal, pop bottles. The strike went on for forty-four days, immobilizing sixty factories in fourteen states. It ended with the partial recognition of the United Automobile Workers, whose membership increased from 30,000 to 400,000 in a single year. Their spokesman was John L. Lewis, first president of the Congress of Industrial Organizations. He emerged a hero, and there was talk of his running for the White House.

The "Sharpeville" of the 1930's was the strike at Republic Steel in Chicago, 1937, when police charged peaceful pickets, shouting "You Red bastards, you got no rights," killing seven and wounding a hundred, with newsreels and press photographers

# GLAMOUR

*You're Mussolini,*
*You're Mrs. Sweeny,*
*You're Camembert.*

(COLE PORTER, in *Anything Goes*)

Mrs. Sweeny, born Ethel Margaret Whigham at Newton Mearns, Renfrewshire, was then (1935) married to Charles Sweeny the golfer. She is now the Duchess of Argyll. She was "Deb of the Year" in 1930, and, despite considerable competition from Lady Bridget Poulett, she overnight succeeded Lady Diana Duff Cooper as contender for the title of Britain's most beautiful woman of the century. She

Margaret Whigham, now the Duchess of Argyll, wearing a Norman Hartnell dress at the Beau Geste Party held at Claridges Hotel in December 1938

was briefly engaged to the Earl of Warwick, who was briefly a film actor; but the Earl eventually married another debutante, Rose Bingham. Other "debs of the year" were Patricia Weigall (1933) and Primrose Salt (1934).

You did not necessarily have to be beautiful to be a "rave" deb. Lisa Maugham, described by contemporary gossip-writers as "the Perfect Debutante", was said by Barbara Cartland to be "well produced"—"as artistically designed as the famous white rooms her mother, Syrie Maugham, had made the apex of fashion." The essential thing was to capture the imagination of press photographers, who would then conspire and compete to give you the full treatment.

Margaret Whigham was (a new word in the 1930s) "photogenic". Her face was symmetrical, her features strongly marked, her skin perfect. She had spent much of her girlhood in America, and this seemed to have given her an extra measure of poise and unaffected vitality. She was not only beautiful—she was fun. At her wedding to Charles Sweeny at Brompton Oratory she was mobbed like a film-star, and her eventful life was followed by a sort of fan-club who were fed by the gossip-writers. She had revived the deb-ballyhoo industry, which reached a climax in Jubilee Year, 1935, when some debs (or their mothers) employed press-agents. After two seasons a deb was said to be out of date, and even referred to as a "bag". The result of all this artificial pressure, which could mean, in the season, five dances a week or more, was early marriage (to Mr. Right, if not the Duke of Right) and often quick divorce. Mothers invited other mothers to luncheon to compare lists of eligible young men (who were graded by a special code—e.g. NST meant "not safe in taxis"), and professional titled bringers-out, who would arrange publicity and presentation, were in great demand.

Primrose Salt, 1934, by Paul Tanqueray

Baba Beaton, Wanda Baillie-Hamilton and Lady Bridget Poullet,
by Cecil Beaton

Margaret Whigham had "glamour"—a Thirties word of great importance. Not all of the girls whose chauffeur-driven cars lined the Mall before a Presentation, encouraged by "Good luck, ducks!" from women on the sidewalks, had it. Too often, one deb's Mum, fumbling for a kind word to say about another Mum's deb daughter, fell back on something like: "She looks so—so sweet—so *fresh*." There they all were, their curtsies rehearsed at Madame Vacani's, their feathers ruffled by the wind, hoping they would not (who was it who *did*?) vomit with fear in front of Their Majesties. Afterwards they would be taken to dinner at the Savoy (Restaurant, not Grill) where it was very bad form to be seen still wearing your feathers. Among more mature beauties were Edwina Mountbatten, the Hon. Mrs. Richard Norton, Viscountess Weymouth and Mrs. Wallis Simpson, dressed mainly by Schiaparelli.

"Glamour" was what women, helped by men, surrounded themselves with as skirts grew longer, governments lost control of nation's destinies, and uncomprehended waves of fear lapped at the shores of countries that believed themselves to be democracies. In Britain, Merle Oberon had it; so had blonde Ann Todd (these two were among my adolescent images of the Ideal Woman).

Glamour was perhaps the only thing they had in common, these girls of the Thirties—the London debs and the Hollywood goddesses—Norma Shearer, Joan Crawford, the new, emaciated Marlene Dietrich (only Ernest Hemingway was allowed to address her as Kraut), Ruth Chatterton, Carole Lombard, Joan Bennett, and—Garbo. Another new pop-epithet was "sophisticated", which meant that they were immaculately groomed and knew that champagne had bubbles in it. They, or their public personalities, were now often "ladies" instead of just (as in the Twenties) girls. Myrna Loy, once a "vamp" and a "bad" girl, now spoke epigrams trippingly on the tongue. Almost alone, Jean Harlow refused to be a lady.

Among the new faces was a bleached blonde on a Chesterfield cigarette poster in 1933, known to her employer Hattie Carnegie as Diane Belmont, supposedly from Butte, Montana. Her real name was, and is, Lucille Ball. Born in Jamestown, N.Y., she was

*(above left)* The Hon. Mrs. Richard Norton
*(left)* Merle Oberon

*(above left)* Norma Shearer
*(above right)* Marlene Dietrich
*(far left)* Carole Lombard
*(left)* Jean Harlow

27

soon to appear as an apparently nude slave girl in Eddie Cantor's *Roman Scandals*, the decencies being protected by knee-length blonde hair. From Hungary came Hedy Lamarr, heroine of the notorious *Extase* (1933), shown only in small cinemas such as Studio One in Oxford Street because Hedy both walked and swam nude in the film which her husband tried unsuccessfully to buy and destroy.

Marlene, for all her slender beauty, whether déshabillée or in male evening dress, under Sternberg's direction made a luminous magic with her lips and hollow cheeks and misty eyes. But how to explain Garbo, the "big dumb Swede" as some of the men who played opposite her called her? "A gaze so deep that every spectator there found what he sought," said one critic. "Garbo's visage," wrote Simone de Beauvoir, "has a kind of emptiness into which anything could be projected." Her most famous shot was in *Queen Christina*, the last figurehead image, which director Mamoulian achieved by asking her to think of—*nothing*. She is not looking at us—she is looking into a mirror. Yet, before the end of the decade, she will make *Ninotchka*, will laugh and make *us* laugh, and we shall see something of the Garbo that Cecil Beaton saw: Garbo saying "You're so beautiful" to *him*; Garbo clowning, and looking like a clown; Garbo doing an imitation of Douglas Fairbanks swinging from a cross-beam; Garbo swimming naked in David Niven's pool.

Foreign faces were fashionable. From France, Simone Simon and Danielle Darrieux. From Germany, the elfin Elizabeth Bergner, the first international film star to turn a cartwheel. From Austria, Marthe Eggerth. So, once again, were bosoms, and it was in these years that we had the first glimpses of Lana Turner. Julia Jean Mildred Frances Turner was spotted in 1936, when she was sixteen, by a talent scout while sipping strawberry-flavoured malted milk. It was noted that she wore no visible means of support underneath her jersey, and so she was publicized as the Sweater Girl.

*(left)* Greta Garbo
*(opposite below)* Hedy Lamarr in *Extase*
*(opposite above)* Ruth Etting and Eddie Cantor in *Roman Scandals*

*(top left)* Simone Simon
*(top right)* Clark Gable and Vivien Leigh
in *Gone with the Wind*
*(above)* Martha Eggerth
*(right)* Princess Pearl

Of "ladylike" beauties, Britain's Vivien Leigh, whose face was given to the world in *Gone With The Wind*, had no near competitor. There were several "sister acts": the Paget Twins; and the three daughters of Sir Charles (Rajah) Brooke of Sarawak, known to the press as Princess Gold, Princess Pearl and Princess Dawn. Gold became Lady Inchcape, Pearl married the bandleader Harry Roy (inspiring a song, 'Why Did She Fall for the Leader of the Band?') and Dawn became Mrs Bob Gregory, wife to an all-in wrestler. Add to these the tall, unconventional Freeman-Mitford sisters, daughters of Lord Redesdale. Deborah became Duchess of Devonshire; Diana married first Bryan Guinness and then Sir Oswald Mosley; Unity became Hitler's "perfect Nordic woman"; Jessica eloped to the Spanish Civil War with Churchill's nephew Esmond Romilly; and Nancy recorded their weird upbringing in her novels.

The girl-next-door, carrying over from Clara Bow the Twenties image of teasing virginity, appeared now as Ginger Rogers, whose publicity made it clear that she lived with her Mum. Aristocracy and intellect, for those who wanted those things, were personified in Elissa Landi, novelist and actress, and (it

'The Mitford Sisters',
(left to right):
Unity, Diana and Nancy

Ginger Rogers and Fred Astaire in *Carefree*

was claimed) granddaughter of the Empress Elizabeth of Austria; and the well-bred looks of Madeleine Carroll were backed by the information that she was a graduate of Birmingham Univeristy. Miss Carroll married Philip Astley, Adjutant of the Life Guards, who had to resign his commission for having married an actress. In *Dante's Inferno* (1935) a dancer named Marguerita Cansino attracted attention: two years later, her face remodelled by Columbia studios, her black hair dyed auburn, she became Rita Hayworth. Three sisters—Loretta, Sally and Pollyanna Young—had appeared in Hollywood like a close-harmony trio, but only one, Loretta, remained. Alone among all these, perhaps because she died so young, Jean Harlow created her never-changing image of the whore with a heart of gold and "platinum blonde" hair.

To say that "anything goes" for fashion in the Thirties—fashion in clothes as well as faces, which, instead of being bored, as in the Twenties, were now alert and pert (like Brenda Frazier, New York's deb-of-the-year in 1939)—is merely to recognize the immense variety of the decade, which is perhaps symptomatic of the underlying insecurity. In general, you didn't buy off the peg; if you couldn't afford a couturier, you ran up a dress yourself on your own sewing machine; but you always followed fashion,

Scene from *Dante's Inferno*

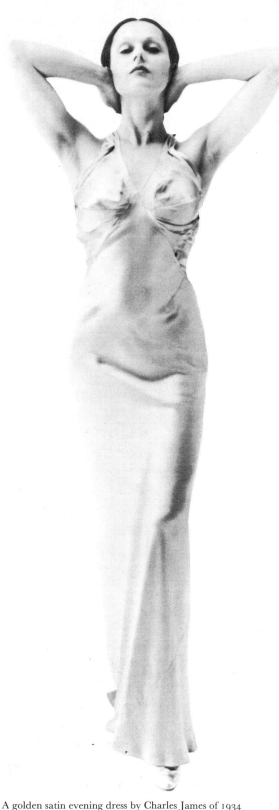

A golden satin evening dress by Charles James of 1934

which still came from Paris, London or New York, rather than from Hollywood. And always there were the key words *glamour*, *sophistication* and—a new one which came from industrial design and hit fashion about 1934—*streamlining*.

Any young man who went to dances in the 1930s will remember the joke, "she was wearing a gownless evening strap." Evening gowns, from around 1931, were long, clinging, almost skin-tight, especially round the bottom, which was splendid for girls with pretty bottoms; and it was a fearful temptation, when you were dancing cheek-to-cheek, to slide your right hand a little too low, as if by accident. The halter neck meant that if that single strap broke while you were dancing with a girl, and she were not wearing a bra, you had to hold the dress up for her till she could get to a cloakroom. *Punch* showed a young man saying to his partner in her sheath dress: "Shall we—er—*can* you sit down?" Other long dresses, whether backless or strapless, overcame this problem by parting, in a filmy fabric, to reveal the leg up to the thigh. "Where is my waist going to be this year?" another *Punch* girl asks her mirror; and young thing, seeing that her

Joan Crawford and Brenda Frazier at the Stork Club, New York, 1939

mother still wears short skirts, says: "I wish you weren't so modern, Mother. It's terribly out of date."

Dresses might plunge at the back, but not yet at the front, in spite of the omnipresent V-neck. at

Folies-Bergère scene from *Nymph Errant*

rehearsals of Cole Porter's and James Laver's *Nymph Errant* (1933) the chorus went on strike against Doris Zinkeisen's low-cut "waistcoat" costumes, and what was not yet called "cleavage" had to be filled up with gauze. "Junoesque forms are fashionable, with round and naturally curved *derrières*," wrote a fashion editor in 1934. There was even a return to Victorian styles: Anne Scott-James, in *Picture Post* (November 1938) noted that "crinolines or petticoats stiffened with whalebone hoops support the new evening dresses."

You could tell what time of day it was, if your watch had stopped, by observing a fashionable woman's skirt-length, which might change three times in one day: to the knee in the morning, to the calf for formal afternoon wear, to the ankle in the evening. This was in London: in New York in summer women went shopping in backless dresses.

In 1938 Paris designers voted Mme. Antenor Patino, wife of the new Bolivian Minister to London, the "best-dressed woman in the world", with the Duchess of Windsor and the Duchess of Kent tying for second place.

It was ill-bred to say "costume": you were supposed to say "coat and skirt" to denote the tailored clothes which became so popular for day wear. Schiaparelli (who went to Russia in 1935, apparently in search of inspiration) gave them square padded shoulders—you see the influence in the clothes worn by Rosalind Russell in her "sophisticated" comedies with Melvyn Douglas—"mannish suits", it has been said, "that looked as if the coathangers had been left in." In Britain the names of Charles Creed, Digby Morton and Victor Stiebel were beginning to be heard. For various occasions, there were tea-gowns (occasionally *pyjama* tea-gowns), house-coats, "activity frocks" and something called a "dinner dress and robe de cinema", most of them looking like close-fitting dressing-gowns. When I remember American girls of the Thirties, I think of ruffled and pleated shirt-waists with jabots.

The Court Dress worn by debutantes followed rigid rules laid down by the Lord Chamberlain's Office: "Long evening dresses with Court trains suspended from the shoulders, white veils with ostrich feathers will be worn on the head . . . gloves must be worn." Veils were to be no longer than 45 inches. Three small white feathers—the Prince of Wales Plume—must be worn slightly on the left side of the head.

Of outdoor clothes, many of which (around Jubilee

Miss Margaret Hoskin (now Mrs. Alan Jenkins), 1939

time) became increasingly military, perhaps the coat that stays longest in the memory was the "swagger coat", sometimes in English moleskin. Foreign furs were rising in price, and Queen Mary let it be known that in the interest of national economy she would buy English moleskin for her next coat. Nevertheless Messrs. Swears and Wells, many of whose furs came from Russia, took huge, crowded full-page advertisements ("amazing reductions") to sell their wares.

For tennis there were sleeveless dresses, divided skirts—and, at last, shorts. Helen Jacobs wore white shorts with shirt and ankle socks, but in the suburbs short pleated skirts were more popular. The short rolled socks fashion was adopted by Mrs. Fearnley-Whittingstall at Wimbledon; Senorita de Alvarez favoured divided or pleated skirts; Alice Marble and Kay Stammers stuck to shorts. From America came "playsuits", beach pyjamas and (influenced by Marlene Dietrich) slacks.

After the cropped Twenties, longer hair meant smaller hats or no hat at all. This in turn meant more hair-washing: a famous advertisement proclaimed "Friday Night is Amami Night" (to look good for the Saturday date). A New Yorker's memory of the Thirties is "hatless girls striding along like young goddesses, their hair tossing behind them." (Who has not followed a hatless girl with wonderful hair, to overtake her and see if her face lives up to the promise of the rear view?) Never had fashion seen such a variety of hats (from these years dates the phrase "a really *hatty* hat")—from the broad-brimmed, deep-crowned Garbo hat to tiny pill-boxes, from the Tyrolese hats that followed the Austrian vogue (started by Dodie Smith's play *Autumn Crocus* in 1931) to the Anne Boleyn hats (started by Merle Oberon in Korda's *The Private Life of Henry VIII*) and the Juliet hat, worn with a page-boy cut. Tiny hats were worn even at Ascot in 1933. Tiny hats, moreover, could be worn at outrageous angles, sometimes with a beauty

Helen Jacobs wearing shorts, 1935

'From America (influenced by Marlene Dietrich) came slacks'

spot on the opposite cheek: a *Punch* drawing shows two girls trying on hats—one of them has hers poised over one eye: the other says "Darling, it's perfect!—you look absolutely blotto!"

Princess Marina, who married the Duke of Kent in 1934, contributed to fashion both pill-box and picture hats (also the famous two rows of pearls). "Berets and velvet Tams. Also Marina hats, from 2/11–12/11," said a 1935 advertisement. Hair-styles began long and loose (swept behind the ears if you had pretty ears), which was Garbo's style in the early 1930's; and slowly progressed towards the swept-up look, sometimes with centre parting, sometimes with snood.

As hats grew madder and war approached, colours grew richer and more daring, often influenced by Royal people and occasions—Margaret Rose, Marina Green, Wallis (Simpson) Blue, Jubilee Blue (1935), Coronation Purple (1937); and the pale blue favoured by the new Queen during that year and almost ever after, in romantic dresses designed for her by Norman Hartnell. And when she and the King paid a state visit to Paris in 1938, her off-shoulder dresses with big skirts made a tremendous impact.

Nylon was still only a rumour from the Du Pont laboratories; rayon (artificial silk) was combined with wool and cotton in stockings, which were made with seams, so that it was very important to have your seams absolutely parallel. In summer girls began to leave off stockings and shave their legs. Princess Marina, being Royal, never did this, but she did make it OK to wear cotton frocks.

It was fashionable to be feminine—down to the finger-nails, which were now enamelled: more and more little bottles appeared on dressing tables. The *Sunday Express* in 1931 noted that 1,500 lipsticks were being sold for every one sold in 1921. In 1932 Barbara Haugwitz-Reventlow, born Barbara Hutton and formerly Princess Mdivani, was seen in London to be wearing black lipstick and black nail varnish. London ladies with bad complexions (Mrs. Simpson was among them) went to a Canadian masseuse, Mrs. Gladys Furlonger. Nails—and, with sandals, toe-nails—were all colours, even blue; eye-shadow went green; lipsticks and powders were available in every colour of the spectrum, and chosen to blend with the general effect of hair and complexion.

Shoes, like hats, grew madder towards the end of the decade: from sandals in bright colours, through squarish walking shoes to wedge heels (from the Italian designer Ferragamo) and what was called the "clumsy look". Many shoes had "peep-toes", a cut-away bit that made it worthwhile to paint your big toe-nail if you weren't wearing stockings. Art Déco was still going on, and its new materials, plastic and chrome, were still used for costume jewellery and ear-rings; but most of the engineering geometry had gone. "Victorian jewellery came into fashion", a fashion correspondent recalls, "and people went slumming in the Caledonian Market to find it." There were bracelets, sometimes a dozen on one arm, jingling sexily, sometimes a single "slave bangle."

Bathing dresses went backless in 1930, so that you could count a girl's vertebrae; then came the two-piece bra and shorts (but not usually exposing the navel). The bikini was still a whole war away. One of the great swimwear firms was (and is) Slix, for whose products, as a young advertising copywriter, I wrote the abominable slogan *Slix Clix with Swimmin Wimmin* around 1938. The Jantzen diving girl appeared on the thigh of woollen swimsuits, and there were rubber bathing caps in fancy designs.

For men, formal fashion trundled along un-

(*above*) Day wear for 1935
(*below*) 'The two-piece bra and shorts'

adventurously, perhaps because the *status quo* was the only stable thing in life. The pork-pie hat still flourished but was thought a little caddish, and the Fair Isle pullover became *déclassé*. There were a few Borotra berets and Oxford-ish bags left over from the Twenties. For leisure wear, shirts and shorts suddenly went gay in primary colours; and often they were cellular, to "let the air get to the skin." You could at last wear suède shoes without having small boys shout "sissy!" after you in the street.

In the City of London few frock-coats were seen, though stockbrokers still wore toppers. The frock-coat, said the *Tailor and Cutter*, was now worn by elder statesmen when attending the funerals of other elder statesmen, and were generally hired from Moss Bros. Except for very formal functions, you could dine in a dinner jacket with a soft white shirt; white tie and tails, however, enjoyed a come-back (especially in New York) after Fred Astaire's film *Top Hat*; but for most occasions the male equivalent of the "little black dress" was the unnoticeably well-tailored dark lounge suit. This, around 1936, acquired a slight "drape shape" which, strangely, went to America, became gangsterized, and returned to the British mass market after the war. "Weekend suits" (*without* waistcoats) in tweed were advertised by Harrods in 1937 "from £6.6.0." The new chalk-stripe flannels of these years were rather daring and worn only by young men. Blazers and tweed jackets (always with *light* grey trousers) were as regular as uniforms, especially for students, worn in winter with sleeveless knitted pullovers. We also wore corduroys, until now the dress of labourers and sculptors. Shirt collars grew longer and more pointed, often with a polka-dotted bow tie. Long ties remained on the whole quiet, except in Oxford and Cambridge: I still have a snakeskin tie which was, in 1934, sufficient reason for a debagging. For swimming, men could now appear naked to the waist in trunks which usually had a belt. The Palm Beach suit of linen, for climatic reasons, made more headway in America than in Britain. Silk handkerchiefs were sometimes worn tucked into the sleeve instead of in the breast pocket: A. J. Alan, in a radio short story, spoke of "the kind of self-confidence that wears its handkerchief up its sleeve."

Under the influence of Ronald Colman, Clark Gable and William Powell small thin moustaches were popular. Sidewhiskers happened at universities, but nowhere else. Hats, if worn at all, were generally

(*above*) 'Small thin moustaches were popular'
(*below*) Mr. and Mrs. Anthony Eden, March 1935

trilbies and "snap brim" felt hats. The fashion leader in hats was Anthony Eden, whose long struggle to save the League of Nations was conducted in a black Homburg-cum-trilby with curled-up brim which inevitably became known as the Anthony Eden hat.

Who cares what a man wears underneath his suit, until one is either married to him or has some other reason for watching him undress? Long woollen underpants were probably unknown in the Thirties, except as an Army term or to elderly gentlemen living in large cold houses without central heating. Now short cellular pants were in (but not yet jockey-style) with elastic tops (the other kind, of wool, had loops for putting your braces through). So were cotton vests (undershirts in America).

Who cared? Well, millions of women did, in thousands of cinemas, in 1934. For, in his famous undressing scene in *It Happened One Night*, in a twin-bedded hotel room where they have registered as man and wife, Clark Gable tells Claudette Colbert that no two men undress alike. He personally always takes off his socks before his trousers. With his hands on his belt-buckle he says "Now it's every man for himself!" But that was not what shocked the audience into embarrassed laughter. It was the fact that, when he took off his shirt, he had nothing underneath. Splendid torso he might have, but he wasn't a gentleman: all decent men wore undershirts.

Not after that, they didn't. All over the United States millions of men, economizing during the Depression, stopped wearing undershirts. The garment trade has never recovered from it.

Claudette Colbert and Clark Gable in *It Happened One Night*

# WORK AND BREAD

The portable gramophone is playing 'Sweet and Lovely'—"sweeter than the roses in May" (Ambrose's Orchestra, with Sam Browne). I am sixteen: sitting in a wet bathing dress outside a beach cabin on the north Kent coast, watching a Thames steamer called the Royal Sovereign discharging day trippers at the end of the pier. Overhead flies a

the pier tonight. Dances nowadays end with a new tune called 'Goodnight Sweetheart'.

In the Sixth form we are supposed to take an interest in Current Affairs. We shall need them for the Open Scholarships which the School is going to throw us into next year, knowing that our fathers cannot otherwise afford to send us to a university. I know

Renate Müller and Jack Hulbert in *Sunshine Susie*

biplane towing a banner advertising Bile Beans. I have just seen a film called *Sunshine Susie*, starring Jack Hulbert and a round-faced German girl called Renate Müller, who sang a song, 'Today I Feel So Happy' ("so happy, so happy; I don't know why I'm happy, I only know I am"). Well, I *am* happy: I have just had my Higher School Certificate results (Distinction in English), and I am going to a dance on

there is a thing called the Gold Standard; I know I ought to feel as relieved as Mr. J. L. Garvin, whose leading article in yesterday's *Observer* was headlined "Thank God for Him!" "Him" is Mr. Ramsay MacDonald, who has just formed a National Government.

It seems to have been Sir Herbert Samuel, the Liberal leader, and King George V who hatched the idea of a National Government with Ramsay MacDonald as Prime Minister, on the theory that the proposed drastic cuts in expenditure (including pay and unemployment relief) would be more acceptable from a Labour Premier. The financial crisis had been going on all the summer. Yet Parliament was taking its usual recess.

"It was quite by luck that Mr. Baldwin did not come to see the King before Sir Herbert Samuel," said Sir Clive Wigram, then the King's private secretary. Mr. Baldwin had been fetched back from his beloved Aix-les-Bains for the second time, but could not be found. The King himself had been fetched back from Balmoral. Neville Chamberlain was on his way back from fishing in the Highlands, as he always was at times of national crisis. Prime Minister MacDonald was expected from Lossiemouth.

America's bankers had been asked for a huge loan which would not be forthcoming until action had been taken to ensure economies. The Labour Cabinet was divided on how those economies should be made—a possible 20 per cent cut in unemployment pay had been suggested. The Cabinet resigned, and so did Mr. MacDonald. But the Cabinet was in for a shock; for MacDonald came back to Downing Street with the news that he had been invited to form a National Government with himself continuing as Premier, and that he had accepted the King's proposal without consulting his colleagues. It meant that the Labour Party would be hopelessly split, and that it would find itself in opposition to those former colleagues who agreed to enter the new Government. "Prime Minister, I think you're wrong," said Herbert Morrison; and henceforth he and many other Labour leaders regarded MacDonald as a traitor to, indeed no longer a member of, the Party he had helped to found.

Gold had been leaving the country at the rate of £2 million a day. In Vienna the Credit Anstalt bank had crashed, followed by other banks in Germany. The German mark had begun to fall. The Bank of England had tried to come to the rescue, but panic had set in. President Hoover hurriedly suggested a moratorium on war debts and reparations, which the British Government immediately accepted while the French took a fortnight to make up their minds. "These awful storms have a way of blowing over," wrote Sir Clive Wigram hopefully to the King; and in his memoirs Sir Samuel Hoare said he "thought of the danger as one of the many that so often came and went in Central Europe."

People thronged Downing Street, watching politicians going in and out of No. 10. They saw, not the Ramsay MacDonald who expected duchesses to kiss him, but a haggard man with cold feet. At the swearing-in of the new Cabinet the King laughed at him for looking so mournful in his black tie and frock coat: "You look as if you were attending your own funeral! Put on a white tie and try to pretend it's your wedding!"

Ramsay MacDonald, July 1936

Philip Snowden's emergency Economy Bill, introduced on September 11, met a deficit of £170 million by imposing £70 million cuts in salaries and benefits and £81 million in new taxation, suspending debt redemption to make up the balance. The King himself took a pay cut of 10 per cent; ("but Mrs. Windsor won't need to take in washing just yet," commented the *Daily Worker*); 10 per cent came off the dole; and somehow teachers' salaries were cut by 15 per cent. The drain on gold stopped at once. Was the crisis over already? But while the Bill was still being debated, 12,000 naval ratings in five battleships stationed at Invergordon refused to obey orders, or perhaps did not understand those orders. Mutiny in the British Navy, it seemed to foreign eyes, could only presage revolution. The withdrawals of gold began again.

What happened at Invergordon has been attributed to the Admiralty's decision, ten years before, to stop lower deck benefit societies, so that grievances could never be properly aired. An officer and naval patrol had been thrown out of a canteen when they tried to break up a meeting which had decided that "all hands should cheer" at daybreak to indicate disapproval of the cut in pay, which was "a bob a day across the board for all receiving the old scale of pay": this could mean 25 per cent to seamen earning 28 shillings a week. The officer concerned thought the mutiny was Communist-inspired. This has been denied by one of the men, Len Wincott, who in his book, *Invergordon Mutineer*, says that the relations between officers and men were good. Mr. Wincott, then twenty-four, was dismissed (with twenty-three other "ringleaders") from the Navy, joined the Communist Party and went to live in Russia.

A wave of patriotism swept the country, or at least all who were in work: people felt braced by the then unprecedented burdens imposed by the Budget, and actually queued at Inland Revenue offices to pay their taxes before they were due. But it was too late to save the Gold Standard, which was abandoned on September 21 (yet Chancellor Philip Snowden had said, only a few weeks before, that if the Gold Standard were not saved, the working class standard of life would decline by fifty per cent). The National Government was confirmed in a general election, which was preceded, on October 13, by the opening night of Noël Coward's spectacular patriotic musical saga, *Cavalcade*.

Did *Cavalcade* influence the vote? It had not been seen outside London, it had little mass appeal, its feelings were mainly middle-class, and its author had always professed to be "bleakly uninterested in politics." *Cavalcade* did *not* end with the famous toast on New Year's Eve, 1929—the sheer rhetoric which Mary Clare, as the spirit of the Marryot family, was required to speak—". . . let's drink to the hope that one day this country of ours, which we love so much, will find dignity and greatness and peace again." There was another scene after this apparent climax—a night-club scene in which the harsh 'Twentieth Century Blues' was sung while dead-faced couples danced mechanically; followed by a darkened stage, with special sound and light effects representing chaos, while slowly a Union Jack, softly illuminated, appeared at the back. It was this

The King and Queen and other members of the Royal Family in the Royal Box at Drury Lane watching Noël Coward's *Cavalcade* on the night after the general election, 1931

magnificent bit of corn that was so irresistibly moving, a theatrical stroke that had the whole audience blinded with tears even before the lights went up and the entire cast turned to the auditorium and sang 'God Save The King'. In the wild cheering that followed, Noël Coward's speech, so often parodied since, was almost an anticlimax, and perhaps he shouldn't have said it: "After all, it is a pretty exciting thing in these days to be English."

The old Duke of Connaught and his ADC, both in their eighties, had difficulty in following the show. As the cast stood at the window, watching Queen Victoria's funeral, the Duke asked: "What are they doin' now?" "Buryin' yer mother," said the ADC. Two weeks later, on Election Night itself, the whole Royal Family went to Drury Lane, Noël Coward was presented to the King in the Royal Box during the second interval, and at the end, during the National Anthem, both cast and audience turned to the Royal Box, where the King "stood there bowing, looking a little tired." But there was no knighthood yet for the

Mahatma Gandhi leaving the Friends' Meeting House, Euston Road, London, September 1931

reformed *enfant terrible* of the British theatre.

To the masses, it was probably Flanagan and Allen who made more appeal, for they were singing a down-and-out nostalgic song, 'Underneath the Arches' ("I dream my dreams away"), which contained Bud Flanagan's boyhood memories of Whitechapel, in the East End, where a strange figure now appeared to make the West wonder about its condition: Mahatma Gandhi, staying with the Quakers at Kingsley Hall, Bow. The Warden of Kingsley Hall, Muriel Lester, described it as "a sort of teetotal pub . . . a social and educational Christian centre where the people ran everything themselves." Here Gandhi slept on a thin mattress on a concrete floor. Two policemen accompanied him on his early-morning walk; and on a Saturday night he attended a local dance at which women shouted to him: "Hallo, Gandhi! Come and dance with me!"

He had come to Britain for the Round Table Conference on India. Everything about him was a gift to cartoonists—his loin-cloth and shawl, his sandals, his goat's milk, his regular hours of prayer (3 a.m. and 6.30 p.m.), his weekly day of silence, his early morning walk at 6 a.m., his very plain English disciple, Miss Slade. He had been offered a suite in a West End hotel, but rejected it in favour of the East End. He had come to ask the Government for *purna swaraj* for India, which to the British meant "complete independence" but to him meant "disciplined self-rule from within," a distinction whose subtlety had eluded the Viceroy, who had recently imprisoned him, and would do so again.

The British, to their own surprise, liked the tiny, emaciated man of sixty-two who had arrived a week before the Gold Standard departed; and some of his admirers gave him two new goats, which turned out to be male and non-milk-producing. His manners, everyone agreed, were superb. Did India really qualify for Dominion Status? The Statute of Westminster had implied that Canada, Australia, South Africa and others could now be separately represented in the League of Nations, could now appoint their own ambassadors, could now have direct access to the Sovereign. But India? Should Gandhi be allowed to meet the King at all? Winston Churchill had called him a "seditious saint striding half-naked up the steps of the Vice-Regal Palace." Lord Birkenhead had sneered at the fact that it had been necessary to open Indian jails to provide enough delegates for the Conference at all. George V, who was always frightened of unknown people until he had actually met them, barked: "What! Have this rebel fakir in the Palace after he has been behind all these attacks on my loyal officers?" His aides added: "With no proper clothes on, and bare knees?"

When, at last, with no modification whatever in his dress, Gandhi stood before him, the King could not take his eyes off those black, bony knees. And as the Mahatma was about to leave, George V, Emperor of India, said severely: "Remember, Mr. Gandhi, I won't have any attacks on my Empire!" Tactfully Gandhi replied: "I must not be drawn into a political argument in Your Majesty's Palace after receiving Your Majesty's hospitality." The Round Table Conference failed: the Moslems began talking about Pakistan, the Princes looked insecure and suspicious, and the Congress Party feared that both Princes and

Moslems might combine against them. So Gandhi went home, determined to start civil disobedience all over again. Four years later Sir Samuel Hoare, Secretary of State for India, after sixty-one days of debate, managed to get a Government of India Bill through Parliament. It gave full self-government to the eleven Provinces, and provided for a central Government. Unexpectedly the Princes denounced the Bill, and George V was so disgusted with them that he wished he hadn't invited them to his Jubilee.

Gandhi had never heard of Charlie Chaplin because he had never seen a film; but Charlie, in London for the first night of *City Lights*, was determined to meet Gandhi. They met in the East End, smiled before cameras, even embraced, but found little to talk about. Each felt deeply for the underdog; but the twain could not really meet.

"He looks like a mendicant; he speaks like Socrates," wrote George Slocombe of Gandhi. "His influence is based on love. . . . He would not prostrate himself at the feet of the Prince of Wales, but if an Untouchable struck him in the face, he would stoop and embrace his feet. . . . He pities the oppressor more than the oppressed. . . . His moral victory was won from the moment he stepped on English

Charlie Chaplin in *City Lights*

shores. . . . He has menaced the very existence of the British Empire." In India Sir Edwin Lutyens's splendid capital at New Delhi, which had been twenty-one years a-building, had just been opened by the Viceroy; in London, the naked fakir was undoing it all, and even saying that the Western world had so ruined Christianity that he called himself a non-Christian.

His was the way of non-violence for three hundred million people. Britain's 2,275,000 unemployed were to learn something from him, but not yet. For the present they were developing the hunger march, successfully tried out in the 1920's, as a weapon of protest. In 1932 a giant National Hunger March of nearly 3,000, bearing a petition signed by a million people demanding the abolition of the hated Means Test, converged on London from the provinces. Half of them were men who had been out of work for five years. One branch took five weeks to march from Glasgow. The march was wonderfully organized, with field kitchens and a squad of cobblers for mending marchers' boots. It was met by 100,000 workers in Hyde Park and Trafalgar Square, and eventually charged by police with batons. Its leader, Wal Hannington, a Communist, was jailed for three months. The Means Test stayed, but the dole went up a little.

Jarrow, on Tyneside, was one of four chief Distressed or "Special" Areas. It had idle shipbuilding yards, iron and steel plants, and coal-mines. Malnutrition was general, the T.B. death rate was double the national average, infant mortality was over eleven per cent. In 1935 Jarrow elected a new M.P., Ellen Wilkinson, small, pretty, impudent and red-haired. She, and Jarrow, decided to try a *small* hunger march of only two hundred. On October 5, 1936, she led them out of the town, marching to mouth-organs, towards London, three hundred miles away. They were blessed by the Bishop of Jarrow, and accompanied for the first twelve miles by the Mayor and Mayoress of the town. They too had a petition. Soon they were joined by other contingents from other cities; but the banner Red Ellen carried said firmly: "Jarrow Crusade."

Some towns welcomed them with hot dinners, eaten sitting down at white table-cloths. Others sheepishly provided tea poured from buckets, and bread and margarine. The marchers entered London in torrents of rain, singing 'The Minstrel Boy', and

43

were led by Ellen to a soup-kitchen in Garrick Street; then to the public gallery of the House of Commons where they heard her present the petition to the House, asking for the Jarrow shipyards to be reopened. Why, she asked Walter Runciman, President of the Board of Trade, could not the Admiralty give Jarrow even two years' work in the new rearmament programme? Both she and he knew the answer: that a company called National Shipbuilding Security Ltd. had bought up Palmer's, the local shipyard, along with many other idle yards, and as long as there was no Government intervention could call the tune about where the orders went.

The marchers were sent home to Jarrow in a special train, to a heroes' welcome, with Ellen as the local Joan of Arc. But their dole was cut because they had been away for a month, and so would not have been available for work if there had been any.

But the march had had an emotional effect on the whole country. And now the lesson of Gandhi—even, perhaps, of the more passive Suffragettes—was learnt. Wal Hannington in 1938 planned a series of dislocating "civil disobedience" stunts to draw attention to the need for extra winter relief for the unemployed. Christmas shoppers in London's Oxford Street saw the traffic lights turn red, and two hundred ragged men lie down in the street, eight abreast, heads to toes, some of them only inches from the wheels of halted buses. They covered themselves with posters bearing the words "Work or

Bread", and chanted this and other slogans. It was at once frightening and comic. Meantime the greatest traffic jam London had ever known was accumulating. A few policemen appeared, and could think of nothing to do except send for reinforcements and try gentle persuasion: "Get up, you fellows, you're holding up the traffic." The reinforcements, of course, were held up in the traffic jam. The police began lifting the inert men one by one off the road on to the pavement; the men simply went back and lay on the road again.

The unemployed sang carols (with new words) outside politicians' houses on Christmas Eve. Processions suddenly appeared, carrying coffins. Demonstrators chained themselves, Pankhurst-wise, to the railings outside the Minister of Labour's house. They pretended to fish in the water-logged trenches which had been dug during the Munich scare.

And one afternoon, Wal Hannington pulled off a brilliant propaganda trick. He sent a hundred unemployed men into the Ritz Hotel, where middle-aged women sat among the potted palms drinking China tea and nibbling cucumber sandwiches, while a trio played selections from musical shows. The unemployed men asked for tea. They said nothing else: just stood there looking at the wealthy women having their tea. The press coverage was excellent. Perhaps it had come too late; for the Depression was waning, production was going up, unemployment was slowly shrinking, as the country prepared for war.

(*opposite above*) Arrival of the first contingent of Hunger Marchers at Hyde Park, October 1932
(*opposite below*) Hunger marchers being dispersed by the police
(*above*) Ellen Wilkinson leading the Jarrow marchers, October 1936

# AT THE ODEON

*When I go to a movie, I don't like to see something that leaves me depressed.*

(WALT DISNEY)

"Amid the fairy lands of Surrey, 600 feet above sea-level on dry, chalky soil swept by sweet air direct from the Southern Seas. . . ." began an estate agent's advertisement for Surrey Downs Estate, Tattenham Corner, some time in 1935; adding the information that "illness is unknown" there because of the pine trees, which were popularly believed to have medicinal properties. By a conspiracy between developers and transport organizations, lubricated by building societies, mortgages, low interest rates and hire purchase, thousands of people were buying their own homes in villages which were about to become suburbs, thus removing the countryside to which the advertisements had attracted them.

To Arnos Grove and Cockfosters and Harrow in the north; to Shenfield, Essex, in the east; to Edgware in the north-west, Stoneleigh Park in the south-west; Tolworth and Chessington and Morden, Purley and Coulsdon in the south, Petts Wood in the south-east, the tentacles of London crept out swiftly, sometimes following the new Underground Railway extensions, sometimes ribboning along the new motor roads begun in the Twenties and nearing completion in the Thirties—Western Avenue, Kingston By-Pass, North and South Circular Roads, Rochester Way. New housing estates, carefully planned with winding roads and "architect-designed houses, all different. . . . Queen Anne, Jacobean, Georgian or Tudor styles available," with shopping parades near stations, soon to have their own Sainsburys and W. H. Smiths and Boots Cash Chemists, arrived with mains drainage and electricity for the new "labour-saving" cookers and vacuum-cleaners that were solving the "servant problem". At Kingstanding, near Birming-

ham, a village known to me in childhood became a vast housing estate.

Depression there may have been, yet in 1934 alone nearly 73,000 houses were built in Greater London, in pleasant roads called Groves, Parks, Rises, Dells, Glades and Vales. For the better-heeled, John Laing offered a detached "Coronation" type house with a round turret in Edgware for £1,145 freehold. In Hayes, Middlesex, Taylor Woodrow were building semi-detached houses at £345 each. Possession of a house could be gained by a deposit of only 10 per cent of the cost. Sometimes the builder would welcome a new houseowner with flowers, a bottle of champagne and a week's supply of groceries, free, left on the kitchen table. Sometimes a new estate would be declared open by variety stars such as Elsie and Doris Waters; and Kid Berg the boxer, assisted by a display of fireworks, personally sold houses at Ruislip. Lord Ashfield, chairman of the Underground Railway Co., was worried in 1934 that a housing density of only twelve per acre would make his new lines unremunerative; three years later a Labour M.P. was worried about overcrowding on the Northern Line—men and women were squashed so close together that "the question of decency arises"; and doctors were worried about a new disease called "suburb neurosis" by which bored housewives, used to the friendly clutter of the mean city streets from which they had emigrated, were liable, on impulse, to put their heads into gas ovens.

To their spiritual rescue came the Supercinema and the Superpub. This was the order of priority. In Edgware, Middlesex, a huge Tudor Railway Hotel had suddenly appeared in 1931, followed immediately by a still huger Ritz cinema, seating 2,120 and incorporating shops, marble staircases, "classical" murals of discreetly nude figures, a tea-lounge and an electric beacon visible for miles around. It was

*(above)* The Astoria, Brixton, designed by Edward A. Stone
*(left)* Elsie and Doris Waters

47

to have been called The Citadel, and it looked like one; for a supercinema must *never* blend with its surroundings.

Fifty years earlier, a new community would have gathered round a church; but there were some new estates that did not get a church until after the war. The church, unfortunately, had no Oscar Deutsch.

Deutsch had realized that the coming of talking-pictures, about to be mass-produced on a scale only imaginable in Hollywood, was the main revolution of the times. It must be possible for everyone to dream that he or she dwelt in marble halls. "I want to ring London with Odeons", said Deutsch; yet his first Odeon Cinema was in the Midlands in 1930 and the first in the London area was at Kingston in 1933; others followed at Harrow, Tolworth, Worcester Park, all seating 1,000–1,500 people. Nine were built at costs between £50,000 and £100,000, in 1934, ten in 1935. Altogether 890 new cinemas were built in Britain between 1932 and 1937, which is more than three a week. Sometimes old buildings would be pulled down to accommodate them, and in 1938 Herbert Farjeon's *Little Revue* contained a song called 'Knocking Down London'—

> . . . for there ain't no money in an Adams house,
> But there's oodles in an Odeon.

And not only Odeons, but Roxys (after the nickname of Mr Rothapfel in America), Gaumonts, Astorias, Ritzes, Plazas, States, Regals, Paramounts, Majestics, Capitols, Dominions, Embassies. Their architects will live for evermore: George Coles, William R. Glen, W. J. King, Edward A. Stone; and their interior décor has been called "Babylonian-Spanish-Cubist with chromium and bakelite trimmings." Only Atlantic liners had hitherto provided such luxury—powder rooms, tea-lounges, sometimes with a band you could dance to; gold-braided flunkeys opening doors for you; warmth; often a stage show; fountains and a ceiling like a night sky; restaurants, comfort, organ music, even a patchouli-type scent which may have been only disinfectant; chocolates, cigarettes, ice-creams, soft drinks served by pretty girls in berets and slacks known as "usherettes". It seemed that the Super-cinema was going to solve all social problems: youth was not delinquent as long as it could neck in the back row, children could be sent on wet Saturday afternoons to matinees for cowboy films and cartoons.

*(above)* Edward G. Robinson in *Little Caesar*
*(below)* James Cagney (left) in *Public Enemy*

The Supercinema was the supreme social centre, the knitter-together of families, even the refuge of the unemployed. By 1938 there were nearly 5,000 cinemas in Britain, 20 million people went to them each week, and 25 per cent of them twice a week or more often.

You don't have to believe me: hear Kingsley Amis on his schooldays: "I would go as far as Streatham Astoria to see Richard Barthelmess or Gary Cooper on the screen, the Paramount Tiller Girls or Troise and his Mandoliers (vocalist: Don Carlos) in the stage show." Gary, Marlene, Shirley—a whole generation of children was named after the stars.

A roaring lion, searchlights sweeping the sky across futuristic skyscrapers, a lady with a torch, a shield with WB on it, the Gainsborough Lady (a Miss Glennis Lorrimer, now seventy-two and living in Surrey), London's Clock Tower with the chimes of Big Ben, a naked-to-the-waist giant (actually Bombardier Billy Wells, the retired boxer) beating a huge gong, a revolving globe—these symbols, each representing a production company, introduced the films. What were those films about? Everything; every trend in films before the post-war Italian school was already happening in the Thirties. It was not all escapist, for Hollywood discovered that a social conscience, in measured doses, could make money too. "Social realism" began with Darryl Zanuck's "gangster cycle": he gave us Edward G. Robinson in *Little Caesar* (1930) and, discovering Jimmy Cagney, *Public Enemy* (1931). For their day, they were violent films, drawing on real-life stories of the lawlessness which J. Edgar Hoover of the F.B.I. was now striving to stamp out. It is said that Al Capone turned down a handsome offer to play himself in *Public Enemy*. "In *Public Enemy*", said Zanuck, "I gave Cagney one redeeming trait. He was a no-good bastard but he loved his mother."

The scene which shocked cinema-goers so much in 1931 showed Tom Powers (Cagney) having breakfast with his mistress Kitty (Mae Clarke) in pyjamas. He is irritable, doesn't want to talk. "Maybe you've found someone you like better," she says. For answer he picks up half a grapefruit and smashes it into her face. There seems to be little doubt that women in the Odeon audiences enjoyed this new kind of brutality, as, in the silent days of the previous decade, they had enjoyed vicarious rough treatment from Rudolph Valentino. In their different ways George

Raft and Humphrey Bogart carried on the tradition. Yet Cagney had a soft centre somewhere: all shot up in *Public Enemy*, he gasped: "I ain't so tough." And in *Each Dawn I Die* he actually burst into tears. In later years, Cagney said "I'm sick of carrying guns and beating up women," and thought that children shouldn't be allowed to see his pictures. But it is for the grapefruit incident, and the sight of his bullet-riddled body falling into his brother's front door, that he is remembered; not for playing Bottom in Hollywood's *A Midsummer Night's Dream* (1935).

Pressure groups and the new Production Code changed the "gangster cycle" into a more justifiable kind of violence, stories in which the tough guys came out on the side of the law, in films like *G-Men* (1935). In 1931 law and order was still losing out in America, but by 1935 it was winning. Now the cops were the heroes. Meanwhile crimes greater than anything Chicago could devise were happening in Nazi Germany, and in World War II violent films became superfluous.

Should films have a message? This was often debated in Hollywood, where, although Communism was fashionable among intellectuals, there was thought to be a risk of radical interpretation. You could make a character talk about "us, the people", meaning people as a whole, not versus any controlling class. So, when Zanuck was making *The Grapes of Wrath* in the last days of 1939, it was all right for Ma Joad to end the film with the reflection that the rich die out if their kids are no good, but "*We're* the people that live. Can't lick us. We'll go on forever." There was another reason why Zanuck made both *Grapes* and, later, *How Green Was My Valley*, both directed by the sure hand of John Ford: whatever their social content, Zanuck saw them both as "human stories about families".

*I Am a Fugitive from a Chain Gang* (1932), based on the autobiography of Robert E. Burns, starred Paul Muni, a character actor of genius who was afterwards seen as Louis Pasteur, Emile Zola and a Chinese peasant in *The Good Earth*. (He, too, was in the "gangster cycle" as Tony Camonte in *Scarface*.) Born Muni Weisenfreund in Poland, he had grown up in Yiddish variety theatres, specializing in old men parts. In *Chain Gang* it is not as the victim of physical cruelty in Georgian camps, or even of social injustice, that we remember him, but as a man somehow defending human dignity. The scene nobody ever

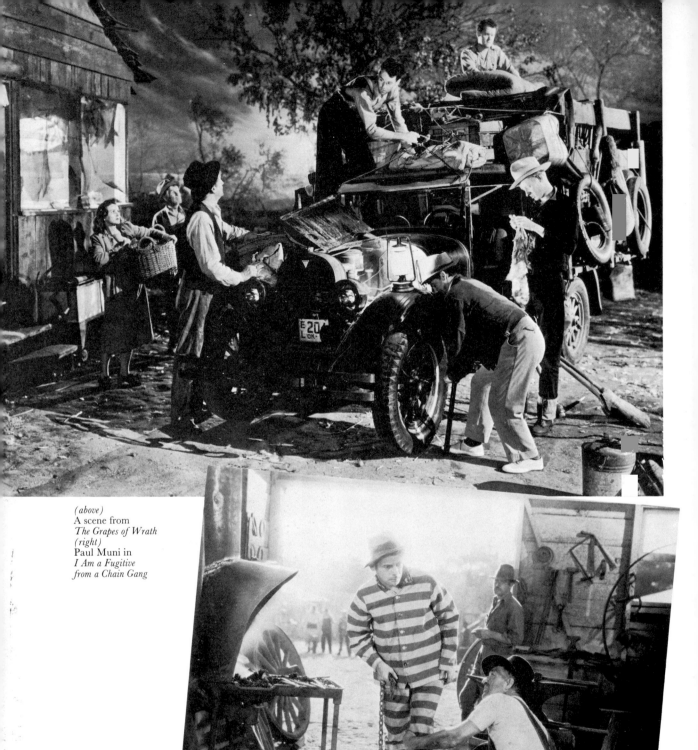

*(above)*
A scene from
*The Grapes of Wrath*
*(right)*
Paul Muni in
*I Am a Fugitive
from a Chain Gang*

forgets is the last. He, a convict who has been on the run for a year, revisits his old sweetheart to say goodbye. "How do you live?" she asks. We see the famous wounded-animal eyes disappearing into the dark night. "I steal", he murmurs.

The film's message succeeded: chain-gangs in Georgia were abolished. It had all been brought about by director Mervyn Leroy's idea of *not* showing actual floggings, but using shadows on the wall—and the horror on the faces of those who watched.

You can also convey a message in a comedy. Robert Sherwood's *Idiot's Delight* (1939), while it didn't quite carry the punch of the original play, was a light sermon against war. But that was not what packed the cinemas: it was Clark Gable, clumsily singing and dancing 'Puttin' on the Ritz'. What are we to make of the Capra comedies? Did they have a message or were they sheer anarchy? In *Mr. Deeds Goes To Town* (1936), Gary Cooper (hitherto typecast as a man of few words, most of them "yup" and "nope"), whose recreation in his home town of Mandrake Falls was playing the tuba in the town band, inherited $20 million but had to go to New York to get it. Gravely and calmly he punches the jaws of people who make fun of him "Because it ain't good manners." He feeds a horse on dough-nuts and is attacked by an unemployed farmer: it is of course in the depths of the Depression. So Mr. Deeds, without either hesitation or emotion, starts giving his money away to dispossessed farmers, clearly the behaviour of a madman.

In the famous court scene, Mr. Deeds defends himself against a charge of lunacy. He points out that the judge himself is "doodling"—which is surely no madder than playing the tuba as an aid to concentration. He cross-questions the two maiden ladies who have been brought from his home town as witnesses that he is "pixilated", in such a way that they admit that to them everyone, including the judge, is pixilated. He is giving his money away from a patriotic desire to help the Government. ... The judge pronounces him "the sanest man who ever walked into this courtroom." And that, in this gentle satire on Babbitt values, is how the words "doodle" and "pixilated" entered our language.

Longfellow Deeds was followed by Jefferson Smith, played this time by James Stewart, in *Mr. Smith Goes to Washington*— another small-town campaigner for a simple and good cause. In the great filibustering scene

James Stewart in *Mr. Smith Goes to Washington*

in the Senate, comedy suddenly becomes drama—he wins his point by fainting. Senator Alben Barkley complained that the film "makes the Senate look like a bunch of crooks." The *Daily Worker* commented "if the cap fits. . . ." And in *You Can't Take It With You* (1938) Lionel Barrymore proclaimed the belief, put into practice by all his family and friends, that everybody should quit work and have fun doing exactly what they want—including non-payment of income-tax because he "didn't believe in it." These comedies wear well, and come up freshly on television.

The Marx Brothers in *A Night at the Opera*

The Marx Brothers, who became a cult—even a left-wing cult—never really appealed to the mass audience in the thirties. Today their pictures are accepted as classics, and certain scenes have a legendary fame, like the cabin scene in *A Night at the Opera* (1935), or Groucho and Chico negotiating a singer's contract by tearing out unwanted clauses until there is nothing left. Frothy light comedy, well-dressed with every line polished to a high gloss, was purveyed by Melvyn Douglas and Rosalind Russell, and by William Powell and Myrna Loy in the *Thin Man* series; and this, with the aid of Central European scriptwriters, was carried to its furthermost possibility by Ernst Lubitsch. He had begun, in Hollywood, with satirical musicals: now the music disappeared, the satire increased—and the victim was romantic love. "They're just apes copulating on a bubble," complained a left wing film critic to me of

*Bluebeard's Eighth Wife.*

And in November 1939, when it was "safe" to make fun of Russia, Lubitsch gave us Garbo in her only comedy role as *Ninotchka*, a Soviet official sent to France to discipline three male emissaries who have plainly become corrupted by the capitalist system. She meets her match in Melvyn Douglas, as a White Russian aristocrat. "Garbo Laughs!" said the publicity, and what makes her laugh is Melvyn Douglas falling off a chair. Thereafter she abandons her belief that "love is just a chemical reaction," buys Paris clothes, drinks too much champagne and . . . but the point has been made.

In Britain, Alfred Hitchcock had found, in films like *The 39 Steps*, *The Man Who Knew Too Much* and *The Lady Vanishes*, a brilliant formula which mixed fear, horror and satire, and when, in 1939, Hollywood finally seduced him, it was to make *Rebecca*. *The Lady*

*Vanishes* (based on Ethel Lina White's *The Wheel
Spins*) brought together Basil Radford and Naunton
Wayne in an unforgettable partnership as a pair of
jolly decent, dim-witted Englishmen.

By now comedy—indeed, all films—had to con-
tend with the new Production Code. In 1934 a
campaign headed by the Legion of Decency led to the
appointment of one Joseph Breen, of the Motion
Picture Producers and Distributors of America, as
censor of Hollywood's output. The effect was a
sweetening of "social realism" by which (with some
glaring exceptions we have already noted) the
American way of life was shown to include a
swimming pool and a British butler as standard
equipment, and stenographers apparently shared
humble little all-electric apartments. Bette Davis,
Frederick Lewis Allen noted, having (in *Dark Victory*)
"given up everything" in exchange for what she
called "nothing", was reduced to "a remodelled
Vermont farmhouse" which must have cost $12,000 a
year to live in.

Among the reasons for the new Production Code
was the scandalous life of certain stars, which
publicity departments now suppressed, substituting
fictional gossip stories. The two great, unliterary
channels for this sort of thing were Hedda Hopper
and Louella O. Parsons of Hearst newspapers. Much
of the Code was concerned with ludicrous measure-
ments of cleavage, durations of kisses, and "avoiding
the horizontal" in love scenes. It will never be certain
what incident started the Code. Some historians say it
was Miriam Hopkins in *The Story of Temple Drake*
(1933) when, as an unrepentent society girl, she
boasted of her liking for "smoking, drinking and
men"; and Anita Loos says it was Jean Harlow in *Red
Headed Woman*—"the trollop in the movie gets the
man, the money and is even decorated by the
President of France at the end. The women's club
raised such a stink that a board had to be appointed."

Censorship had not yet been applied to personal
politics. Nobody was yet asking: "Is Shirley Temple a
Soviet agent?" Hollywood was not exactly Red, but
it was certainly pink, led by the intellectuals who had
left New York for California and, since the Wall
Street Crash, had been professing Communism.
Donald Ogden Stewart once told me they had all
been "converted" by a single book, John Strachey's
*The Coming Struggle for Power*. Yet certain moguls were
disturbed, and in October 1937 Hal Roach, producer

Scene from *The Thin Man*

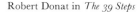

Robert Donat in *The 39 Steps*

of Laurel and Hardy, invited Vittorio Mussolini, bomber of Ethiopian villages, to Hollywood—why? to help international understanding? or to show Hollywood a strong political system that seemed to work? Here is Roach's view of "one of Hollywood's leading Communists." He is "one of the four or five cleverest, most competent film writers. He gets 3,000 a week, and is outwardly a gay dog with a cynical, suave manner. Inside of him, though, he is bitter; he hates Hollywood and the producers and, because of his dependence on the picture industry . . . is not overfond of himself. He finds a curious satisfaction in posing as a Red, in uttering Marxist phrases and ideas while holding a long-stemmed cocktail or champagne goblet at some large Hollywood party; in writing out a cheque for $1,000 and handing it to the Communist Party."

For several years it was hardly possible, in America, to see a British film unless you went to some back-street flea-pit. There weren't enough of them; they weren't good enough, being usually produced on shoe-string budgets; and anyway the British accent was incomprehensible. Of course it had to be a Hungarian with a genius for borrowing money, Alexander Korda, who dragged British films out of their futility. In the spring of 1932 London Film Productions set up shop in eight rooms at 22, Grosvenor Street, opposite Molyneux the dressmaker, in a building which had once been known as Earl's Temperance Hotel.

It could not have been less like Hollywood. "Standing on the feet of René Clair," wrote Caroline Lejeune, film critic of the *Observer*, "with Robert Sherwood towering over you, and Robert Flaherty's vast bulk filling up the doorway, you would argue with Robert Donat about his next play or discuss history with A. E. W. Mason." Korda drew his staff largely from Paramount British, which had suspended production after the failure of *Lily Christine*, an attempt to commit Michael Arlen's novel to celluloid. Korda picked and developed four starlets, Diana Napier, Wendy Barrie, Joan Gardner and Merle Oberon (whom he eventually married). His brothers Vincent and Zoltan were responsible for set-designs and cutting, and another Hungarian, Lajos Biro, drafted the script of Korda's first film, *Wedding Rehearsal*, in which Merle Oberon got her first starring part because Ann Todd, who was to have starred, was injured in a motor smash. Neither this film nor its

Charles Laughton in *The Private Life of Henry VIII*

successor, *Men of Tomorrow* (about Oxford), earned much money; there were debts, more borrowings, and a constant search for a really good "British" story. Then, one day, Korda hailed a taxi whose driver happened to be singing "I'm 'Enery the Eighth, I am."

The result, *The Private Life of Henry VIII*, starring Charles Laughton, was the first British film to score an equal success in both America and Britain. Its two most famous scenes were probably Merle Oberon, as Anne Boleyn, going to her execution ("such a pretty little neck"), and King Henry gnawing a whole chicken in his hands and throwing the bones over his shoulder.

"A bold, heroic enterprise, born of a strong faith in the creative future of the cinema" was the *London Mercury*'s verdict on Korda's—and H. G. Wells's—*The Shape of Things to Come* (1936)—although "many people, surrounded just now with fears of actual war, may not much care to buy seats in order to watch the wiping out of civilization with air bombs on the screen." The film appeared just as Hitler was reoccupying the Rhineland. It showed that favourite dread of the Thirties, undeclared gas warfare. The few survivors beget a race which builds all its cities underground, finally (in A.D. 2054) shooting a boy and a girl into space (with a gun, not a rocket) to look at the other side of the moon.

"This is the Night Mail crossing the border /

Bringing the cheque and the postal order / Pulling at Beattock, a steady climb, / The gradient's against her but she's on time." Not W. H. Auden at his best, but part of his commentary to *Night Mail*, one of about forty short documentary films, some with music by Benjamin Britten, made by the Post Office film unit which were perhaps Britain's chief contribution to the art of the cinema. Something of the same technique was used by Pare Lorentz in *The River* (1938), which had a commentary in Whitmanesque free verse on the Mississippi—"New Orleans to Baton Rouge, Baton Rouge to Natchez, Natchez to Vicksburg. . . . Ill-clad, ill-housed, ill fed—and in the greatest river valley in the world."

More journalistic, and better known to the Odeon audiences, was America's *The March of Time*, introduced by a toastmaster-voice, which treated such news subjects as football pools and cancer research in some depth. There were also Gaumont-British Instructionals, about bird-watching and other "secrets of nature"; and all these were encouraged by the British Film Institute, which had been established in 1933. Ponderously funny were the cliché-ridden Fitzpatrick Travelogues, each ending with the same phrase, sometimes chanted by the audience—"so it is with regret that we leave colourful Tahiti."

Fantasy took several forms: the "singies" of Jeannette MacDonald ("the Iron Butterfly") and Nelson Eddy (called by a certain critic "the singing capon"); the child-world of Shirley Temple, Deanna Durbin and the sixteen-year-old Judy Garland in the *Wizard of Oz* (1939); the world of Walt Disney; monsters; and girls—masses and masses of girls.

MacDonald and Eddy, with their frustrated ambitions (she to sing at the Met., he to be a comedian) sang their way, in full-tonsilled close-up, through 'Ah, Sweet Mystery of Life', 'Indian Love Call', and (from *Maytime*, 1937) "Sweetheart, sweetheart, sweetheart . . . / Will you remember the day / When we were happy in May?" (If you catch a revival on TV, try switching off the sound—the vision is sidesplitting).

"Infancy with her is a disguise, her appeal is more secret and more adult." Thus Graham Greene, reviewing a Shirley Temple film in *Night and Day*, a British counterpart to the *New Yorker*, in October 1937. He went on to write about Shirley's performance in caustic terms, which impelled the production company to bring a libel action and obtain $9,800 damages. This ruined the magazine.

Miss Temple fared no better with American critics. Seeing her in *Poor Little Rich Girl*, Frank Nugent of the *New York Times* wrote: "Short of becoming a defeated candidate for Vice-President, we can think of no better method of guaranteeing one's anonymity than appearing in one of the moppet's films." Darryl

Shirley Temple in *Poor Little Rich Girl*

Zanuck guaranteed Nugent's temporary anonymity by hiring him as a script-writer at three times his old salary.

Deanna Durbin was a little older, and really could sing. And does anyone remember that Britain tried to find an answer to Shirley Temple? Her name was Binkie Stewart, she was half Shirley's age (3), made nine films (one was called *Little Dolly Daydream*), and is now a nightshift operator at Reading Telephone Exchange. Dimples were also part of the charm of Sonja Henie, a good deal older than either of these, who skated.

Colour was coming in, but only in cartoons was it really successful. The Silly Symphonies, animating flowers, birds, bees and animals, mocking well-loved pieces of classical music, using the freedom of design and line and colour to create funny, moving, dramatic and sometimes terrifying effects, are probably Walt Disney's masterpieces. Mickey Mouse, the dog Pluto, the Three Little Pigs were added to, and often borrowed from, the world's folk-lore. "Who's Afraid of the Big, Bad Wolf?" took on a special meaning from the threats in Hitler's speeches. As for *Snow White and the Seven Dwarfs*, a reputedly hard-boiled and widely syndicated American columnist, Westbrook Pegler, thought it "the happiest

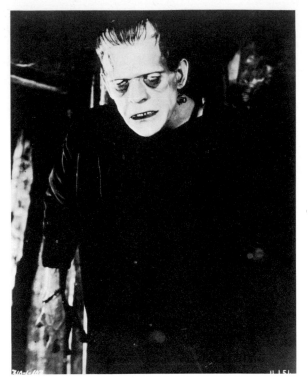

Boris Karloff in *Frankenstein*

thing that has happened in this world since the Armistice."

Monsters? We had Bela Lugosi ("I never drink—*wine*") in *Dracula* (1931), Boris Karloff in *Frankenstein* (1931), followed by Bela Lugosi in *Son of Frankenstein* (1939), and the eternal wonder of Fay Wray's screams in *King Kong* (1933), where the monster was a model ape, animated by Disney techniques, who was finally shot down from the top of the Empire State Building by fighter aircraft. Was the Empire State a phallic symbol? Was the monster a symbol of revolt against the machine age? Theories abound. Scenes of King Kong eating people were cut, but the film has left such an imperishable legacy of horror that in England, for 40 years after it was made, it was banned by Surrey County Council, even after it had been shown on television on Christmas Day. In the end, people are always sorry for monsters.

Almost alone, Charlie Chaplin went on making silent films—silent except for sound effects, background music and a nonsense-song in an invented foreign language, which was what happened in *City Lights* (1931). Probably no Chaplin film is more

revealing of his clown's soul than this one. An unknown "bathing belle", Virginia Cherrill, played the blind girl with whom he falls in love. He was to play the little tramp in only one more film, *Modern Times* (1936). Already Hollywood was ganging up on him, with charges of "moral turpitude" and "Communist sympathies". *Modern Times*, which shows the little man crushed by machinery, inhuman labour conditions and the stultifying monotony of mass-production, was indeed a film of hilarious protest; but ever after, somebody had it in for Chaplin.

To relegate *Gone with the Wind* to Hollywood's "history cycle" would be an insult to this 3¾-hour epic of the American Civil War. The Civil War, as a film subject, was generally thought to be bad box-office, but when the book became a best-seller, David Selznick drew lots with the other studio heads for the film rights. Selznick, who had just broken away from his father-in-law, Louis B. Mayer, was not at first too concerned about who should play Scarlett O'Hara. What mattered was Rhett Butler, and it had to be Clark Gable. But Gable was under contract to Sam Goldwyn. Bette Davis desperately wanted to play Scarlett, but when Warner Bros. offered Selznick both Davis and Errol Flynn as a package deal, Davis refused to play opposite Flynn. Eventually Selznick made a vast deal with MGM to get Clark Gable, and then started looking seriously for a Scarlett O'Hara.

Should an unknown girl be "discovered" for this bitchy role? Fourteen hundred girls were interviewed and ninety screen-tested. No good. So eight established stars who were known to want the part were considered. Katharine Hepburn was thought to be not sexy enough. Norma Shearer's fan-club didn't want to see her in an unladylike role. Scarlett O'Hara was only sixteen in the story: this didn't matter so much, because most of the great Thirties female stars were "mature": so there seemed to be nothing extraordinary in testing Miriam Hopkins (35), Tallulah Bankhead (34), Joan Crawford, Jean Arthur and Irene Dunne (all in their early thirties). Joan Bennett, Paulette Goddard, Lucille Ball, Lana Turner—well, she *was* sixteen, but showed too little understanding of the part—Loretta Young.... It was getting ridiculous. Paulette Goddard came nearer to Scarlett than any other candidate, but her name had been linked with Chaplin—better not risk it.

When David Selznick's brother Myron, a leading agent, suddenly produced Vivien Leigh (25) Selznick went into a "I-took-one-look" routine. She had a clipped English accent, but managed to acquire a Southern drawl in three days. She had greenish eyes, just as Margaret Mitchell had said in the book (she had read the book, too). And she could express blazing emotions without fluttering her eyelashes. GWTW, which won the Oscar for the best film of 1939, cost an apparently ruinous $4,250,000 to make; to date, with TV showings, it has grossed $125 million.

In back-street "art" cinemas, and in the plushy fauteuils of the Marquis of Casa Maury's new small cinemas in London, and George Hoellering's Studios One and Two, we saw French and other foreign films, and they became fashionable among the *cognoscenti*, who loved criticizing the English sub-titles. The French did not create new stars—they used established figures of the theatre. Guitry, Jouvet, Alerme, Danielle Darrieux, Françoise Rosay; Fernandel, Barrault, Jean Gabin, Michèle Morgan, Charles Boyer. René Clair, in *Sous Les Toits de Paris*, lets his camera pan over the Montmartre steps and the chimneys and the lives of ordinary people in the

*King Kong*

Photograph showing the making of *Sous Les Toits de Paris*

streets, and gave us humour, poetry, satire. Guitry gave us episodic films featuring himself in several parts with his own voice narrating over-shot. Duvivier's *Un Carnet de Bal* traced what had happened to all the young men on a girl's dance-card: the girl, approaching middle-age, sees that even her memories of the waltz tune were an illusion. The most terrifying scene, shot at an angle of 30 degrees, enters the world

Peter Lorre in "*M*"

of an abortionist who is also an epileptic. . . . I can't go on: I've seen it eight times, and for me it is the greatest of all French films.

Jacques Feyder's *La Kermesse Héroïque* (1937), set in the Netherlands of the 17th century, shows a town deciding, under the influence of the women, not to resist the invading—and more virile—Spaniards, but instead to welcome them as friendly occupiers, extending the hospitality of board and, of course, bed. The modern parallel was inescapable: this was defeatism, yes, with Hitler screaming about his "territorial demands", and pacifists seriously debating whether it wouldn't be better, after all, to lie down and try to enjoy it.

From Germany came Fritz Lang's "*M*", with Peter Lorre as the Düsseldorf murderer; and the guiltily-admired work of Leni Riefenstahl, whose silent pictures *The White Hell of Pitz Palu* and *The Blue Light* had already penetrated the film societies. Now, in *Triumph of the Will* (1935) and an overwhelming record of the 1936 Olympic Games, she showed a new young Germany, frightening hypnotizing—propaganda, as the Russian films of the Twenties had been, yet (in the jargon of the time) "pure cinema".

To hell with pure cinema. This was not what millions went to the Odeons and Roxys and Astorias to see. The ultimate escape-dream was based on such stuff as girls, spectacle, music and dancing. Films like *Gold Diggers of Broadway* (1930), whose advertising claimed (I quote verbatim) that it "exceeds in pretentiousness and beauty anything which has yet appeared on the screen." The early "all-talking, all-singing, all dancing" pictures had been content to show a chorus line high-kicking as they did on stage, and the public grew tired of them, so much so that some managers with a straight film felt obliged to put a poster outside saying: "This is not a musical."

But *42nd Street*, barely four years later than *The Broadway Melody*, was something different. Girls as harps, girls on roller skates, girls reflected to infinity in mirrors, girls in revolving pyramids, girls in star-formation photographed either in swimming pools or lying on the studio floor, girls playing neon-lit violins, girls in ascending rows, in hanging gardens, in waterfalls—the screen had never been used like this before. This was the "girl geometry" of ex-Lieutenant William Berkeley Enos, thoroughly accustomed to arranging military spectacles, and now known as Busby Berkeley. He was said to choose three hundred out of five thousand girls for his chorus—some said by faces, ankles, knees and elimination, though he himself claimed he went for eyes—"because they mirror the soul."

The "angel" who backs the show because the understudy has got her big break and her boy-friend the song-writer turns out to be the son of a millionaire—or maybe all that backwards—the plots don't matter. *42nd Street* was followed by *Gold Diggers of 1933*, with a number called "Pettin' in the Park" in which a rainstorm leads to all the girls undressing behind semi-transparent screens. *Flying Down to Rio* had Fred Astaire and Ginger Rogers stealing the show from the principals, Dolores del Rio and Gene Raymond, in the dance songs 'Carioca' and 'Music Makes Me' ("... do those things I never should do.")

Fred and Ginger emerged to make their own films, and gradually to dispense with masses of girls. No weird camera angles: the whole stage, the whole bodies of the dancers visible so that you could see their balletic movement, even in tap dancing. Here, in films like *Roberta, Top Hat, Follow the Fleet, Swing Time* and *Shall We Dance?* was the Astaire elegance, with songs by Irving Berlin, Gershwin and Kern, and interludes of uproarious comedy: in *Top Hat*, Edward Everett Horton asks Eric Blore (the unvarying, disapproving English manservant) for a steak to put on his black eye. Blore serves it grilled, with the appropriate sauce. . . . And the songs—ah, the songs! 'Isn't This a Lovely Day to be Caught in the Rain?'—'Top Hat, White Tie and Tails'—'Cheek to Cheek'. . . .

George Arliss and Anna Neagle being historical in, respectively, *The House of Rothschild* and *Queen Victoria*; epics of World War I, of which *Hell's Angels* stays in the memory, if not for the aerobatics, then for Jean Harlow's "Do you mind if I slip into something more comfortable?". . . . Marie Dressler and Wallace Beery, being lovable in *Min and Bill* and *Tugboat Annie*; Mickey Rooney being Middle America's plug-ugly ideal of American boyhood in *Love Finds Andy Hardy*. . . . The enthronement of two screen-queens, the electric, hyperthyroid Bette Davis, by no means lovable in *Jezebel*, and Katharine Hepburn, hailed by *Vanity Fair* as "Bryn Mawr's celebrated alumna", whose "luminous portrayals" in *A Bill of Divorcement*, the Oscar-winning *Morning Glory*, and *Little Women* "have enhanced the screen". . . . All this, and Bernard Shaw's final capitulation to the cinema by allowing Gabriel Pascal to make *Pygmalion*, with Wendy Hiller and Leslie Howard. . . .

The total production of films during these years defies statistics. Darryl Zanuck alone, while at Fox-Movietone-City, reckoned that he "read, revised, cast, filmed, cut, assembled and released one picture every 12 days." There were 'A' pictures, 'B' pictures, first and second features, and, in Britain, "quota quickies"; and practically everyone in Britain and America saw practically every one of them. "They were the kind of movies you went to before you could afford a psychiatrist," someone said. "They drained away your guilt. They absolved you." Today, television networks, despite all the trendy, class-conscious new scripts and Liverpudlian voices, are baffled by the fact that old movies are still the biggest draw at "peak viewing" times. Why? Because, you fool, they don't make movies like that any more.

# GROVES OF ACADEME

I am eighteen. I am going up to Oxford in a motor-coach, because it is cheaper than the train. My trunk and bicycle have gone, in advance by rail, to Oxford (L.M.S.) Station. My requited love for Oxford had begun in another motor-coach, five years ago, on a school outing to a city which, we were told, had been written about by Matthew Arnold and Compton Mackenzie, Max Beerbohm and Beverley Nichols. If you have grown up in Birmingham, you have seldom seen an old or a beautiful building. The sight of New College gardens and the staircase at Christ Church was too much for me. I must win scholarships; I must get here somehow!

In motor-coach and ecstasy, trundling gently through towns and villages with warm, southern names—Shipston-on-Stour, Long Compton, Great Rollright, Chipping Norton, Woodstock—lunch at the Red Lion, Stratford-on-Avon—I watch the hawthorn-hedged Warwickshire pastures and russet-bricked cottages give place to straggling villages and meadows walled in yellow Cotswold stone. My first sight of Oxford, as the huge motor-coach slithers on fallen leaves, is dusky, frosty, autumnal.

It had so nearly not happened. Three weeks before, for want of £40 a year, I was destined for Birmingham University—an excellent institution, but I would have had to be a home student. Then, out of the blue, came an exhibition worth £42 a year. This, added to my County Major scholarship (£90 a year and a maintenance grant) gave me £162 a year for everything. My father would come to the rescue if necessary up to an absolute limit of £50 a year. I was to have a bank account, and my uncle gave me, as a birthday present, a life membership of the Union (£11).

Coming up at short notice means that there is no room in college for the first year. My digs in Headington Road are awful: I go to bed by candlelight; there is no bathroom; the landlady coughs and is probably consumptive. I am intensely lonely, until I discover one priceless social asset which cuts across all barriers and makes me, a beady-eyed suspicious grammar-school boy, acceptable in all milieux: I can sing for my supper: I can play jazz on the piano. Soon this will help my financial situation too; so that I need no longer give up a bread and cheese lunch in order to buy a secondhand book: I can earn 10s. a night as relief pianist in local dance-bands, and I am not too proud to be paid for playing at people's parties. After about a year I am accepted by the University dance-band, The Bandits. I write special arrangements, I become locally famous—accounts of parties in the *Isis* gossip column end with—"and Mr Alan Jenkins was at the piano." The band, in neat, white mess-jackets, plays at women's college dances and the Eights Week Ball, and acts as relief band to Jack Jackson or Marius Winter or Arthur Salisbury at Commemoration Balls in vast marquees in college quadrangles. Occasionally we go to Cambridge for exchange dates with their university dance-band, the Quinquaginta Ramblers. We introduce the rumba, played for the first time at the St. Hilda's college dance (I refer to my Oxford diary) on May 24, 1934. We play for the Hunger Marchers (Lancashire contingent) as they lie exhausted on the floor of the Corn Exchange; but they don't like our "hot" 'Tiger Rag', and ask for 'Lily of Laguna'—something they can sing.

In my second term the Union, on February 9, 1933, carried its notorious resolution "that this House will not fight for King and country." For months afterwards we were drunk with glory: Oxford was news! The debate, in retrospect, was confused: the proposer saw war as furthering "the selfish wishes of a class"; his opponent, a true-blue Tory, "would be proud to defend his King"; a third speaker found it a matter of getting guidance from God (he was a

The Oxford University dance-band, *The Bandits*

Buchmanite). Then came the heavy visiting guns—Mr. Quintin Hogg thought that refusing to fight would actually cause war; and Professor Joad, after making the House laugh, asserted that "a single bomb from an aeroplane could poison every living thing in an area of three-quarters of a square mile." He gave gruesome details of war-wounds and the effects of gas—the fear-propaganda that never failed—and women in the gallery were seen to be clasping their foreheads as if about to be sick.

*The Times* thought, in a leading article entitled CHILDREN'S HOUR, that we were not symptomatic of Britain's decadence—we were just too young to know better. The *Daily Express* said we were "woozy-minded Communists and sexual indeterminates", and Beachcomber, their humorist, started a series of paragraphs about undergraduates who used scent in their baths and belonged to the "Oxford Onion". The *Daily Telegraph* accused us of "foul-minded disloyalty"; Winston Churchill made a speech saying he was nauseated by "the abject, squalid, shameless avowal made in the Oxford Union"; 275 white feathers were sent to the President, Frank Hardie. The St. John's College Boat Club marched in the following week and tried to tear the resolution out of the minute book. Randolph Churchill, Lord Stanley of Alderley and fifty life members of the Union came down to propose that the resolution be expunged; stink bombs were let off during the debate; the motion was defeated by 750 votes to 188. Meanwhile the Reichstag had been set on fire, Hitler was about to seize power, and German propaganda was preparing to say that the British officer class, exemplified by a

few hundred undergraduates, had lost its morale.

Yet had not Mr. Baldwin spoken of the "monstrous wickedness of bombing the women and children of another country lest they should bomb yours first?" The Cambridge Union was more positive: they voted in favour of fighting "for the League and sanctions."

The Union at this time was dominated by the Left Wing. We were pinkish-red because it seemed to us that there was nothing else to be. It was possible to call oneself a Communist but also be President of the Labour Club. The October Club, its meetings sometimes banned by proctors, sometimes broken up by "hearties", had a difficult existence. Deciding that I ought to learn something about politics, and reading in the *Isis* that the Labour Club was "the jolliest club in Oxford", I paid 2s. 6d. and joined. I never for one moment knew what was going on. The disunity of the Left at this time was so great that there were several Labour Parties, and the Club seemed unable to decide to which it wanted to be affiliated. John Stafford Cripps, Tony Greenwood and others struggled with a polyphony from the floor which generally included a rich Tyneside voice from Ruskin College bellowing "What about the Means Test?" We called each other "Comrade", sang 'The Red Flag', and then went on to the Carlton Club for drinks. There was a Study Group, run by Professor G. D. H. Cole and Bill (now Sir William) Nield. Cole was one of the main influences on a generation of undergraduates, equipping them with basic Marxism and the theory of dialectic materialism. Sometimes we sang songs like—

*Redshirts, Blackshirts, everybody come!*
*Join the Oxford Labour Club and make yourselves at home.*
*Bring your Marx and Engels and squat upon the floor,*
*And we'll teach you economics as you never heard before.*

Michael Foot was still a Liberal—"the Liberals' last hope", quipped the *Isis* when reporting Union debates. His earnest, rasping voice had been heard in a maiden speech as long ago as his first term in October 1931: two years later he was President. In February 1935 came the dramatic news that he had joined the Labour Party, influenced, it was said, by John Cripps. Talent-spotters at the Union, and sternly critical *Isis* reporters, noted Angus Maude, Giles Playfair (apt to do his imitation of Lloyd George at the drop of a hat), Derek Walker-Smith; "I am

Caricature of Michael Foot by W.R.N.

cheaper clubs, such as the extremely fashionable Fencing Club, and a Russia Club, run by a White Russian Countess, which used to give exhibitions of Russian folk-dances: I was once roped in to take part in them, singing Russian words which I didn't understand but learnt phonetically. Prince Franz Hohenlohe tried to continue the gaiety of the Twenties by giving a Kiddy Party; he also (with Baron von Einem) ran an Austrian Club where people did Tyrolese dances in *Dirndl* and *Lederhosen*.

The Oxford University Dramatic Society (OUDS) was as much social as dramatic, with its own club-room and bar. By tradition it generally adhered to Shakespeare and Marlowe, since the ability to speak verse resonantly in college gardens covers a multitude of acting deficiencies, and to "Smokers" at which members played and sang their own songs and acted in their own Coward-inspired sketches. (We *all* wrote songs which owed recognizable debts to Gershwin, Coward and Porter). A notable production of *Dr Faustus* (on an Elizabethan stage) with Primrose Salt, 1934's Deb of the Year, as Helen of Troy, moved on from Oxford Town Hall to the Salzburg Festival. Nevill Coghill produced *Hamlet* with Peter Glenville, whom one critic thought "better than Gielgud". Leontine Sagan, famous for her film *Mädchen in Uniform*, was called in to produce *Richard III* in the cloisters at Christ Church, the audience sitting in the middle with the battle raging all round them.

In this brilliant little pond young men made great local reputations: what happens to Presidents of the O.U.D.S. after they have gone down? You may perhaps correctly forecast that the President of a Boat Club will become a Bishop; but with student actors you cannot be sure. One or two made their names in theatre, films and television; one joined the BBC and became the Mayor of Toytown in Children's Hour; one ended up as a male "man of distinction" model in New York; and one became a "presenter" of detergent commercials.

Within the University argument raged about the position of women students. They, too, were in mild revolt against rules such as the one at Lady Margaret Hall which said that "undergraduates may not telephone women students except between 2 and 3 p.m." They managed to found their own club, the Pentagon ("men may be entertained on Sunday between 3.30 and 6 p.m. on condition that their names are entered in a book provided for the purpose

getting terribly tired of Mr. Max Beloff' . . . "Mr. Beloff is improving—he was really quite witty"; "Mr. Peter Pain must do something about his trousers". Later, in 1937, "Mr. E. R. G. Heath (Balliol) made an extremely forcible and able maiden speech . . . he must be careful not to appear too aggressive . . . he says 'Now, Sir,' rather too often." (Mr. Heath's wittiest speech was in derision of Neville Chamberlain's visits to Germany to avoid war—"If at first you don't concede, fly, fly again!") Mr. J. H. Wilson (Jesus), destined to play Gladstone to Mr. Heath's Disraeli, seems never to have spoken at the Union at all.

Despite the recent influx of hardworking scholarship boys, whose grants would be taken away from them if they were demonstrably idle, Oxford was still largely a social community. There were expensive social clubs, all-male, like the Carlton, which had a wine-steward named Roby and blackballed coloured students (even the brilliant Dosoo Karaka, first Indian President of the Union); the Bullingdon, whose Grind was "still one of the best point-to-points in the country"; and the Gridiron, whose members must have been to Public Schools. There were

and the Club Hostess is in the building"). They also started their own magazine, *Lysistrata*, which was edited by Sally Graves: it contained contributions by Virginia Woolf, Naomi Mitchison ("a Marxist love-poem") and Marghanita Laski, then an undergraduette at Somerville. In March 1935 undergraduates paraded in beards and bathchairs at an Oxford Union poll (including life-members) to decide whether women should be allowed to be entertained at the Union: the right was won by only twenty-five votes. The idea that there could ever be a woman President never entered anyone's head.

Oh, well, we managed somehow. If you wanted to meet girls unchaperoned you could join Phyllis Frames's dancing school in Boswell House (where I played the piano on Tuesday evenings in exchange for free tap-dancing lessons); and in summer there were punts moored in leafy backwaters of the Cherwell, and the murmuring of portable gramophones in the long grass near St Hilda's College gave no hint of what was actually going on there. The proportion of men to women undergraduates was roughly seven to one. Any reasonably attractive girl could reckon on getting engaged two or three times during her academic career.

Nearly all life was social, every detail recorded in the *Isis* gossip column:—

"I hear that make-up is not being worn in Schools this summer. It will be considered *tout outré* at Vivas . . . The Marquis Julio de Amodio has taken up fencing . . . Miss Anne Scott-James, of Somerville, makes all her own clothes . . . The Prince of Wales was beaten at squash by the President of Magdalen J. C. R. . . . Mr. Ossia Trilling gave a most enjoyable sherry party with potato crisps . . . Mr. Adolf Schlepegrell has given up his Rhodes Scholarship and is returning to Germany to join the Storm Troops . . . Mr. Joseph Cooper, Organ Scholar of Keble, has made a record of his new song . . . Mr. Peter Glenville is back in Oxford after a week's recuperation from the effects of his party held the Sunday before last . . . Mr. William Douglas-Home was seen driving a phaeton in The High . . . Mr. John Profumo gave his celebrated imitation of Douglas Byng . . . Mr. Stormont Mancroft is interested in goldfish, canaries and concertinas . . . Max, genial head waiter at the George, has moved to the Town and Gown . . . The recent kidnapping of Miss Renée Houston is unfortunately typical of undergraduate irresponsibility today . . . The Guy Fawkes festivities this year were quite tame. Seventeen arrests were made by the police, while one member of the Force retired to hospital with a damaged stomach."

"The sound of the English county families baying for broken glass" (*Decline and Fall*, page 2) was not quite dead; in sober St. Edmund Hall there was one last room-wrecking during my time—the victim (now a judge) had been heard expressing Socialist opinions at dinner. But in general we reserved our violence for politics and polemics. A Communist in my college spent two days in jail and had his scholarship taken away for shouting anti-Empire slogans in a West Country cinema. (He is now Russian Affairs correspondent of our Toriest daily newspaper.) Two Ruskin College men published books—Roger Dataller's *A Pitman looks At Oxford*, and John Brown's *I Saw For Myself*, a disillusioned account of Russia where he had been sent at Lord Nuffield's expense. A strange symposium, *Red Rags*, "Essays of Hate from Oxford", edited by Richard Comyns Carr, included a contribution from Mr. Quintin Hogg. Keith Briant

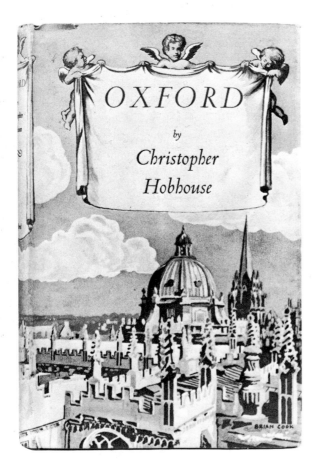

'Street Scene', 1933–9, by Barnett Freedman

wrote *Oxford Unlimited* which was remembered for one sentence: "It is doubtful if more than 20 per cent of undergraduettes have intercourse during their University life." This was headlined in a Sunday paper—"Girls' Orgies in Men's Rooms."

Undergraduate novels were fashionable: Tangye Lean, editor of the *Isis* and afterwards Controller of the BBC's European Service, wrote *Storm Over Oxford*, which features a room-wrecking and a duel. Shamus Frazer, who affected a monocle and a straw-boater, wrote *Acorned Hog*, a Waugh-type farce about the nationalization of Oxford by a Socialist politician named James Laxative. Frazer became a local hero: Lean was thrown into the Cherwell.

We felt guilty at enjoying Oxford so much. We liked to think of ourselves and Cambridge as decadent: had not Sir Michael Sadleir, Master of University College, recently said that Oxford in the next few years would "yield pride of place to London and lesser universities"? After us the deluge. Cambridge appeared to us more liberated (they could drink in pubs), more committed to action instead of theory. This was the Cambridge from which Philby and Burgess had recently come down. There, being—not just pretending to be—homosexual was a form of protest, inherited from the "Apostles" tradition of Maynard Keynes and Morgan Forster. Cambridge did not only talk; Cambridge *did*, Cambridge was committed to political action. Goronwy Rees saw this going on in the mind of Guy Burgess, whose "hatred of capitalism . . . was that of a disappointed and embittered imperialist who rejects it because of its failures." Tom Harrisson, who had left Cambridge after a rebellious year and had then organized an Oxford University expedition to Borneo, published a notorious *Letter to Oxford* in 1933 in which he tried to define the difference between Oxford and Cambridge: "Cam produces men with bigger bodies than brains, rather honest and English, reasonably intolerant, without intellectual conceit, vocally louder . . . less suddenly enthusiastic than Ox, with less intrinsic respect for politics and men . . . Cam talk is beertalk. Oxconversation is Sherryconversation." Harrisson, who in those days had a beard and red toenails on his bare feet, became a world-famous anthropologist and, when war came, was parachuted into Borneo to organize guerrillas before the Allied landings. Maybe he did us good.

About Cambridge, Sir Geoffrey Jackson has nothing but happy memories of innocent pleasures—records by the Hot Club de France, girls in punts in polka-dot silk dresses, young pacifists who were also putting in time at the University Air Squadron, a total unsnobbishness about money, wearing his father's 30s. dinner jacket, swimming to Grantchester and back, singing madrigals in punts on the Backs, and a leather-jacketed John Cornford, leader of the Federation of Socialist Societies, who was to die in Spain. Sir Geoffrey lived on scholarships worth £160 a year—£2 less than I had.

Though rebellious, we accepted proctorial discipline (the Union in 1938 even voted for the retention of the proctorial system). The reason was probably the comparative liberty after the rigid incarceration of school. Yet this was the decade in which so many public schoolboys committed almamatricide—in novels and by direct action. An unhappy youth called Richard Rumbold wrote *Little Victims*, a novel about homosexuality at public schools, in a style heavily influenced by Richard Aldington: the two unforgettable lines of dialogue, which we used to chant over our beer-tankards, were "Honour thy father and mother—what bloody cant!" and "I'm in love at last—and with a *woman!*" And Derek Walker-Smith wrote a much better-balanced public-school novel, *Out of Step*.

Boys, some of whom achieved notoriety, ran away from school. Giles Romilly, second cousin of the Mitford girls (of whom Jessica too had, and eventually used, her "running away money"), and nephew of Winston Churchill, ran away from Wellington at the age of fifteen and went to London, where he edited a magazine called *Out of Bounds*, selections from which became a best-selling book. "Winston's Red Nephew" was joined by his brother Esmond (who "ran away" with Jessica to the Spanish Civil War as correspondent for the *News Chronicle*) and also by Philip Toynbee (who became President of the Oxford Union in spite of running away from Rugby at the age of eighteen). *Out of Bounds*, which was praised by Bernard Shaw and the *New Statesman*, had a circulation of three thousand and correspondents in all leading public schools, and its manifesto began: "We attack the vast machinery of propaganda which forms the basis of Public Schools, and makes them so useful in the preservation of a vicious form of society . . ."

Making fun of public schools, sometimes enviously,

'The Tennis Player'. Art Deco figure in bronze and ivory by Frederick Preiss, about 1932

was now stock material for cabaret entertainers. On one level the broadcasting Western Brothers were singing 'Play the Game, You Cads!' and occasionally interjecting 'He Was Drunken and Magdalen'; on another, Ronald Frankau, brother of Gilbert and uncle of Pamela ("I'm the only *intentional* comedian ever produced by Eton"), much of whose material was too "hot" for the BBC, was singing—

*Eton and Winchester, Rugby and Harrow,*
*What's bred in the bone must come out in the marrow;*
*Charterhouse, Clifton, Marlborough, Repton—*
*How wet are the pillows the new boys have wept on!*
*. . . For I'm terribly, terribly British,*
*And that's what I like about me . . .*
*I haven't got any emotions at all,*
*'Cause I'm terribly British, you see—*

These were the schools that Hitler admired, on which he was said to be basing his own "youth castles", and which had now betrayed themselves at the Oxford Union.

In America, the American Student Union had followed Oxford pacifism in a resolution "not to support any war which the Government may undertake" (1936), yet by the following year it was urging "repeal or modification of the Neutrality Act." And earlier, in 1934, 25,000 American students had left their classrooms in a Strike Against War, many of them sacrificing their academic careers to do so. To presidents and deans it was "bad manners". Roger Chase, editor of the *Columbia Spectator*, said that American students had "come of age after the infantilism of the 1920's." A year later, 175,000 students struck, saying that "American colleges are going to continue to supply real leadership in the campaign against national involvement, by profit-seeking bankers and businessmen, in the forthcoming European war."

The President of the National Student Federation of America in 1930 was Egbert Roscoe Murrow, better known as Ed, whose first radio programme, with Chet Williams of CBS, was *University of the Air*. The Federation had grown out of the Intercollegiate World Court Congress which had met at Princeton in 1925. Ed Murrow organized cheap tours to Europe for American undergraduates, and visiting debating teams from Oxford and Cambridge. Often the Americans attended the Confédération Internationale des Étudiants in Brussels, where they

were considered either too idealistic or downright frivolous. They were bewildered by the nationalism of European students, who were generally older. At congresses in Prague, Rome, Budapest and Brussels it was the new nations that were most difficult—Czechs and Poles arguing over Teschen, Poles and Lithuanians over Vilna, Hungarians and Romanians over Transylvania, Poles and Germans over Danzig. At least the Americans learnt what was wrong with the Treaty of Versailles.

Yet Murrow, and his friend Professor Stephen Pierce Duggan, who taught political science at the City College of New York, believed obstinately in "international peace through education". They rescued persecuted students and intellectuals from Europe—no easy task in the Depression with five thousand American Ph.D's unemployed—and by January 1934, after seven months' work, an interuniversity "emergency committee" had placed fifty-three refugee scholars in thirty-eight universities, including the theologian Paul Tillich, and eventually Martin Buber, Herbert Marcuse and Jacques Maritain.

Doing, not merely talking or dreaming. Were there American students who, like us at Oxford, wanted to stay at university for ever, taking new degrees every other year, anything rather than venture into the cold, jobless world outside? Wearing our blue Russian shirts and sandals, our teddy-bear and coonskin coats, our velvet trousers; listening to Richard Crossman's account of how he was converted to Socialism by his own lectures on National Socialism, or to a man called William Joyce, one day to become famous as "Lord Haw-Haw" on Hamburg Radio, at the Fascist Club, surrounded by men with knuckle-dusters, saying exactly the opposite; seeing R. C. Sherriff, who had used his sudden wealth after the success of *Journey's End* to send himself to Oxford at the age of thirty-three, coaching the New College boat; watching the freshmen tubbing in front of large mirrors to study their own style ("Just remember that you work the oar as if you were turning your mother's mangle backwards"); Dennis Price, a future film star, in his Noël Coward dressing-gown, drinking champagne for breakfast ("So decadent, dear boy!"); a chamber-pot, placed at unthinkable physical risk, on the top of the Radcliffe Camera; the conviction that most of us would be dead in five years' time; we knew, even then, that we should never have it so good again.

# CHAPTER
## VII

# HOT AND SWEET

The word is "crooner". It comes from a Dutch verb meaning to groan or whimper, and it was used to describe a kind of vocalist who was developed by radio and the use of microphones in dance-halls. It was a gentle style which went with the new "sweet" music—one of the two broad divisions in popular music of the 1930's, the other being "hot", applied to certain jazz elements which were creeping into otherwise "commercial" dance music. Our elders, concerned with the virility of the race, thought crooning effeminate, enervating, decadent. It was all right for mothers to croon their babies to sleep, but quite unsuitable for declaring one's love to a girl. Our elders also thought the new "scat" singing of Louis Armstrong and Cab Calloway decadent because it was savage; and anyway they were Negroes, weren't they?

In America there were Rudy Vallee, Russ Colombo, and Bing Crosby, who would soon out-sing both and become a forty-year wonder. In Britain we had Al Bowlly, Sam Browne, Denny Dennis (né Pountain) and Jack Plant: Al and Sam sang mostly with London bands, but Jack and Denny toured the country's dance-halls as well. Listening to them on old 78s today, it is hard to understand what all the fuss was about. Sometimes they spoke the words rather than sang them: their diction was good (it had to be, for song-lyrics were getting sophisticated, with internal rhymes in the Lorenz Hart–Coward–Porter manner, and new cross-rhythms); and they developed a trick of seeming to lag behind the time and then catching up with it by the end of the phrase, with minor alterations and improvisations which gave each tune their own stamp of personality. They were bringing a new element of interpretation into the popular romantic song, something of the *diseuse* in French cabaret. All this was new in the Thirties.

Harry Lillis Crosby, born in Tacoma, Washington, in 1904, owed much of his success to his old school,

The Boswell Sisters

Gonzaga High, Spokane, a Jesuit establishment where oratory and elocution were stressed: this developed the art of phrasing which made his singing so clear. Because of his fondness for a comic strip called *Bingville Bugle* (or possibly because as a boy he was given an electric toy streetcar with a bell that went bing-bing) he acquired his first name. At Gonzaga University, where he read law, Bing joined a band known as the Musicaladers. Meeting up with Harry Barris and Mildred Bailey's brother Al Rinker, he formed a trio called the Rhythm Boys.

They specialized in "close harmony", which was becoming high fashion and was about to give the Boswell Sisters, the Mills Brothers and other trios and quartets to the world. The Boswells were led by the eldest sister Connie, who, though paralysed from the waist down and confined to a wheel chair, produced a contralto "blues" voice of astonishing power from her small, thin body. The Mills Brothers—John, Herbert, Harry and Donald—had begun as "Four Boys and a

Kazoo". One night they forgot the kazoo, and John imitated it by humming through his cupped hands. Soon they were imitating muted trumpets, saxophones and sousaphone (John doing the deep bass pom-poms). Their phrasing and smooth *crescendi* were a joy to hear. When John died their father, John Snr., a barber, took over his part in the family act.

The Rhythm Boys were heard in Los Angeles by Paul Whiteman, whose orchestra was creating what he called "symphonic jazz". (Jazz it never was, but no matter.) And the Rhythm Boys made their first nation-wide appearance in *The King of Jazz* (1930), one of the first film musicals. To Bing's eternal disgrace, it was in Seattle, in his home state of Washington, that he was fired by Whiteman "for not having a serious attitude about his work." It is true he sometimes forgot the words and had to sing "boo-boo-boo" till he could find a piece of lyric he could remember. Worse still, the audience often liked the boo-boo-boo more than the words, especially when he did a little throat-shake on the last boo.

The Rhythm Boys disbanded, and Bing married Dixie Lee, a rising movie starlet at Fox. He made a few short films for Mack Sennett, and then, one day in 1932, his brother Everett, now his business manager, sent a record to William Paley, President of Columbia Broadcasting System. The record was 'I Surrender, Dear', as Bingy a song as ever was. It got him to the Paramount Theater, New York, for an unheard-of run of twenty weeks. The Bing baritone was instantly successful in Britain, as the Vallee tenor had never been, in 'Please', 'When the Blue' (shake) 'of the Night' (shake) 'meets the Gold' (shake) 'of the Day', 'Swinging on a Star', 'Home on the Range', and 'Once in a Blue Moon'. Meanwhile he had met Jack Kapp, head of Decca Records, who is credited with having both toned down Bing's style (not so many boo-boos) and extended its range by making him sing *any* kind of song, including 'Ave Maria' and hymns.

To Hollywood in *Mississippi, Pennies from Heaven* and many another film, yet still faithful in his fashion to CBS, which he did not leave until 1936, when the prospect of starring in NBC's "Kraft Music Hall" proved irresistible. In this radio monument to cheese he stayed for ten years, taking time off to make more films—*Waikiki Wedding, Sing You Sinners, Eastside of Heaven*. Not until the 1940s did he team up with Bob Hope in the famous *Roads to . . .* series. But his musical reputation was already secure: in 1937 Gonzaga

Jack Payne, 1937, by Edmond X. Kapp

Jack Hylton

Guy Lombardo and his Royal Canadians

University made him an honorary Doctor of Music.

It was the golden age of the Big Band and the gorgeous arrangement, when freelance orchestras could command high fees and need have no doubts about whether a phrase was too difficult, so high was the standard of execution among dance-band players. In an era of two few and badly paid jobs in symphony orchestras, it was tempting for graduates of academies of music to join dance-bands. Thus Jack Payne had Eric Siday and Jean Pougnet as violinists, and Jack Hylton had a viola-player named Harry Berly who, had he not died young, might have rivalled Lionel Tertis. Lew Stone, whose band was at the Monseigneur Restaurant in London, had a classical pianist named Monia Liter, and—if he so desired, and he did—could score a chorus for three flutes in addition to the normal band equipment.

Each big band had to have its own instantly recognizable sound. In England Henry Hall, now in charge of the BBC Dance Orchestra, had "thick" orchestrations, not very sensitive to the tone-colour of each instrument. Carroll Gibbons, at the Savoy, was unmistakeable—the velvet piano touch, the moving thirds inside the right-hand octaves, the left-hand tenths rolling backwards. Jack Jackson at the Dorchester—well, the brass, and Jack's own trumpet, told you at once. Roy Fox—did ever a man play a muted trumpet more sweetly? Like all the big bands, he introduced himself with a "signature tune": 'Whispering'.

America, too, had "sweet bands", like Eddie Duchin's and Victor Young's; Ray Ventura's and Leo Reisman's; and above all, Guy Lombardo's Royal Canadians, billed as "the sweetest music this side of Heaven." The four Lombardo brothers, Guy (violin), Carmen (saxophone), Lebert (trumpet) and Victor had formed the nucleus of their band in London, Ontario, as long ago as 1917. If you were in any doubt about their identity, you listened for the sound of the two pianos.

But there were new big band sounds on the way. "Hot" and "sweet" were beginning to mingle, white players were learning from black as the segregation rules were relaxed to allow them to play together; and the new synthesis was labelled "swing", which meant different things to different people. The younger historians of popular music, especially those who write sleeve-notes, date the Swing Era variously from 1935–45 to 1939–49. Yet we were talking about

Swing long before that, and Duke Ellington, using his wa-wa mutes, had given us 'It don't mean a thing if it ain't got that swing'. Swing was attacked in the *Radio Times* by Percy Scholes, the musicologist, and furiously defended by a young freelance named Alan Jenkins—the year was 1936.

You could "swing" a number, taking "swing" to mean a quality of rhythm (precise and light, the slapped double-bass instead of the mushy sousaphone), without having a big band. Yet Swing became identified with big bands, especially bands that one went to hear without necessarily dancing to them or demanding any other entertainment on the bill. So December 22, 1935, is a key date: this was the night when the Paramount Theater, New York, booked Glen Gray's Casa Loma Orchestra. Other theatres followed this wild success: there were hardly enough bands to fill them, all over America.

In May, 1936, a twenty-six-year-old clarinettist named Artie Shaw (formerly Arthur Arshawsky) gave a "swing" concert at New York's Imperial Theater, leading a curious group consisting of himself, a string quartet, bass and drums which played, among other things, a composition of his own, Interlude in B Flat. This group became the nucleus of a bigger band at the Lexington Hotel, and later at the Lincoln and the Pennsylvania. Eventually he dropped the string quartet and built the band conventionally around brass and saxophones, using new arrangers as if he wanted to respond to every new trend. He played unwritten jazz with his "little band", the Gramercy Five: his big band by now, said his trumpeter Billy Butterfield, was "not a jazz band—just a nice, pretty band." Shaw's clarinet style was quieter, more sinuous and romantic than Benny Goodman's—"loud isn't hot", he used to say—and numbers like 'One Night Stand', 'Traffic Jam' and a best-selling arrangement of 'Begin the Beguine' show what he meant. Artie Shaw, having made a great deal of money and married several times, announced his retirement in 1939, saying that he had really always wanted to be a writer. He had been for three or four years the idol of American youth, whom he now called "the morons". "Goodman swung," one member of his band summed up, "but Shaw was more modern."

Goodman, meanwhile, was not to be outdone. Teenagers were queueing at six o'clock on the morning of March 10, 1937, outside the Paramount

Benny Goodman and Gene Krupa in 1938

Theater to hear his concert of Swing, the police vainly trying to control them. Once inside, nearly 3,700 boys and girls milled around, listening, cheering, jitterbugging (a new word which, like "alligator", "in the groove", "boogie-woogie", and "jam session", had just entered the language). Even greater was the success of the Carnegie Hall concert on January 16, 1938. To the stars of Goodman's own orchestra—Gene Krupa, drums; Jess Stacy, piano; Harry James and Ziggy Elman, trumpets—were added guest soloists: Count Basie, Teddy Wilson, Lionel Hampton doing impossible stick-juggling things with the vibraphone, saxophonists Johnny Hodges and Harry Carney and trumpeter Cootie Williams from Duke Ellington's band.

This enormously long concert was recorded for posterity. One recording went to the Library of Congress; another Goodman took home with him and forgot about for twelve years until his daughter.

found it in a cupboard. It was taped and transferred to two long-playing records. Whether with his full orchestra or his trio, Goodman made a tremendous impact on both highbrow and lowbrow music-lovers; and it was said that he was leading his fans back to the classics. Did not some of his improvisations remind one of the forty-eight Preludes and Fugues? Did he not take refresher lessons from Reginald Kell, the Yorkshireman who was then reckoned to be the finest clarinet player in the world?

What's bigger than the Carnegie Hall? The open air. So it came about, in the spring of 1938, Randall's Island, New York, was thrown open to a "Carnival of Swing", with twenty-five bands and two thousand three hundred jitterbugs in a performance lasting nearly six hours.

"Swinging the classics", intending no disrespect, was fashionable. Tommy Dorsey ("the Sentimental Gentleman of Swing") did an arrangement of Rimsky-Korsakov's *Chanson Hindoue*. The British jazz pianist Arthur Young set Shakespeare's lyrics to new tunes. A blind pianist named Alec Templeton composed a kind of syncopated fugue, 'Bach Goes to Town'. A coloured musician of great versatility, Reginald Foresythe, much more popular in America than in England, tried to develop a kind of jazz chamber music, using only reed instruments (including bassoon), piano and drums, in strictly written arrangements with offbeat "sophisticated" titles like 'Serenade for a Wealthy Widow' and 'Dodging a Divorcee'. Music critics thought they detected in his "new music" the influence of Erik Satie. In France, the Hot Club of Paris, unimpressed by big bands, followed the precedent of Joe Venuti's Blue Four and concentrated on brilliant classics-inspired improvisation with Stéphan Grappelly's violin and Django Reinhardt's guitar.

In Britain, we waited eagerly for Duke Ellington to arrive. During the Depression years there were labour laws allowing British and American musicians to play in each other's countries only on an exchange basis, and for the same rates of pay. When the Ellington band finally got to London and went on tour, "serious" musicians joined the young audience to study Barney Bigard's clarinet technique, and Constant Lambert, from 'Mood Indigo' onwards, had begun to hail the Duke, not only as a jazz artist, but as "an American composer". A careful distinction was drawn between the true Duke (Creole Rhapsody) and the commercial Duke ('Drop Me Off at Harlem', 'Ducky-Wucky', 'Sophisticated Lady'): like many band-leaders, he sometimes used his "hot" reputation to sell "commercial" records to non-connoisseurs, strictly rationing the jungle sounds. On stage, the Duke used a new effect: Adelaide Hall, in almost total darkness, leaning against the side of the proscenium, silhouetted as she sang 'Stormy Weather'—you never saw her face till the lights went up.

Claude Hopkins, Bob Crosby, Chick Webb—black bands, white bands, hot bands, sweet bands—and towards the end of the Thirties, something new happened to Swing: it "went sweet", some said, and the sounds of Glenn Miller and Woody Herman began to be heard. The Glenn Miller sound—which those who didn't like it compared with a cinema-organ—was achieved by mixing reeds, "clarinets on top", hitherto considered "bad arranging". It had started by accident when high trumpeter Pee Wee Erwin left the band and his replacement couldn't hit top notes sweetly and *legato*; so a B-flat clarinet was slipped in to take the high melody line. The formula, rigidly applied—and it was no use working for Miller if you couldn't accept discipline—was immensely successful for five years. "Let people *see* you're enjoying the music," Miller told his musicians. Part of a number which had once been known as 'Moten Swing' when it was played by Bennie Moten's Kansas City Orchestra now became the hypnotically repetitive 'In The Mood' (1939) and sold two million records. Miller too, at a time when it was reckoned that America was spending ninety million dollars a year on listening to bands, gave concerts at the Paramount Theater, the keening reeds and the ooh-wah brass occasionally interrupted by vocalists Marion Hutton and Ray Eberle, and a close-harmony group, the Modernaires. 'Tuxedo Junction', 'Chattanooga Choo-Choo' (a million and a quarter records) and the famous signature-tune, 'Moonlight Serenade'—these are among his memorials.

It seemed that there was room for any kind of band, any soloist with a new style—the slap-tongue, breathy *vibrato* of Coleman Hawkins on tenor saxophone; a straight four-in-a-bar club pianist with a crippled left hand named Charlie Kunz; a pianist called Gerald Bright who led Geraldo's Gaucho Tango Orchestra; a coloured blind pianist named

(above) Woody Herman
(left and opposite) Glenn Miller in *Sun Valley Serenade*

(below) Art Tatum and Mildred Bailey

Art Tatum who could read music only in Braille, could span twelve notes with his left hand and was watched for hours by Vladimir Horowitz to see how he could play Chopin with wrong fingering.

Into ballrooms came new dances. The rumba rhythm was introduced by Charles B. Cochran in his 1931 Revue with a song of complicated structure, 'The Pea-Nut Vendor'. Soon bands were equipping themselves with strange new instruments, maracas, claves, bongos and gourds, and slowly the new dance entered the ballrooms to tunes like 'Piccolo Pete' and 'Yuba and his Tuba'. Another jollier dance called the Conga, which demanded that everyone hold on to someone in front and progress round the floor in a giant serpent, followed it. The Continental, an energetic, hopping, together-and-apart dance with lifts and turns, introduced by Fred Astaire and Ginger Rogers in *The Gay Divorcée* (1934), had a brief vogue, but was too complicated for most people. Much easier to do was the Big Apple, a sort of

'The Big Apple'

square-dance invented by Carolina students.

From Europe, a new style of intimate singing, well suited to radio—that of "continental cabaret", with Greta Keller ('*Eine Kleine Reise*'—'Just a Little Ramble'— sung in two languages on one record), Jean Sablon ('Le Fiacre'), Charles Trenet ('Boum!'), Lucienne Boyer, afterwards reviled for singing to German officers, who sang 'Parlez moi d'Amour'. The Corsican Tino Rossi, falsetto-tenor ('Un Chaland qui passe'); to know them was to be a connoisseur.

Something was happening to the lyrics of Anglo-American songs. The complex rhyme schemes of Lorenz Hart, Coward and Porter were finding imitators such as Eric Maschwitz, who with composer Jack Strachey wrote 'These Foolish Things' (1936)—

> *The smile of Garbo and the scent of roses,*
> *The waiters whistling as the last bar closes,*
> *The song that Crosby sings—*
> *These Foolish Things remind me of you.*

There were hints of promiscuity in 'Gather Lip Rouge While You May' and 'I'm Young and Healthy—and So Are You'; and Sophie Tucker disturbed a number of people in 1930 with Jack Yellen's lyric,

> *. . . get his clothes and help him pack:*
> *If your kisses can't hold the man you love,*
> *Then your tears won't bring him back.*

As for Coward and Porter themselves, the one self-made from boy-actordom onwards, the other a playboy born so rich that in 1930, dissatisfied with the Japanese train service, he hired a special train to take his party to Kyoto, they were extending the whole scope of the show song that became the standard hit for years to come. Coward wrote his shows as a whole; Porter was hired by producers to provide songs after the main outline had been settled. Porter, staying the weekend with Mrs. Vincent Astor, heard his hostess complaining that a gutter needed mending—"that drip, drip, drip is driving me crazy." So was born the opening verse of 'Night and Day'—"the drip, drip, drip of the raindrops"—leading to a refrain that was sixteen bars too long, out of vocal range, and, Cole said, was "inspired by a muezzin calling the faithful to prayers in Morocco." In 'The Physician' (epiglottis, pelvic girdle, medulla oblongata etc.) he wrought miracles of medical double-entendre, claiming that he had taken a course in anatomy before writing it. And *Anything Goes* (1935) yielded two songs that contain the whole of Cole—'I Get A Kick Out of You' (bored playboy) in which "I get no kick from cocaine" had to be changed to "...from champagne" for popular consumption, and 'You're the Top!' which, like 'Let's Do It', lent itself to endless parody and topical allusion. In New York it contained jokes about Rockefellers and Roosevelts, but in Britain most politics were banned for fear of offending the Dictators. In the fresh lyrics written for London, "Bendel bonnet" became "Ascot bonnet", "dress from Saks" became a "dress by Patou", and "Irene Bordoni" was changed to "Tallulah Bankhead". I do

not understand the obituarist of Porter who said that "his lyrics got worse as his tunes got better."

Noël Coward went on producing ever-more ingenious lyrics to deathless tunes, in shows that seemed to get shorter runs. Thus *Words and Music* (1932) yielded 'Mad Dogs and Englishmen', first sung by Beatrice Lillie in New York in 1931, 'Mad About the Boy' and 'The Party's Over Now'; *Conversation Piece* (1934) had 'I'll Follow My Secret Heart'; and *Operette* (1937) contained 'The Stately Homes of England.' In *Private Lives* and *To-night at 8.30* he did his parlour-trick of introducing songs into otherwise straight plays—'Someday I'll Find You', and 'Play, Orchestra, Play!'

Cole Porter and Peggy Mann

Richard Rodgers and Lorenz Hart, in *On Your Toes*, produced two numbers in one show that went round the world, 'There's A Small Hotel' and—a novelty for 1936—the second-act ballet, *Slaughter on Tenth Avenue*. And one of Hart's lyrics, from *The Boys from Syracuse* (1938) could be said to sum up, better than any other poetry of the decade, the New York attitude towards love in the insecure Thirties:—

*Falling in love with love*
  *Is falling for make-believe . . .*
*Learning to trust is just*
  *For children in school.*

(Cole Porter said it another way in 'Just One Of Those Things'.) In all this romance, the symbols—"sophisticated"—were cigarettes, champagne, cocktails for two, evening dress. Maschwitz's cigarette showed "a lipstick's traces"; another writer imagined 'Two Cigarettes In the Dark'; there were 'Cocktails for Two'—or, for teetotallers, a soft drink extracted from a Mexican plant:

*Would you like to take a walk?*
*Mm-mm-mm*
*How about a sarsaparilla?*
*Gee, the moon is yella!*
*Something good'll come from that!*

In America, Sammy Cahn and Johnny Mercer were up and coming; and in Britain, Jimmy Kennedy and Michael Carr, whose mothers may or may not have come from Ireland, saw red sails in the sunset, sang of Mexico way, south of the border, where they had never been, ordered the covered wagon to roll along and begged to be carried back to green pastures. Love was in bloom; lovers encounter one another in the Isle of Capri; and a lot of people were 'doing the Lambeth Walk'.

What was known in Britain as "good" music was reaching a wider public, on both sides of the Atlantic, without producing any major new talent (young Ben Britten seemed versatile and prolific, but you couldn't yet predict his staying power). William Walton's *Belshazzar's Feast*, incorporating what were thought to be "jazz" rhythms, had a sensational debut at Leeds Festival in 1931, and Vaughan Williams produced a Fourth Symphony in 1935. His great *Serenade to Music*, celebrating the Henry Wood Jubilee in 1938, was famously recorded with sixteen star soloists. Arnold Bax's Fifth Symphony? Romantic waves

pounding, Celtic-eclectic, harmonies thicker than Delius's. Ravel's *Bolero?* It had been composed in 1928, but it didn't hit the Promenade Concerts till a few years later, and, while it was wildly applauded, many people thought it was a joke. Walton's long-awaited Symphony, full of disturbing counter-rhythms, ominous discords and echoes of Sibelius, was first performed in 1934, without the last movement, because he couldn't finish it in time.

It seemed that all the great composers (except Sibelius) were dead. Elgar, Delius, Holst had all gone, within a few months of each other, in 1934. Ravel and Gershwin died in 1937, both of brain tumours. There was still Sibelius, thank heaven; but would he stay sober enough to complete an 8th Symphony?

Rarely does Britain produce links between classical and popular music, but in these years there were two: Spike Hughes and Constant Lambert. Hughes, son of a music critic, had written about jazz and won a good deal of appreciation for it. He had also composed and recorded (with Benny Carter's Orchestra) some attractive numbers in the Ellington tradition. When he composed a whole jazz ballet, *High Yellow*, Ernest Newman, *Sunday Times* music critic, exploded: "Spike Hughes? No doubt we shall soon be hearing of Two-Gun Walton."

Lambert, composer, conductor and music critic of the *Sunday Referee*, published in 1934 a witty, analytical and sometimes irreverent book which was read by people who did not normally read books about music. The subtitle of *Music Ho!* was *A Study of Music in Decline*. Lambert looked for revolution, and found none since 1914, not even in George Antheil, who had written something for sixteen pianos, an electric buzzer, an aeroplane propeller and a pneumatic drill. Of John Cage, whose Construction I (1938) used piano strings played with felt-headed sticks, he had not yet heard. Why was there no contemporary *Sacré du Printemps*, *Pierrot Lunaire?* Poetry, painting and sport were mixed in his metaphors, from Baudelaire to Borotra by way of Debussy. We were in one of art's "neurasthenic periods". After the "deliberate silliness" of the 1920's, Stravinsky was creating a fashion for boredom. English composers were burdened by their "Anglo-Irish melodic line" and their love of folk-songs—whoever heard a bus-conductor whistling folk-songs? Now that Elgar was dead, there was no

English composer, not even vaughan Williams, who could address an international audience. Sibelius alone in Europe could do that; and perhaps, in America, Duke Ellington, "the most distinguished [composer of] popular music since Johann Strauss . . . I know nothing in Ravel so dextrous in treatment as the varied solos in the ebullient 'Hot and Bothered', and nothing in Stravinsky more dynamic than the final section." 'Mood Indigo', like Cole Porter's 'Love for Sale', could stand beside Alban Berg's Lyric Suite and Sibelius's 7th Symphony as world masterpieces.

The classics were becoming hackneyed because people listened to the radio too much. Unhelpful was the *Gebrauchsmusik* attitude of Hindemith, who said that a composer should only write when asked to. Bartók was just navel-staring. Prokofiev was "bourgeois". Schönberg's cerebral tricks were sometimes "as childish as the prep-school puns in *Anna Livia Plurabelle* . . ."

London now laid some claim to be the centre of the musical world, if only because Germany and Austria

Sir John Reith, 1932, by Sir William Rothenstein

were in decline. Sir Henry Wood's long white baton still swished audibly at the Promenade Concerts, and he introduced at least a dozen new works each season among the well-loved 'lollipops': in 1937 there were compositions by Germaine Tailleferre, Malipiero, Constant Lambert, Kodály, Rubbra, Walton and Alan Bush. Sir Walford Davies broadcast little talks on "this Symphony business". Indeed BBC sponsorship was keeping alive both the Proms and one of the country's two leading symphony orchestras: the other was the London Philharmonic, founded by Sir Thomas Beecham in 1932. How Sir Adrian Boult got the jobs of Director of Music at Broadcasting House and conductor of the B.B.C. Symphony Orchestra is told in these words from the Director-General, Sir John Reith, in 1931:

"I don't care whether my music director plays the comb, the trumpet or what, as long as he plays the music. But if I phone him in the afternoon before a concert I don't want him unobtainable . . . They tell me that the orchestra plays better for you than any of the other blokes they've worked with."

In 1937 Sir Adrian took the Orchestra on its first European tour. In Vienna they played a piece by Schönberg which had never been given in Vienna (Schönberg's birthplace) before: the audience hated it. Afterwards the President of Austria asked Boult: "But who *is* this Schönberg?"

American broadcasting had from the outset been largely in the hands of commercial sponsors; and so "good music", following the pioneer work of NBC in the 1920's, was sponsored by manufacturers of cigarettes and mouthwashes and cars. Philco, who made radio sets, backed the Philadelphia Orchestra. CBC in 1930 began offering the New York Philharmonic on Sunday afternoons. On Saturday afternoons you could get the Metropolitan Opera from NBC, who, around Christmas 1937, got Toscanini to conduct weekly concerts, with a studio audience whose programmes were made of satin so that they wouldn't rustle. The Ford Hour offered the Detroit Symphony Orchestra on Sundays, and in 1938 was the fifth most popular programme.

In 1939 there were 270 symphony orchestras in the U.S.A., sixteen times as many as there had been a quarter of a century before; and it was claimed that the combined radio audiences for the Metropolitan Opera, New York Philharmonic and the Ford Hour was $10\frac{1}{4}$ million families a week. America's answer to

(right) Sir Henry Wood, 1939, by E. Fairhurst
(below) Caricature of Sir Adrian Boult, about 1937, by Ernest Forbes

Walter Damrosch

Sir Walford Davies was Walter Damrosch, whose NBC Music Appreciation Hour was heard by seven million schoolchildren. So far from competing with the phonograph, radio helped record sales to increase sixfold in the years 1933–38. One station, WQXR New York, specialized in "good" music. These years also saw the founding by Koussevitzky in 1937 of the annual Berkshire Festival at Tanglewood, Mass.

Notice, in all this, the prominence of opera, helped by films with singing stars—and perhaps by Gershwin's *Porgy and Bess*, which in 1935 bridged the gulf between, say, *Carmen* and *Show Boat*, and changed a young Negro named Todd Duncan, who sang Porgy, from an obscure professor of music at Howard University, Washington, into the first male Negro ever to sing in opera.

In Britain, Philip Snowden, Labour Chancellor of the Exchequer, entered into partnership with the BBC to subsidize opera by putting up £17,500 of Government money a year for five years. This drew scorn from the *Daily Express*, to whom opera was "a form of art which is not characteristic of the British people." Covent Garden was temporarily saved, until Neville Chamberlain, least operatic of Chancellors, withdrew the subsidy in 1932, leaving the BBC to go it alone. Alone? Well, there was still Sadlers Wells, built in 1931, where you could get into the gallery for a shilling.

So we were not to get a State Opera. What we did get was the mad, undemocratic, glorious phenomenon of Glyndebourne, which from 1934 onwards caused people to leave Victoria Station in full evening dress at 3.10 in the afternoon while the midday headlines were still screaming "Hitler Speaks!" and "Insurgents Take Santander".

Captain John Christie, M.C., a former Eton science master with a game leg and blind in one eye, whose family manufactured cinema organs, believed two things: that quality was more important than quantity, and that it was the duty of landowners to create employment in the surrounding district. His Tudor manor house "nestling in the Sussex Downs" had for some years been the scene of musical house parties at which single Acts of Wagner and Mozart operas were performed with piano, organ, singers and sometimes a small orchestra without brass. Christie himself played no instrument but occasionally sang and obliged on the cymbals. One of the visitors, to whom he paid £5 a week (twice as much as she had earned with the touring Carl Rosa Opera Company), he married: Audrey Mildmay. Glyndebourne—the press called it a "Pocket" or "Village" Opera House—was designed for 311 people to cater for "good opera at high prices rather than bad opera at low prices." Sometimes the audience followed the Austrian fashion of *Dirndl* and *Lederhosen*, but generally Christie "recommended" (i.e. insisted on) evening dress for the "English Bayreuth". Sir Thomas Beecham never bothered to answer his letters, but Fritz Busch, director of the Dresden Opera, responded and brought with him two producers, Carl Ebert and Rudolf Bing. "Do you realize what all this will cost?" asked Ebert when Christie told him his plans for the 1935 season (*Walküre, Siegfried, Rosenkavalier*, perhaps *Meistersinger* with a chorus of 200). But Christie seemed willing to lose £7,000 a season until the money ran out.

At the Lewes Petty Sessions in April 1934 Christie applied for a licence for singing, dancing and the sale of alcoholic liquor, and was told by the magistrates that, while opera could not be performed on Sundays, *Parsifal* might be given on Good Friday. There was some discomfort in having to gobble your dinner in time for curtain-up, but (even in the rain) you could attempt to picnic in the car or on the grass, trailing your white wine in the stream to cool it; or else (according to Christie's new rule) "patrons may also bring their own refreshments and consume them in the Dining Hall, and . . . if they wish, be waited on by their own servants." Was evening dress really appropriate, asked *The Times*? Lady Diana Cooper was not ashamed to be seen in "a blue and white printed day dress and a straw hat".

There were problems: bad acoustics; cheerful amateurism; failure to give musicians a proper contract so that they were sometimes playing elsewhere; the lack of an English coloratura to sing Queen of the Night; Sir Thomas Beecham saying nastily "Mozart needs no Busch!"; crises of casting which once necessitated asking Childs, Christie's batman-butler, to take a non-speaking part in Mozart's *Il Seraglio* (always called by its German name *Die Entführung aus dem Serail* at Glyndebourne); and Christie's tussles with his artistic staff as he discovered that he who pays the piper cannot always call the tune. There were complaints about giving so much work to foreign singers (the work-permits had been arranged by the poet Humbert Wolfe, who was a senior civil servant in the Ministry of Labour), and a row when Audrey Mildmay sang at the Nazified Salzburg Festival (Rudolf Bing called it "shaking hands with murderers").

But the family atmosphere prevailed. The trumpet call from *Fidelio* told you when to finish dinner in time for curtain-up. The wine list explained, as to children, what *Riesling* and *Auslese* meant. You did not show any surprise at seeing restaurant waiters suddenly appear on stage as soldiers in Verdi's *Macbetto* or (in July 1939, amid an explosive international situation) when Christie himself announced from the stage that Harrow had beaten Eton at Lord's for the first time since 1908. The programme gave unusual credits, for example: "Head Gardener: F. Harvey". How to explain the ineffable charm of Glyndebourne? Let Spike Hughes sum up: "A good dinner, a walk in somebody else's garden, and a sight of the orchestra playing croquet."

*(right)*
Visitors to Glyndebourne, 1934

*(opposite)*
W. H. Auden, by William Coldstream

# OVERTURES TO DEATH

I am twenty-three, unemployed, and staying in a room in Soho: 60, Frith Street, owned by a writer named Stephen Graham and let to impoverished or out-of-work journalists. I have actually not eaten for thirty-six hours; tomorrow I shall sink my pride and write to my father for money. So this is the *vie de Bohème*, these are the *Povertätsjähre*. . . . There is a tradition that Lytton Strachey once had an assignation with Carrington in this house. If so, I wonder how they coped with the bugs: one puts kerosene along the wainscot and drives them into the house next door, then the people next door put down kerosene and drive them back.

Soho in 1937 had all-night café-bars full of mandolines and Italian voices, and pubs where one could see poets and unreal characters with names like Count Potocki de Montalk, Ironfoot Jack and Overcoat Joe, waiting for some English Damon Runyon to make a book about them. Mostly the poets went to pubs north of Oxford Street—the Fitzroy Tavern and the Wheatsheaf—but at The Pillars of Hercules, in Greek Street, Dylan Thomas is on view, already drinking whisky. We have nothing in common except the fact that my father's family come from South Wales. I sit with my half pint of bitter and we talk about Dickens. Dylan thinks Dickens was only half an artist because Victorian prudery wouldn't let him write the whole truth. "If only," Dylan booms, "he could have given us all the piss and shit!"

I cannot, like so many others, boast that Dylan was sick on my carpet: I couldn't afford a carpet. He had published *Eighteen Poems* (1934), been hailed as a genius by Edith Sitwell, and followed them up with *Twenty-five Poems* (1936). Not yet the childhood sketches and orotund radio voice that reached the wider public. The interest of our unimportant meeting was simply that we were *not* talking about Spain. For Soho was full of young writers and out-of-

work film extras who were asking each other: "Have you seen Tony? He's been *under fire*." And then: "Aren't *you* going? Why not—are you a Trotskyist or something?"

In the Twenties most people had said: Life is bloody, politics is useless, there's nothing I can do about it. Now, since the Depression, some were saying: Yes, there *is* something I can do: I can join the workers, or possibly even the Communist Party—it might be the only way of actually meeting any workers. And if you felt like this, it stood to reason that you had to take sides, and the right side was the Left, the Republican, side, since a defeat of fascism in Spain might deter the Dictators, who were using Spain as a proving ground for their own weapons. Also it would be useful to learn the art of irregular warfare in case there was a revolution at home. We can see the Spanish Civil War, indeed the whole crescendo of fear before the Second World War which began in 1936, from many viewpoints, but most interestingly through the eyes of poets, to whom it seemed as big as the French Revolution had seemed to Wordsworth.

Dylan was labelled "difficult". Others—Auden, Spender, MacNeice, Day Lewis—all with a public-school-university education, now saw it as their duty to be understood, even if it meant producing a kind of verse-journalism. It has been said that Georgian poetry (Rupert Brooke and after) came to an end quite suddenly in 1930 when W. H. Auden published his first *Poems*. Let us stop moaning about the war and the dead, he seemed to be saying, and see what we can do to salvage civilization. From now on, poetry was to be about action, poems were to be pamphlets, they didn't have to be beautiful any more, they had to be loud and clear; and poets went abroad to see for themselves, in Berlin, China, Abyssinia. Just before he was killed in the 1914–1918 War, Wilfred Owen

*(opposite)* 'The Surrender of Barcelona', 1934–7, by Wyndham Lewis

had said that "poets can only warn". This was not enough for the new generation of poets: poetry must now report the true conditions of the masses, exhort society to action as Hugh McDiarmid had done, in Scots vernacular, in his *First Hymn to Lenin*. "Evolution the dance, revolution the steps"—Day Lewis's line became a slogan. Anthologies with titles like *New Signatures*, *New Country*, *Poetry and the People*, *Poems for Spain* appeared, and Geoffrey Grigson edited *New Verse*, which stamped its personality on the times but seldom sold more than a thousand copies.

Of the two thousand or so British volunteers who joined the International Brigade and fought on the Republican side in Spain, most were workers, generally unemployed miners. Auden, having written, in *Spain*,

> What's your proposal? To build the just city? I will.
> I agree. Or is it the suicide pact, the romantic
> Death? Very well, I accept, for
> I am your choice, your decision. I am Spain.

*(above)* Christopher Isherwood and W. H. Auden setting off for China, January 1938
*(below)* T. S. Eliot
*(opposite)* Devastation at Toledo during the Spanish Civil War

joined the crusade as a stretcher-bearer for two months, and when he came back, he said little. Other young men in Britain (but far fewer) fought for General Franco, and sometimes, at parties in London, one met people who in Spain had been trying to kill each other. I once asked a young Irish Guards officer why he had fought for Franco when it was perfectly clear that Franco represented fascism. He replied: "Well, I'm a Catholic, y'know. The Reds have been raping nuns. Nuns don't care for it, y'know."

Stephen Spender, having been invited to join the British Communist Party by its Secretary, Harry Pollitt, went to Spain on an assignment for the *Daily Worker*—"a fruitless hunt", Christopher Isherwood tells us, "for information about the interned crew of the Russian steamer *Komsomol*." "Spender's adventures," Isherwood adds, "as an amateur intelligence agent, snooping around Gibraltar and Tangiers, would make a great satirical novel." Returning, Spender wrote an embarrassingly honest article for the *Daily Worker* on his discomfort with the Party, especially its approval of the Moscow Trials, so that the Party treated him coldly ever afterwards.

The older poets, T. S. Eliot, Walter de la Mare, the Sitwells, wrote less, nodding cautious approval of the young, but seeming incapable of taking part in the movement; and John Masefield, the Poet Laureate,

wrote hardly at all in verse. Edith Sitwell, in 1936, making fun of Geoffrey Grigson's "brass Band of Hope", welcomed four new voices, William Empson ("his mind is deep, vital and well-stored . . . [but he is] an absolute victim to S's and soft C's"), Ronald Bottrall ("a poet with the finest mastery over technique, and with a definite and terrifying apprehension of the modern world"); Dylan Thomas, of course; and America's Archibald MacLeish, whom she did not like ("facile . . . surface prettiness . . . garrulous"). Miss Sitwell graded them according to their response to the Machine Age, which demanded "flawless mechanism, whose rhythms are hard and brilliant."

Cecil Day Lewis, a card-carrying member of the Communist Party, for some years seemed to swallow

Edith Sitwell, 1937, by Pavel Tchelitchew

its propaganda whole. He had the good fortune, in 1934, to be the subject of a gossip paragraph in a daily newspaper which reported that T. E. Lawrence had recommended Day Lewis to Winston Churchill as a poet of the future. "The telephone bell started ringing in the office of the Hogarth Press. Leonard and Virginia Woolf . . . had covered the stack of unsold copies" of Day Lewis's three books of verse "with chintz . . . and were using it as a settee." The settee, Day Lewis said, gradually subsided until the Woolfs were forced to sit on the floor. In 1938 he published *Overtures to Death*, some poems of which Byronically celebrated the cause of Republican Spain, such as *The Nabara*, a poem about a gallant Government trawler; using cadences that in another age would have been applied by a Newbolt or an Austin to deeds of Elizabethan derring-do, he wrote:

> *Freedom is more than a word, more than the base coinage*
> *Of statesmen . . .*
> *The year, Nineteen-thirty-seven: month, March: the men,*
> *    descendants*
> *Of those Iberian fathers . . .*

The role of the Poet as Hero fell to a Spaniard, Federico Garcia Lorca, poet and dramatist, executed by a Falangist firing squad at Viznar, Andalusia, in August 1936; and to John Cornford, a kind of Red Rupert Brooke, son of a Cambridge don (and of Frances Cornford who wrote "O fat white woman whom nobody loves"), poet, history scholar, winner of a double-first and a research scholarship, revolutionary and fighter, who personified all that it was to be a thinking, feeling student in the Thirties, and died at Cordova aged twenty-one:

> *Nothing is ever certain, nothing is safe . . .*
> *Everything dying keeps a hungry grip on life,*
> *Nothing is ever born without screaming and blood.*

"The sun may shine no doubt," wrote Louis MacNeice in *Autumn Journal*, a long poem full of the uneasiness of 1938 after Munich, "but how many people Will see it with their eyes in 1939?" Lying awake at night he feels shame; then—"Listen: a whirr, a challenge, an aubade—It is the cock crowing in Barcelona."

But to get the immediate smell of Spain, we must go to prose writers. George Orwell, issued with a forty-year-old Mauser rifle, fought with the P.O.U.M.

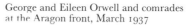

George and Eileen Orwell and comrades
at the Aragon front, March 1937

George Orwell, July 29th, 1935

(Marxist militia), was wounded in the neck by a sniper, and, being told that the P.O.U.M. was regarded by the Communists as a fascist "fifth column", escaped to France. "I had come to Spain with some notion of writing newspaper articles, but I had joined the militia almost immediately because ... it seemed the only conceivable thing to do." In Barcelona "it was the first time I had ever been in a town where the working class was in the saddle. Practically every building of any size had been seized by the workers and draped with red flags or with the red and black flag of the Anarchists . . . Almost every church had been gutted and its images burnt. . . . Even the bootblacks had been collectivised. . . . There were no private motor-cars, they had all been commandeered. . . . The bread queues were hundreds of yards long. . . . In the barber's shops were Anarchist notices solemnly explaining that barbers were no longer slaves. In the streets were coloured posters appealing to prostitutes to stop being prostitutes."

Wounded members of the International Brigade returning to London, March 1938

Arthur Koestler, correspondent for the London *News Chronicle* but also apparently working for *Agitprop* in Paris, was condemned to death as a spy by Franco's army, kept in solitary confinement for four months while hearing other prisoners being led away to execution, saved from execution by being exchanged for the wife of a Franco air pilot, and lived to write one of the best books on Spain, *Spanish Testament* (1937).

Ernest Hemingway, although he had said "no European country is our friend" and wanted America to stay out of other people's wars, became, early in 1937, chairman of the Ambulance Committee for the American Friends of Spanish Democracy. In a Madrid hotel, hit more than thirty times by shellfire, he wrote a bad play called *The Fifth Column* and a lot of excellent dispatches, most of which could be (and some were) turned into short stories by simply changing the titles.

In Paris, Anaïs Nin, sharing a house with Henry Miller and various visiting firemen, heard the stories brought back by artists who had gone to fight, or at least to look: how could one distinguish facts from propaganda? How could one not weep at the news?

"Blood. Massacres. Blood. Tortures. Cruelty. Fanaticism. People burned with gasoline. Stomachs ripped open in the shape of a cross. Nuns stripped naked. French surrealists have gone to Spain to fight. . . ."

It could be said, perhaps, that the British Government was right after all in refusing visas to volunteers for Spain, and even to delegates to the Communist-organized International Writers' Conference at Madrid in 1937 (Stephen Spender attended it with a forged passport provided by André Malraux), if it genuinely believed that the problems of Spain were simply not understood by naive British intellectuals (*lumpenintelligentsia*, someone called them) who seemed to think that Andalusia, Catalonia, Asturias, were constituted like Lancashire, Surrey, Devon. "I found the Catholics . . . supported Franco, thinking of him as the upholder of religion," said Christopher Hollis. "Public opinion at large opposed him, imagining that the so-called Loyalists were the defenders of the constitution. It is hard, as things have turned out, to decide which opinion was the more ridiculous." Everyone was motivated by fear: fear of

Russia on the Right, fear of fascism on the Left.

Yet there had been unofficial British intervention which, in a sense, had helped to set the war in motion; for General Franco, who had been Governor of the Canary Islands, had been conveyed from Las Palmas to Morocco and from Morocco to Spain to lead the "Nationalists" by aeroplanes financed and piloted by Englishmen.

Historians are still busy trying to reconstruct what actually happened in Spain. Twice as many people (800,000) were said to have been executed as had been killed in battle. True or false? Those prisoners massacred at Badajoz: was it in the bull-ring, and were there really 4,000 of them? Jason Gurney, sculptor, a figure of 1930's Chelsea, lost the use of a hand in the fearful battle of Jarama, in which, he said, less than 20 per cent of the men in his international unit had ever held a gun before. Gurney was later attached to the American Lincoln Battalion, which he found more efficient and more democratic than his British unit: that unit had been commanded by Wilfred Macartney, who had been in Parkhurst for spying for Russia and had written a best-seller about prison life called *Walls Have Mouths*. He was assisted by Tom Wintringham, afterwards hailed by the Left as an expert on guerrilla warfare. Gurney says that the middle-class intellectuals weren't much use, and praised the guts of East End youths and the Negroes of the Lincoln Battalion.

At Guernica, near Bilbao on the north coast, on April 26, 1937, the Condor Legion of the German Air Force, apparently as an experiment in total annihilation, wiped out a town of 7,000 people plus 3,000 refugees, at 4.30 p.m. on market day. Guernica, calling itself "Holy City of the Basques", became a symbol of terror. Lord Robert Cecil called its destruction "the most savage act in history". Certain Right-wing papers suggested that the Basques were all Communists and had blown up the town themselves for propaganda effect. Picasso painted his picture, which may have done some good; but indignation was overcome by fear, fear of what might happen to London in a future war.

Some of the idealism about Spain collapsed when, in January 1939, Auden and Isherwood left for America. We who were young felt betrayed; yet Cyril Connolly, believing that artists should stand aloof from wars, even from wars that had not yet begun, called it "the most important literary event since the outbreak of the Spanish War."

What did they find in America? American poets were mostly otherwise engaged. The Depression, producing much more violent effects in America, had given them anxieties which were not yet international. The America of Hart Crane was already in the past. Crane, alcoholic and aggressively homosexual, had been rescued from a career in advertising by Otto Kahn the banker so that he could work full time on *The Bridge*, a mystical view of America, past, present and future, which took him six

'Guernica', 1937, by Pablo Picasso

years to write. Crane felt that he was speaking to Whitman, Poe and other figures of American literature. As Whitman had been fascinated by the old Brooklyn Ferry as a symbol, so Crane regarded the new Brooklyn Bridge: "A bridge," he said, "is begun from the two ends at once. . . . I skip from one section to another now like a sky-jack." He apostrophized the bridge as "O thou steeled Cognizance, whose leap commits the agile precincts of the lark's return." It belonged to the new age of machinery, aeroplanes, automobiles, radio; it linked these somehow with Pilgrim Fathers, horse and buggy; and, like Edith Sitwell, he sought a technique by which "poetry can absorb the machine," and even the New York Subway, where he suddenly sees Edgar Allan Poe: "Why do I often meet your visage here . . . below the toothpaste and the dandruff ads.?"

Max Eastman accused him of making a "cult of unintelligibility," but Waldo Frank thought he was "in the great tradition". In 1931 Crane went to fashionable Mexico with the idea of planning another long poem which would do for Latin-America what *The Bridge* had done for the United States. A more un-Latin temperament would be hard to imagine. Returning to New York the following year on the S.S. *Orizaba*, he threw himself overboard, so fulfilling his own prophecy of his end—"Sleep, death, desire, Close round one instant in a floating flower."

Stephen Vincent Benét, two years older than the century, a popular poet known in every American home and school for his *John Brown's Body* and *A Book of Americans*, now spoke with the new, rasping voice of the Depression:

*Is it well with these States? . . .*
*These are your tan-faced children,*
*These skilled men, idle, with the holes in their shoes.*
*These drifters from state to state, these wolvish,*
*                              bewildered boys*
*Who ride the blinds and the box cars from jail to jail . . .*
*Now they say we must have one tyranny or another*
*And a dark bell rings in our hearts.*

The only thing he has in common with Crane is that this is part of an imaginary verse conversation with an old poet, in this case Whitman.

No, it is not well with these States. Look at the titles of poetry books, as poets become more political and social. *Land of the Free: U.S.A.* and *America Was Promises* (Archibald MacLeish). (MacLeish, by

Ezra Pound, 1939, by Wyndham Lewis

publishing *Conquistador* in 1933, seemed to have used Crane's idea.) *The People, Yes* (1936), Carl Sandburg's socio-poetic testament in which he seems to have lost a little faith in democracy but hails the power of the people to go forward somehow.

From Ezra Pound, forty-one more Cantos, blaming Usury above all for the ills of mankind: "With usura hath no man a house of good stone/each block cut smooth and well fitting/. . . no picture is made to endure nor to live with/but it is made to sell and sell quickly. . . ." And prose books on money and culture in *ABC of Economics* and *Guide to Kulchur*. From Robert Frost, now in his late fifties, very little: more at home on the farm, uncertain whether the world would end in fire or ice, he had always distrusted systems, and seemed out of touch with the Thirties, which he spent largely in accepting prizes and gold medals for his past poetry.

In a stone tower at Point Sur, Carmel, California, which was part of a house he had built with his own hands, Robinson Jeffers surveyed the world, his thoughts laced with the learning of his Latin, Greek, French, German, medicine and forestry, acquired in Europe and at three universities. "Ecstatic pantheist", he had been called; and "poet of moral despair": the hawk his symbol of man's savagery, the stone his symbol of the ageless earth, in a world where nature would be better off without man, for man was a dying race. He had been moved by Spain, and saw clearly where it would all lead, in *Sinverguenza* (1936):

*They snarl over Spain like cur-dogs over a bone, then*
  *look at each other and shamelessly*
*Lie out of the sides of their mouths.*
*Brag, threat and lie, these are diplomacy; wolf-fierce,*
  *cobra-deadly and monkey shameless.*
*These are the masters of powerful nations.*
*I wonder is it any satisfaction to Spaniards to see that*
  *their blood is only*
*The first drops of a forming rainstorm.*

And when the guilty fear of the Thirties whimpered into a second World War, he wrote, (not great stuff, but journalizing the feeling of the time):

*Foreseen for so many years: these evils, this monstrous*
  *violence, these massive agonies: no easier to bear.*
*We saw them with slow stone strides approach, everyone*
  *saw them; we closed our eyes against them, we looked*
*And they had come nearer. We ate and drank and slept,*
  *they came nearer. Sometimes we laughed, they were*
  *nearer. Now*
*They are here.*

(below) The stone tower at Point Sur, Carmel, California, built
by Robinson Jeffers
(right) Robinson Jeffers

# FASTER, FASTER!

Back to May, 1930. I am listening to one of Mr. Vernon Bartlett's radio talks on Current Affairs, as we have been told at school to do. Mr. Bartlett is warning us of what may happen in Germany when Allied troops leave the country, and how odd it will be if, as seems likely, Prince Carol of Romania succeeds his young son as King. Suddenly there is a perceptible catch in his voice as he refers, quite unpolitically, to "a slim girl who, at this moment, is flying alone to Australia. . . ." He does not actually speak of "British grit" or "prestige" or "sportsmanship"—Lord Wakefield of Castrol will say all that, both personally and in advertisements for his automotive products—but nobody would have thought it either pompous or inappropriate if he had.

In Denmark Street, London, a music publisher named Lawrence Wright who composes songs under the name of Horatio Nicholls with a lyric writer named Jos. Geo. Gilbert is putting the finishing touches to a song called 'Amy' which will be released if, or when, the "slim girl" touches down on Australian soil. It goes like this:

*Amy, wonderful Amy!*
*How can you blame me*
*For loving you?*

Amy Johnson, twenty-seven, daughter of a Hull fish merchant, had been flying for eighteen months. Her Gipsy Moth *Jason*, bought secondhand from Air Taxis Ltd. with £300 provided by Lord Wakefield and £300 from her father, had a special petrol tank in the passenger seat so that she could carry 79 gallons. She had started from Croydon at breakfast time on Monday, May 5, arriving at Aspern aerodrome, Vienna (the word airport was not yet used) 800 miles away "at tea-time". Next day she made Istanbul, another 800 miles, again by tea-time, sustained by sandwiches and a thermos flask of tea, and doing her own maintenance in the evening. She had a loaded pistol and had learnt ju-jitsu in case she met hostile natives anywhere. She carried letters of introduction to important people in various countries, and on presenting one to Turkish officials, seeking permission to fly over the Taurus mountains, was told: "We regret to inform you that His Excellency is in prison."

The next hop, to Baghdad, was disastrous. She rose from 5,000 to 7,000 feet trying to avoid a sandstorm in the desert near Aleppo. Her petrol pump leaked and the fumes made her vomit. To use the reserve tank she had to pump at the rate of 40 strokes per gallon. The engine coughed, the Moth dropped 2,000 feet into the sandstorm: somehow she managed to land it. The wonder is that it didn't catch fire and that she was able to swing the propeller two hours later, using her handkerchief to keep sand out of the tank, and take off again.

She was already the most famous woman in the world when, at Jhansi, India, out of petrol, she made a forced landing on a barracks square, ruining a guard-mounting ceremony, having so far beaten Bert Hinkler's Britain-Australia speed record by two days. At Insein, Burma, she mistook a football field for Rangoon race-course and ran into a ditch, breaking her propeller and an undercarriage strut, and tearing a tyre. This was the only time she burst into tears. At Singapore on May 18 Flight-Commander Cave-Brown-Cave received her like Royalty, surrounded by the entire British Colony, the women waving their parasols as if at a garden party. Over the Java Sea, after an emergency landing on a sugar estate (more wing damage, repaired by sticking plaster) she lost her bearings, found them again, looked in vain for the oil-tanker which had been instructed to see her safely across the shark-infested Timor Sea and the cannibal-infested mainland, became semi-delirious as she whiled away the time reciting poems learnt at

Amy Johnson being driven through the streets of London on her return from Australia, August 1930

school and counting aloud in French and German, and somehow, on May 24, after nineteen and a half days, landed at Darwin.

She was awarded the C.B.E. She was a new Joan of Arc, she ought to be made a peeress. The Australians too composed a song about her, 'Johnnie's In Town'. When she sailed back to England there was a triumphal procession for her arranged by the *Daily Mail* which paid £2,000 for her exclusive story and later gave her a £10,000 cheque for her "British courage and endurance." She made a publicity marriage—to Jim Mollison, two years her junior, a bit of a drunk and not such a good pilot. He had however made the solo trip Australia–England in a

Puss Moth in only nine days (beating the existing record by two days) and then flown England–Cape Town in four days seventeen hours. Amy beat this record by ten hours in 1932. They were the first husband-wife team to fly the Atlantic, though they crashed in a Connecticut swamp. But they were divorced in 1938.

There were more flying clubs than there had been in the Twenties, and for those who could not afford them, gliding clubs; yet this was the last decade in which adventure flying, with clapped-out old planes and advertising sponsorship and "trophies", was the great thing—the age of the Schneider Trophy, the Gordon Bennett Cup, the King's Cup Race. Com-

petitions would continue, but the future lay in scheduled passenger flights and military aircraft. But there was plenty of amateurism while it lasted. In 1937 Jean Batten cut the Australia–England solo flight time down to 5 days 18 hours 15 minutes (she had done it in just under fifteen days three years before). The MacRobertson England–Australia race had been won by C. W. A. Scott and T. Campbell Black in a De Havilland Comet in 2 days 23 hours. Amelia Earhart in 1932 was the first woman to fly the Atlantic solo (Newfoundland–Ireland) in 13½ hours. She differed from other women aviators in that she had a serious interest in commercial flying. In January 1935 she flew solo across the Pacific from Hawaii to California. Two years later, accompanied by Lieut. Commander Fred Noonan, she attempted a round-the-world trip in a twin-engined Lockheed, but disappeared near Howland Island in the South Pacific.

The round the world trip had already been done by Wiley Post in his Lockheed monoplane *Winnie Mae*, experimenting with automatic pilot equipment and in July 1933 circling the earth in 7 days, 18 hours and 49 minutes, beating his own 1931 record when he had had Harold Gatty as navigator. Post was killed in 1935 with the American humorist Will Rogers, whom he had taken as passenger on a flight over Alaska. Howard Hughes, three years later, flew round the world in 3 days, 19 hours, 8 minutes and (the photo-finish seemed not far off) 10 seconds. Of curiosity value was Douglas Corrigan, who, in the traditional old plane, started to fly from New York to California, but found himself in Ireland; and Blossom Forbes Robertson, who eloped with Mr. F. G. Miles and helped him to build up the Miles aircraft factory: their Sparrow-Hawk did the fastest time in the 1935 King's Cup Race.

The Schneider Trophy by 1931 had become too expensive for most nations: it was won for the third time by Flight-Lieut. J. N. Boothman who reached 340 m.p.h. in a Supermarine after the Government's refusal, during the financial crisis, to finance an R.A.F. entry: the situation had been saved by Lady Houston, "the richest woman in Britain", to whom the necessary £100,000 was a fleabite.

It might have been thought that the R.101 disaster in 1930, followed by the Akron in 1933 and the Macon in 1935, meant the end of the airship as a form of transport for either passengers or freight. There

The Schneider Trophy

was still a mooring mast for airships on top of the new Empire State Building, whose directors believed that in a few years' time Zeppelins would set up transatlantic, transcontinental and transpacific services, and that New York might become the terminal of a South American airship service. Dr. Eckener's 'Hindenburg' offered the only transatlantic passenger service until it too caught fire in 1937, which left its sister ship the new *Graf Zeppelin* undergoing trials in 1938 and Germany the only obstinate believer in its safety.

In America the crash in a thunderstorm over New Mexico of a plane killing eight people was regarded as a setback for transcontinental air transport, and the ban on night flying was a serious obstacle for some time. Nevertheless there was a pioneer air service in conjunction with the Pennsylvania and Santa Fe railroads. You took a night train from New York to Columbus, Ohio; then flew to Waynoka, Oklahoma; then by night train to Clovis, New Mexico; and so by air to Los Angeles, completing the journey in two days flat. Airmail was now standard.

In June 1936 coast-to-coast sleepers arrived, in the form of 200 m.p.h. Douglas DC.3s. In October the China Clipper had flown to Manila and back, and both Pan-Am and Imperial Airways were experimenting with flying-boats, which seemed likely to be

*(opposite)* Amelia Earhart
*(opposite top right)* Howard Hughes
*(opposite above right)* Jean Batten

the largest, fastest and safest aircraft for the next few years. The giant Short took twenty-four passengers in a "flying hotel" from Southampton to Sydney in nine and a half days. Pan-Am in 1939 flew the first transatlantic Clipper service for passengers, from Long Island Sound to France and England, using 41-ton planes with a wing-span of 152 feet. Britain, for whom the routes to the Southern Hemisphere had always been simpler because of large land masses and short sea crossings, had had a through service to India since 1929 which was extended to Singapore in 1933, a Cape Town service opened in 1932, and the first London–Australia through service began in 1935.

Yet astonishingly few people had ever flown, unless it was in one of Sir Alan Cobham's "five-bob flips" (ten shillings for looping the loop). In 1929, there had been 152,809 air passengers; in 1939, there were still only 210,400, or about $\frac{1}{2}$ per cent of the population. The future seemed wonderful, if only war could be avoided. An American aviation correspondent in 1936 saw the North Atlantic being carved up by air powers seeking routes, just as the Congress of Vienna had carved up Europe after Napoleon. America had the equipment and skill, but Britain held the aces of this poker game, for "without her consent nobody can move in the North Atlantic, which is a British pond." At Bridgeport, Connecticut, a steady stream of Sikorsky Clippers was flowing. At Short Bros., Rochester, Kent, the first of a series of seventeen-ton four-engined flying boats had completed its trials: its name was *Canopus*. France had had bad luck: her thirty-seven-ton flying boat *Lieutenant de Vaisseau Paris* had been wrecked by a Florida hurricane. . . .

'Faster, Faster!' was a song by Vivian Ellis and A. P. Herbert in Cochran's 1934 Revue *Streamline*: "step on the gas, boys, and let's save some time!" it sang ironically; for the Thirties saw themselves as an age of crazy speed. Faster, higher, farther, deeper, by all kinds of vehicle, from Professor Piccard (who ascended ten miles in a "pressurized gondola" and introduced us to the word stratosphere) to William Beebe, a versatile biologist who in 1934 descended over three-quarters of a mile into the sea in his bathysphere. American inventiveness, British pluck, call it what you will—it was desperately necessary, in times of depression with no major war to bring national glory, that records should be broken. So Major Sir Henry Segrave was killed on Lake

Programme for *Streamline*

*(opposite above)* Composite seaplane, invented by Major R. H. Mayo, tried by Short Bros. in 1937

*(opposite below)* Streamlined steam locomotives of the South Pacific Railroad, 1937

*(right)* Tilly Losch, wearing a dress designed by Charles James, for 'Harmonia Mobilis' in *Streamline*

The dances by MR. JACK HOLLAND and MISS JUNE HART, the two American artists, are among the most popular numbers of "STREAMLINE," at the Palace. On the first night they were called and called again, and at every performance the applause their acts produce holds up the show for an appreciable time. The dances, "You Turned Your Head" and the dance in the cabaret presented in "The Starving Rich," are both speedy and extremely graceful, though acrobatic. Miss Hart uses her voluminous skirts with amazing skill and swings and swirls them

Windermere in his speedboat *Miss England II* after touching 101 m.p.h. The boat was salvaged and driven by Kaye Don on a river near Buenos Aires at 103 m.p.h., and on Lake Garda at 110 m.p.h. It eventually sank when an American competitor, Gar Wood, cut across its bows, some said deliberately. On land, the stern hero who seemed to have a holy mission to break records was Malcolm Campbell in his *Bluebird*. In 1935 he reached 301 m.p.h., his ninth world record since 1924; and in 1939, even as the air raid shelters were being built, he too took to the water and in his *Bluebird* speedboat achieved 141.74 m.p.h. on Coniston Water. His own land speed record had been broken in 1937 by George Eyston (312.2 m.p.h.) and in 1939 by J. R. Cobb, who touched 369.7 m.p.h. in a Railton Special at Bonneville Salt Flats, Utah.

For the average motorist the speed limit, which nobody observed, was 30 m.p.h. Few people in Britain wanted to drive at more than 50 m.p.h. Motoring, sighed the romantics who had learnt to drive in the Twenties, was becoming mere transportation, craftsmanship was being lost in mass production and advertised gimmicks like radios and heaters. You no longer lovingly polished brass lamps: instead there was chromium plate, which theoretically stayed bright but actually rusted. In America, Britain, Germany and France the assembly line was taking over. America, of course, was ten years ahead of other countries: one tenth of her population was now employed, directly or indirectly, by the automobile industry, and thirty-five per cent of all private cars were made by General Motors (including Vauxhall in England and Opel in Germany), Chryslers were being made at Kew, and Buicks and Chevrolets (advertised as "Empire-built") were imported into Britain from Canada.

Malcolm Campbell in Bluebird

When the Depression began, used cars were at a premium. Later on, you could get a ten-year-old car for $10–20. By 1936 there were nearly three and a half million car owners in America. Commuter suburbs were being laid out with garages. Note that the Joad family, in *The Grapes of Wrath*, trek west searching for work in their own jalopy. Camden, New Jersey, had the first drive-in cinema in 1934, and Los Angeles had the first drive-in bank in 1937. Percy Shaw invented cat's eyes in 1933. The multi-storey car park and the parking-meter, invented by a Mr. C. C. Magee in 1935, had also arrived. As design-consciousness converted square boxes into streamlined bombs and reptiles, the admen grew more lyrical and aggressive. Hudsons had something called "axle flex", the Studebaker gave you a "miracle ride", there were no words in the language to describe "the dazzling beauty and power of the Dodge Six." The new hydraulic brakes enabled you to "stop on a dime". Packard's door handles were "lovely as heirloom

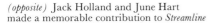

*(opposite)* Jack Holland and June Hart made a memorable contribution to *Streamline*

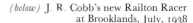

*(below)* J. R. Cobb's new Railton Racer at Brooklands, July, 1938

silver". The Prince of Wales drove a Buick, Stalin was rumoured to own a Packard. The 1936 Buick, a "drawing room on wheels", had a boot or trunk which could accommodate "two teenagers and a great Dane".

If you were extremely rich, you had a "dream car" like Harley Earl's 1938 Buick convertible with electric hood and windows and "pop-out door handles"; or Gary Cooper's 1931 long Duesenberg "Tourster"; or Father Divine's 15-foot "throne car", believed to have cost $17,750; or the 1937 Pierce-Arrow Formal Sedan with "rear-seat privacy". (Too bad that Pierce-Arrow went bankrupt in the following year.) Only Fords seemed to lag behind, often at the expense of safety, despite the resounding success of the V.8. (Yet John O'Hara's modest dream, after the success of *Appointment in Samarra*, was to buy "a Ford phaeton of my own, and a new suit, and some razor blades.")

By 1936 Britain had one private car to every forty-four people and forty-one different makes, though the big six were Morris, Austin, Ford, Rootes, Standard and Vauxhall. You could get a Morris 12 which did up to 70 m.p.h. for £205, or a Hillman Minx for £180 or less. From 1931 onwards there was the Morris 12, and from 1937 the Vauxhall 10. The highly successful Austin 10 had arrived in 1932. In 1934 came the best-selling Morris 8, the sensation of that year's Motor Show. Two baby cars, the Morris Minor and the Austin 7, survived from the 1920's (it was smart to individualize your Austin 7 with Gordon England fabric bodywork). In 1938 Austins introduced the "Big 7" alongside the Baby Austin, eventually to replace it. Austins were considered conservative and slow compared to Morrises, which went in for safety features like hydraulic brakes and could add at least 5 m.p.h. to Austins' top speed of about 65 m.p.h. The Morris Isis combined stateliness with speed for £370.

Perhaps the most typical British middle-class car, comparable to the Buick in America, was the Hillman Minx, which could do about 56 m.p.h., and one version of which, the Melody Minx, was so-called merely because it had a built-in radio. Yet comfort, the present idea of car as extension of house, was a long time coming. Even in a £1,000 car there was no heating, and to demist the screen in winter you used a hot-water bottle.

In Britain, too, the adman was at work; the 12 h.p. Armstrong-Siddeley was promoted "for the daughters of gentlemen" with "plenty of room for your bridge partners or your tennis set", and in 1931 the Hillman Wizard was launched as "the car of the Moderns . . . the voice of the modern world can be heard on all sides calling out for still finer achievements at the hands of man": the de luxe saloon model cost £299. The phrase "the £1,000 look" was already being used to promote cheaper cars. The Armstrong-Siddeley 20 was a "car of aircraft quality". A modest family two-seater had, it was claimed, "room in the boot for four sturdy kiddies". Although Britain was a land of slow drivers, the aggression fantasy was beginning in car names like Hornet, Rapier, Viper, Hawk.

Among luxury cars—Alvis, Lagonda, Bentley, Daimler, Jaguar, the 1935 Rolls-Royce Phantom III (£3,100)—a subtler form of advertising was word-of-mouth about who owned what. Queen Mary had a Double-6 Daimler (there was a story that the Royal Family boycotted Rolls-Royce because she had once been offered a free car by them). Rolls, anyway, unlike Daimlers, were designed for owner-drivers as well as for chauffeurs. The Armstrong-Siddeley Atalanta saloon was favoured by both the Danish Royal family and, incongruously, Neville Chamberlain. The Duke of Gloucester loved the Sunbeam 25 (£875). "Nobility again chooses the Cadillac," said a series of advertisements, dropping the names of the Duke of Bedford, Lady Ribblesdale and President Roosevelt.

Of several popular sports cars, the curious little Morgan three-wheeler suddenly, in 1936, took a wheel at each corner and became the almost changeless, uncomfortable Morgan 4/4 which has been revived. "Styling" and the streamline fashion hit sports cars too, and to beautify the Humber Vogue in 1933 a dress-designer, Captain Molyneux, was hired. But the most popular of all 1930s sports cars, in several countries, was the famous MG at about £220.

Italy, trying to export ninety per cent of her car output, produced two outstanding cheap light cars, the Fiat Millicento and Topolino ("Mickey Mouse"): The Topolino was one of the few foreign (other than sports) cars to be imported into the United States (because it was so "cute"). In France, there was competition between two main firms in the family car market, safe, solid Renault and experimentally-minded Citroën. Citroën, in 1936, designed (but did not yet launch) a kind of Mini-Beetle since known as the Dustbin or "umbrella on

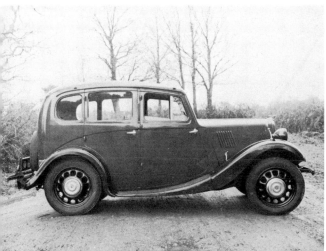

(*above*) The Ford Prefect in 1939
(*left*) The Morris 8, 1934
(*below*) Vauxhall 10, 1939

*(right)* The Morgan 4/4, 1939. Car rallying and hill climbs became increasingly popular during the 1930s
*(below)* The Daimler, 1939

*(above)* The Jaguar, 1939
*(below)* The Rolls-Royce Phantom III, 1937–8
*(bottom)* The Lagonda, 1939

four wheels". With *traction-avant* (front-wheel drive) and a one-piece removable unit that made it exceptionally easy to service, it might have become the People's Car that Hitler failed to deliver to the millions of Germans who had saved up for it. Some of its features were present in the 1934 7.CV.

America already had highways with clover-leaf underpasses over which motorists cruised at 60 m.p.h. Pedestrian crossings (lighted, in Britain, by orange globes known as Belisha Beacons after the Minister of Transport who introduced them) had arrived. Pennsylvania had the first modern motor road, made by converting a disused railway line. British road-building made little progress: accidents were regarded as being due to the stupidity of pedestrians, and anyway, said Neville Chamberlain when he was Chancellor of the Exchequer, "if you make more roads you make more opportunities for accidents." Anyone over the age of seventeen could drive, if he declared himself physically fit. New drivers, from 1935, had to pass tests. A British "highway code", based on good manners but not compulsory, was introduced; more popular was a spoof version, *You Have Been Warned*, by a humorous writer, Donald McCullough, and the *Punch* artist Fougasse. Solemnly labelled "all pianola rights strictly reserved," it was dedicated to someone called Straight-Eight Lincoln, and to the hope that "driving by the people, through the people and over the people may shortly perish from the earth." Speed cops, excruciatingly polite in England (there was a song, 'Gertie the Girl with the Gong') tried to make drivers obey speed limits and road discipline generally by sounding a gong and shouting through loudspeakers "Will the gentleman in the black Hillman Minx kindly pull into the kerb, please. We should like to speak to him."

In August 1935 Lord de Clifford, who had married one of the daughters of Mrs. Meyrick the "nightclub queen" and did endurance tests in small cars for publicity, was charged with the manslaughter of a Mr. Douglas George Hopkins of Hoxton by driving in a reckless and negligent manner on the Kingston By-pass. He elected to be tried by his peers, a thing which had not happened for thirty-four years. Arrayed in their robes, they reminded Chips Channon of *Iolanthe*: at any moment they might sing 'Bow, bow, ye lower middle classes'. Motorists almost to a man, they unanimously acquitted Lord de Clifford.

Transatlantic ocean liners, with never a hope of

(*left*) Bell boys being inspected aboard the *Queen Mary*
(*below*) The dining-room aboard the *Queen Mary*
(*opposite above left*) The Brighton Belle, June 1934
(*opposite above right*) The Silver Link, September 1935
(*opposite below*) The Flying Scotsman and other trains at King's Cross, August 1934

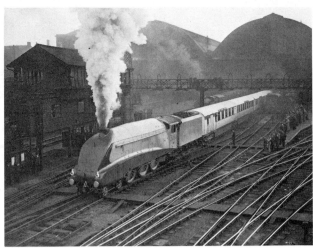

competing in speed with the coming air routes, could still offer luxury and entertainment. Yet it was still prestigious to be able to clip a few hours off the Europe—New York run. Britain, France and Germany were in endless competition for the Blue Riband. North German Lloyd's *Europa* could make 28 knots. France's *Normandie*, launched at St. Nazaire in 1932, longer and heavier, cruised at 31.2 knots. Cunard White Star (the two shipping lines had just merged) in 1934 launched the Cunarder N. 534, the *Queen Mary*, named by the Queen and helped by a Government subsidy of £9½ million. Two years later on her maiden voyage she recaptured the Blue Riband from the *Normandie* with a mean speed of 31.7 knots. The same company's *Queen Elizabeth*, launched in 1938 during the Munich crisis by Queen Elizabeth herself, accompanied by the two little Princesses Elizabeth and Margaret, did not make her maiden voyage until 1940, and then in conditions of secrecy. A year later she was a troop transport, carrying 811,324 soldiers 492,635 miles in five years of war.

"Where is the race to end, and can all these floating hotels be made to pay?" asked a shipping correspondent in June 1936, hinting that the supply of luxury transport was already exceeding the demand. A new dock had been built at Southampton to accommodate the *Queen Mary*, which had two churches and a synagogue on board, and "special quarters for dogs, with a promenade deck of their own. . . . The decorations, designed by some of the most celebrated British artists, resemble those of a large country house." This was the kind of thing that seemed to please the millionaires and business men who formed most of its clientele, and who would be the first to desert it when the Atlantic Clippers really got into their stride. Never mind. The *Queen Mary* was good for British prestige, which wasn't up to much in 1936; and it was consoling to reflect that, if up-ended, she was three times as tall as St. Paul's Cathedral, only few feet shorter than the Chrysler Building, and fifty feet higher than the Eiffel Tower.

With this glamour railways could not compete. In design, they moved with the times, streamlining and embellishing themselves with duralumin and stainless steel (America's Burlington Zephyr was the first in 1934), electrifying themselves over medium-length stretches such as London to Brighton, and longer hauls in America, notably the Pennsylvania railroad's New York–Washington and Philadelphia–Harrisburg lines. Not too much, though, for it now looked as if the diesel locomotive might turn out cheaper. Railways too yielded one or two faster-faster records: it was thought remarkable that a Great Western Railway express attained 78 m.p.h. in 1931, and a worthy tribute to their Majesties that the Silver Jubilee train should reach 112 m.p.h. in 1935.

To celebrate George VI's Coronation the LNER started a "Coronation" service (London–Edinburgh in six hours), but it was the rival LMS which scooped the publicity, helped by a popular tune, with the Coronation Scot (London–Glasgow in six and a half hours).

There was one line in Britain where a maximum speed of 30 m.p.h. was allowed. Technically part of the London, Midland and Scottish Railway, it was reserved for the last private train in the country. Its owner, the fifth Duke of Sutherland, a deafish retired naval officer, kept it at Dunrobin Castle, Sutherlandshire. He had his reasons for disliking speed: his sister Rosemary, Lady Ednam, had been killed, with the Marquis of Dufferin and Ava, in an air crash at Meopham, Kent, while returning from Le Touquet (favourite weekend resort of private aircraft owners) in a plane piloted by harum-scarum Colonel George Henderson, whose party trick was flying under the Tower Bridge. The Duke's private train was used for the last time in 1938, and it entered the history of nations because on that occasion it brought Neville Chamberlain back from a fishing trip at Brora, on one of the several weekends when Hitler had moved too fast for him.

# CHAPTER

## X

# THEATRE WORLD

In December 1931 a play called *1931* by Paul Sifton was put on briefly at the Mansfield Theatre in New York. It appears to have been the kind of documentary afterwards known as "living newspaper", and a critic said kindly of it that "Adam, the lead, was excellently played by a young man named Franchot Tone, who is said to be a millionaire's son and a radical, feeling in real life much as he acts in his role of a jobless worker." Mr. Tone, who afterwards went to Hollywood and married and then unmarried Joan Crawford, had just graduated to Broadway from a stock company and had accepted five such parts since the end of 1930. He was a symptom of the suddenness with which the Depression had hit America.

It was several years before anything like that happened in Britain. True, we had *Cavalcade* to cheer us up for the loss of the Gold Standard, but the typical West End offering of 1931 was probably *Springtime for Henry*, by Benn W. Levy, sometime managing director of a publishing house and a future Socialist M.P., which rose above the trouser-dropping level of much British farce by suggesting that what keeps a marriage going is a mistress, as long as she doesn't meet your wife, and threw in some neat social criticism about the private life of capitalists and their tendency to regard women as sex-objects: it was as if Noël Coward had been *thinking*.

The "living newspaper" proper grew out of America's Federal Theatre Project, established in 1935 as part of the Works Progress administration to give employment to actors, and to introduce drama to millions of people who had never before been to a live theatre as opposed to the talkies which were threatening to swamp all but the commercial theatre. The Project lasted four years, was accused (largely because of the "living newspapers") of being Communist-inspired, and died. The British counterpart, if there was one, was a number of back-street

theatres that put on plays like Odets's *Waiting for Lefty* (1935), a plea for trade unions which used the auditorium as part of the stage. Lefty was a Communist leader, almost a Christ figure who, when he at last arrived, was shot. Chief among them was the Unity Theatre near Euston Station, whose most notable contribution, its bitterly satirical pantomime, *Babes In The Wood* (1938, just after Munich), starred Vida Hope, delivering fierce political jibes in filthy French against Neville Chamberlain, the villain, and his sidekick Daladier. Her own part was the Fairy Wish-fulfilment:—

> *I'm the Fairy Wish-fulfilment,*
> *I'm in love with Godfrey Winn,*
> *I'm the Fairy Wish-fulfilment—*
> *Beverley Nichols is my sin.*

There was, in this sort of thing, something of the self-mocking social criticism of *Pins and Needles*, a revue performed entirely by garment workers and produced in America by Labor Stage Inc.—its hit song was called 'Sing Me A Song with Social Significance'. Opening in November 1933, it ran, through three editions, for 1,108 performances.

Three poets, Auden, Spender and MacNeice, wrote "left" plays which were produced by the Group Theatre at the Westminster Theatre; but the Unity, considering them to be bourgeois writers out of touch with the workers, would have little to do with them. In three plays, *The Dog Beneath the Skin*, *The Ascent of F.6* and *On The Frontier*, Auden collaborated with Isherwood. People for the most part went to these plays as to a sort of Marxist church, to be whipped up into class-hatred, not to experience or enjoy the theatre. Of these, perhaps only *F.6* (about a mountaineer-hero who symbolized many contemporary strivings) could be revived today. *Frontier*, produced at Cambridge in February 1939, anti-

Mad masks in the Red Light District of Ostnia; scene from *The Dog Beneath the Skin*, 1936

cipated war between an imperialist power and a dictatorship, and was greatly helped by its incidental music, composed by the little-known Benjamin Britten. More in the Unity tradition was *Where's That Bomb?* by Herbert Hodge, a London taxi-driver, author of three chirpy books about his own life, *It's Draughty in Front, Cab, Sir!*, and *Cockney on Main Street*. His play was about a worker poet refusing to sell his soul to Capital and False Patriotism by writing advertising verses on lavatory paper. Stephen Spender's *Trial of a Judge* (1938), an attempt at political tragedy in verse, was hailed as "sincere": the Judge, representing the intelligent middle class, is imprisoned with the very revolutionaries he detests when the Fascists come to power.

Nobody reads these plays today, as few were published, and very few people ever saw them: they now belong to sociology. The West End took calculated risks on two "working class" plays, *Love On The Dole* (1935), adapted from Walter Greenwood's best-selling novel (mill girl, played by Wendy Hiller, becomes bookie's mistress to earn money for her unemployed

family), and *Rhondda Roundabout* (1939), by Jack Jones, which brought a little Welsh humour into the misery of the mining valleys. *Love On The Dole* ran for 391 performances at the Garrick.

Less self-conscious, more virile, were the American plays reflecting the Depression. At the time it was argued primly that it was "the loose sexual mores" of the characters that drew packed houses to see *Tobacco Road* at the Masque Theater, New York, where it ran for an incredible 3,182 performances; but there was enough dramatic quality in this adaptation of Erskine Caldwell's novel of a family degenerating through poverty to enable audiences to identify themselves with the characters, and perhaps to feel socially fashionable for so doing. By contrast, Maxwell Anderson's *Winterset*, a study of social injustice, ran for a mere 179 performances, but was successfully translated to the screen. Odets's *Golden Boy*, which appeared to some people to be a left-ish statement, ran for 250 performances at the Belasco in New York and 109 at the St. James's in London: it was a tragic farce about the clash of idealism and money-getting in the soul of a violinist, Joe Bonaparte, who abandons the concert hall for the prize ring. Of course he breaks his hands so that he can never play the violin again; one of his opponents dies after a knockout, and he himself is killed when his Duesenberg car, his status and security symbol, is wrecked. Today it seems melodramatic and its language inflated; but it impressed the *London Mercury* critic in August 1938 because Odets's "characters have an abounding vitality that carries immediate conviction . . . the acting has an American drive which cuts into a situation as if it were the first time that such a thing had ever happened to anyone before."

Somewhere in the centre, eyes looking wistfully right, stood Robert E. Sherwood, a New-Dealer (he was writing some of FDR's speeches) with a feeling for crumbling old Europe, shown in the comedy *Reunion in Vienna* (1931) which reached London in 1934. As Europe crumbled still more, he gave us *The*

(*above*) The American company of *Golden Boy*, St. James's Theatre, London
(*left to right*) Lillian Emerson, Luther Adler and Roman Bohnen

(*below*) Lynn Fontanne and Alfred Lunt in *Reunion in Vienna*

*Petrified Forest* (1935), a melodrama about local (and by implication international) gangsterism, and *Abe Lincoln in Illinois* (1938), an historical appeal to his country to remember what democracy really meant. But it was his *Idiot's Delight* (1936) that is truly of the Thirties. At the time it was thought defeatist—the educated middle-class artist saying, "but of course war's unthinkable. . . ." Its sentiments—"They're all jittery. So they get bigger cannons and sharper bayonets. . . . You can refuse to fight! Have you ever thought of that possibility?"—were seized upon by the Peace Pledge Union when the play was produced in London (March 1938, ten days after Hitler had invaded Austria). In an apparently neutral hotel are Harry Van, an American entertainer not unreminiscent of Fred Astaire; a French idealist trying to save the world by Communism; Achille Weber, an armaments king in the classical mould, with his "assistant" Irene; an Englishman on honeymoon; and a German, Dr. Waldersee, who is working on a cure for cancer. As war creeps nearer, the Englishman goes home to "do his bit", Waldersee goes back to Germany to work on bacterial weapons, and the curtain falls on Harry and Irene, bombs all round them, singing *Onward Christian Soldiers*. Harry Van was played by Alfred Lunt in New York (with Lynn Fontaine as Irene), by Raymond Massey in London, and, on tour, by Vic Oliver, an Austrian comedian-musician who married Winston Churchill's daughter Sarah.

The liberating effect of the Depression on America was to be seen in the sheer anarchy, and licence to turn America upside down, of shows like George Kaufman and Moss Hart's *Once In A Lifetime* (sending up Hollywood), *You Can't Take It With You*, and the musicals *Of Thee I Sing*, about a President and Vice-President of the United States named respectively Wintergreen and Throttlebottom, and *As Thousands Cheer*, with Clifton Webb doddering on as J. D. Rockefeller, Ethel Waters singing 'Heat Wave', and an irreverent but strangely prophetic sketch about George V, Queen Mary, and a recalcitrant Prince of Wales.

Among "long runs" were *The Barretts of Wimpole Street*, with Katharine Cornell touring 225 American cities as Elizabeth Moulton-Barrett (the part was played in London by Gwen Ffrangçon-Davies); Marc Connelly's *Green Pastures*, an all-Negro play about Bible stories seen through the eyes of Southern Negroes (one of the great scenes, captured in a Steichen photograph, was the march of Moses and the Israelites to the Promised Land, which is visualized as a huge eternal fish-fry); and Claire Boothe's *The Women* (New York, 1936), a satirical comedy without men which, though considered "cruel" by British standards, did the West End a power of good in the months before War was declared.

Were women really so awful? Well, perhaps American women were. . . . More to Aunt Edna's taste were the family comedies, always sure-fire box-office, like Dodie Smith's *Dear Octopus* and Esther McCracken's *Quiet Wedding*. What was there about *George and Margaret*, by Gerald Savory, which ran for 799 performances at Wyndham's, that made me see it four times? Jane Baxter, probably. A Hampstead Garden Suburb family named Garth-Bander who have sausages for breakfast, Noel Howlett as a vague father who is always meaning to go to the British Museum—"haven't been since I was a boy"—John Boxer as a pompous scoutmaster who falls from grace by getting the maid with child, and Irene Handl as a new maid called Beer who only appears for one minute and says something inaudible—and George and Margaret, never seen at all, "who were so kind to your Father in Singapore". . . . Damn it, it *is* funny, and I'm laughing as I write this!

Or Terence Rattigan's *French Without Tears*, seeming to run *for ever* at the little Criterion Theatre (you could have a snack at the underground Brasserie Universelle next door for a shilling before you went in), which for me was a continuation of Oxford escapism. . . . At Professor Maingot's school for fledgling diplomats on the Riviera three young men, one of whom is loved by the Professor's blonde daughter, are distracted from their studies by the arrival of a vamp, Diana Lake (played by Kay Hammond), and a rather older (at least 30) naval commander Rogers (played by Roland Culver). Diana eventually makes the *raisonneur* of the piece, the Hon. Alan Howard (Rex Harrison when I saw it), fall in love with her . . . And somewhere, among all the fourth-form jokes about English people not being able to speak French (*elle a des idées au-dessus de sa gare* and "*qu'est-ce c'est—un* Belisha beacon?"), there are moments of pure Thirties, such as the fact that Alan has written an unpublishable novel about people who go to a desert island to avoid an annihilating war.

(*above*) Scene from
*Quiet Wedding*
(*left to right*) Clive
Morton, Anne Firth,
Elizabeth Allan, Marie
Lohr, Marjorie Fielding,
Wyndham's Theatre,
1938

(*left*) Kay Hammond,
Rex Harrison,
Roland Culver and
Robert Flemyng
in *French Without Tears*,
1936

113

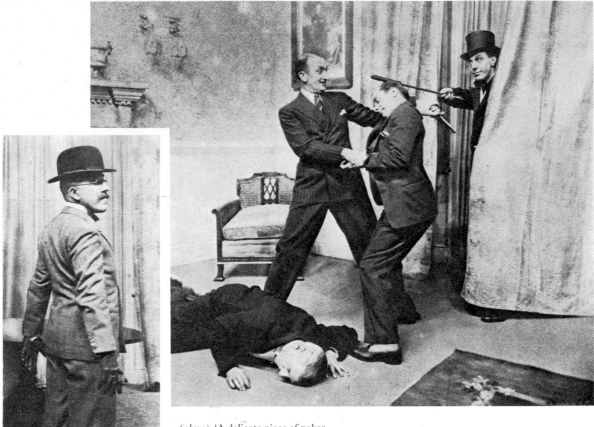

(above) 'A delicate piece of poker-work', from *A Night Like This*, Aldwych Theatre, 1930
(left) 'Victim of a trouser-robbery', Robertson Hare as Tuckett in *A Night Like This*
(right) Caricature of Leslie Henson by Rouson, in *Going Greek*
(opposite) Bobby Howes and Cicely Courtneidge in *Hide and Seek*, London Hippodrome, 1937

At the Aldwych, Ralph Lynn, Robertson Hare, Tom Walls, a race-horse owner whose April the Fifth won the Derby, Mary Brough and Winifred Shotter kept up the splendid tradition of underwear-losing farce which enabled *Punch* to say, of *A Night Like This*, by Ben Travers, "Miss Shotter had very little to do—or undo." At the Gaiety, in its last days, native musical comedy survived in shows like *Going Greek*, with Leslie Henson and Fred Emney; and other theatres gave us *Jill, Darling!* and *Hide and Seek*, both sustained by Vivian Ellis's music—Louise Brown and John Mills singing *I'm On A See-Saw*, and Bobbie Howes singing *She's My Lovely*.

A baby-faced Welsh actor, Emlyn Williams, wrote as his tenth play, an outstanding thriller, *Night Must Fall*, based on a recent murder case, with himself as the murderer, and followed it with *The Corn Is Green*, a tribute to the devoted village schoolmistress (played by Sybil Thorndike) who had made it possible for him to go to Oxford. Margaret Kennedy's *Escape Me Never*, a sequel to *The Constant Nymph*, exploited the elfin appeal of Elisabeth Bergner, a Jewish refugee from Germany for whom Sir James Barrie wrote his last, disastrous play, *The Boy David*. Miss Bergner, a classical actress in Austria and Germany, was always required, in Britain, to be elfin. J. B. Priestley, having

(*above*) Emlyn Williams and Sybil Thorndike in *The Corn Is Green*, Duchess Theatre, 1938
(*right*) Elisabeth Bergner in *Escape Me Never*, Apollo Theatre, 1933

(*opposite*) Programme for *Reunion in Vienna*, designed by Rex Whistler

GILBERT
MILLER
PRESENTS

*Alfred Lunt*
&
*Lynn Fontanne*

IN

# REUNION
IN
VIENNA

*By*

ROBERT E. SHERWOOD

## LYRIC THEATRE

Lessees:
S.J. & L.LTD.

SHAFTESBURY AVENUE, W.1.

Licensed by the Lord Chamberlain to
THOMAS H. BOSTOCK

the theatre guild presents

idiot's delight

by robert e Sherwood

with lynn fontanne & alfred lunt

written in 1932 a thoughtful but highly dramatic conversation piece *Dangerous Corner* (which ran longer in New York than it did in London) gave the family play an entirely new dimension by applying the time theories of J. W. Dunne in *Time and the Conways* and *I Have Been Here Before*. He was writing almost a play a year, and was a director of both the Duchess and the Mask Theatre Company. The plays were translated and performed in many other countries, and some of them, such as *Laburnum Grove* and *Eden End*, have stood the test of time and television. I have a special affection for *Johnson over Jordan*, which didn't run very long: it was a kind of modern Everyman, with Ralph Richardson as Robert Johnson examining his own life in retrospect (with a lot of Priestley in him).

Bernard Shaw now had his Malvern Festival from which *The Apple Cart* had come to the West End in September 1929. A wordy play, but strangely prophetic: King Magnus, a rubber-stamp king whose mistress wants him to be a *real* monarch, with herself as queen; Boanerges the trades unionist, ambitious to be first president of the republic; and a roll-about fight on the floor between Magnus and Orinthia, a whole year before Elyot and Amanda did it in *Private Lives*. Shaw had still a handful of plays in his head, *tours de force* of talk such as *In Good King Charles's Golden Days* performed at Malvern 1939.

At the Glasgow Citizen's Theatre a Scottish Shaw had now appeared, James Bridie with his *Tobias and the Angel*, produced in London with Henry Ainley, *Jonah and the Whale* and Robert Donat in *The Sleeping Clergyman*. Scottish, too, was the inspiration of *The Wind and the Rain*, Merton Hodge's long-running comedy of Edinburgh Medical School, the first to exploit the infinite funniness of medical students.

Dorothy L. Sayers, creator and lover of Lord Peter Wimsey, wrote a religious play, *The Zeal of Thy House*; so did T. S. Eliot, in his treatment of the Becket story, *Murder in the Cathedral*, first given in London at the tiny Mercury Theatre in Notting Hill Gate.

The Eugene O'Neill event of the decade was the vast *Mourning Becomes Electra* trilogy (1931), which was not liked by Dilys Powell, reviewing it in the *London Mercury*. "Just as nowadays the most foetus-like novel succeeds if only it is long enough," she wrote, "so Mr. O'Neill's clutch of plays draws large audiences. America has given us the Dancing Marathon and the epic of pole-squatting. The next thing is a play which *never* stops."

(*above*) Ralph Richardson and Richard Ainley in *Johnson over Jordan*, New Theatre, 1939
(*below*) Photographed at the Malvern Festival; Laura Knight, the artist, Barry Jackson, the producer, and Bernard Shaw

(*opposite*) Programme for *Idiot's Delight*

Two tableaux: *(above)* 'Lalique Lady',
*(below)* 'Time will Tell', Windmill Theatre, 1934

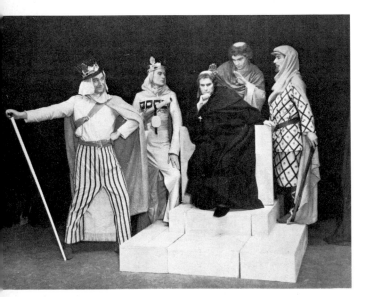

Robert Speaight as Becket, with Knights, in *Murder in the Cathedral*, 1935

Two young playwrights, Ronald Mackenzie (*Musical Chairs*, 1932, with John Gielgud as a war-scarred, piano-playing neurotic refusing to take an interest in the family oil well) and Rodney Ackland (*After October*, 1936) were both being hailed as "English Chekovs", and an eccentric youth of eighteen named Ustinov was convulsing audiences at the Players Theatre late-night Victorian music-hall in a monologue, *The Bishop of Limpopoland*.

Music hall was dying fast, variety theatres were being turned into cinemas, the Alhambra suddenly became known for ballet seasons including in 1933 Colonel de Basil's Ballets of Monte Carlo, before being demolished in 1936 for a big black Odeon.

Yet you could still catch Lily Morris or Randolph Sutton at the Metropolitan, Edgware Road, and one or two other places; there was still a full variety bill at the Holborn Empire, the spiritual home of Max Miller, and the Palladium; and perhaps the only relatively new, first-magnitude variety stars of these years were Gracie Fields and George Formby Jr., both from Lancashire. At London's Prince of Wales there was "non-stop revue", and Revudeville at the Windmill Theatre, where there were also static nudes. Chorus girls wore less, and one troupe in 1939 was billed as "Fifty Nifty Naughties". Music hall was perhaps the inspiration of the Cockney musical at the Victoria Palace, *Me and My Girl*, in which Lupino Lane introduced the famous Lambeth Walk, and which ran for 1,646 performances.

At the Little Theatre and the Gate, carrying on the tradition of the Cave of Harmony of the Twenties, were "intimate revues" such as Herbert Farjeon's *Nine Sharp* (1938), friendly as if they were guests in one's own drawing-room, with a touch of amateurism, purveying cosy middle-class satire and nostalgia, but no politics (all political satire was forbidden for fear of offending the Dictators or the statesmen who were trying to cope with them). Of this tradition only Hermione Gingold, Hermione Baddeley and Joyce Grenfell, the English Ruth Draper, whose monologues were first heard in Farjeon's *Little Revue*, remain. Without politics, what butts were left? The press, the BBC, the frailties of nannies and hotel receptionists, the boredom of other people's holiday snaps, a suburban tea-party ruined by an argument about which bus the guest should have come by; or the new craze for ballet in a song, "When Bolonsky danced Belushka in September 1910."

(below) Léon Woizikovsky in Les Présages, Massine's Symphonic Ballet. Colonel de Basil's Ballets Russes of Monte Carlo, Alhambra Theatre, July 1933

Joyce Grenfell as the village mother (left) and (below) as herself in the Little Revue, Little Theatre, 1939

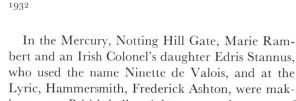

Ninette de Valois and Anton Dolin in *Douanes* Vic Wells Ballet, 1932

In the Mercury, Notting Hill Gate, Marie Rambert and an Irish Colonel's daughter Edris Stannus, who used the name Ninette de Valois, and at the Lyric, Hammersmith, Frederick Ashton, were making a new British ballet. Ashton created one out of William Walton's *Façade* for the new Camargo Society, and de Valois choreographed *Job* to Vaughan Williams's music. At Sadler's Wells, at the unfashionable top of Rosebury Avenue, attainable only by tram, Underground or No. 19 bus, a new, Odeon-shaped people's theatre was arising under the hand of Lilian Baylis, manager of the Old Vic in Waterloo Road. Miss Baylis lured Ninette de Valois (and certainly not with money) to the Old Vic to lead a new ballet school stiffened with professionals; so that Anton Dolin, for one season, found himself dashing over the river to dance in Jack Buchanan's *Stand Up and Sing* at the Hippodrome, and dashing back to complete his work at the Old Vic.

Robert Helpmann and Margot Fonteyn in *The Sleeping Princess*,
Vic Wells Ballet, 1936

the Monte Carlo ballet by an advance box-office sale of $65,000. The Monte Carlo ballet, reorganized by Colonel de Basil from the remains of the Diaghilev entourage and the ballet schools of Paris, with Massine as choreographer, set Brahms and Tchaikovsky symphonies dancing as well as reviving Diaghilev ballets. In London what was headlined as "Royal Accolade for British Ballet" happened in 1939 at a Gala performance conducted by Constant Lambert at Covent Garden in honour of President Lebrun and his wife, who, escorted by Yeomen of the Guard and glittering ceremony, saw the Vic-Wells Ballet Company with a nineteen-year-old prima ballerina named Margot Fonteyn (Peggy Hookham) in *The Sleeping Princess*.

Shakespeare was well-treated: notably by John Gielgud, producing himself in *Hamlet* (1934), the play's second longest run on record, and himself and Laurence Olivier in *Romeo and Juliet* (1935), the two of them swopping the roles of Romeo and Mercutio halfway through the run, and Edith Evans almost stealing the show as the Nurse. Gielgud's Hamlet was praised for being "an actor's interpretation of the part", untrammelled by "too much reading in the bottomless Hamlet literature". He had played

The old balletomanes of the "Bolonsky" school might sneer at the idea of leggy English girls and boys prancing in tights ("'oppin' about in their coms" was the North Country version), but ballet was mesmerizing the young. It was a wonderful, fairy-tale escape from politics and fear; it was both *avant-garde* and nostalgic; watching it, you could enjoy with a clear conscience hackneyed romantic music like *Invitation to the Dance* and workaday Tchaikovsky. In January 1931 Sadlers Wells opened, with Markova (Alice Marks) as prima ballerina in 1932, a new British home for plays, opera and ballet, only a shilling in the gallery and coffee and sandwiches for queueing, hungry students. De Valois choreographed *The Rake's Progress* (1935) (sets by Rex Whistler after Hogarth) and *Checkmate* (1937) (music by Arthur Bliss, sets by McKnight Kauffer the poster-artist), and Constant Lambert conducted.

America's first School of Ballet had meanwhile been founded financially by Lincoln Kirstein and artistically by Georges Balanchine whom he had persuaded over the Atlantic in 1933. New York, like London, was suspicious at first of native talent, though it was quick enough to set a record in 1938 for

John Gielgud as *Hamlet*, New Theatre, 1934

(above) June Brae as the
Black Queen in *Checkmate*,
Vic Wells Ballet, 1937
(left) Laurence Olivier,
Edith Evans and John
Gielgud in *Romeo and Juliet*,
New Theatre, 1935

Evelyn Laye in bed in *Helen!* Adelphi Theatre, 1932

Shakespeare's Richard II, and would play it again; but in 1932 Gordon Daviot (Elizabeth Mackintosh) gave him a sensitive art-loving king in *Richard of Bordeaux* which, after a trial at the Arts Theatre, brought history back to the West End by running for a year at the New Theatre.

More offbeat were Tyrone Guthrie's productions of *The Tempest* at Sadlers Wells (1934) and *The Taming of the Shrew* (1939) at the Old Vic—"Mr. Guthrie has gone frankly slapstick." There were plans for a National Theatre: Mr. Granville Barker wrote a book about it, saying it should be "like a public school or university . . . covering its running expenses by its receipts." A Jubilee Appeal for £500,000 was launched in 1935. The Government would not help. It was hoped to buy a site near the Victoria and Albert Museum. . . .

On both sides of the Atlantic the stage designer was coming into his own. Thus C. B. Cochran called in Oliver Messel to design *Helen!*, a new version (book and lyrics by A. P. Herbert) of Offenbach's *La Belle Hélène*, with Evelyn Laye, in white, and Cecil Beaton to design some scenes in his revue *Follow the Sun*; and in New York the success of *The Barretts of Wimpole Street* and *Winterset* owed much to the sets of Joe Mielziner, as *Victoria Regina* did to Rex Whistler's, and as *Reunion in Vienna* did to Aline Bernstein.

The Coward-Cochran partnership had had two triumphs in *Private Lives* and *Cavalcade*. But with Noël Coward's new one-man revue *Words and Music*, for which the author and composer dictated casting, production, designer and almost everything else, it began to split. *Words and Music* (1932) was not young and light-hearted, in Coward's 1920's manner; it was bitter and Depression-conscious—"a Coward revue but not a Cochran revue," C. B. said. Some of its material was used in *Set to Music*, starring Beatrice Lillie, at New York's Music Box in 1939. In London *Words and Music* had a modest run, but yielded three immortal songs, 'Mad About the Boy', 'The Party's Over Now' and 'Mad Dogs and Englishmen'. Thereafter many Coward shows were announced with "John C. Wilson presents. . . ." Wilson had already produced, in New York, *Design for Living*, a comedy which, described by a New York critic as "an erotic hotch-potch", did not reach London until 1939. In 1936 Coward undertook the risky experiment of playing (with Gertrude Lawrence) in nine one-act plays of his own, grouped in threes for different nights, under the title *Tonight at 8.30* (7.30 in the provinces).

In *Conversation Piece* and *Operette* he created two tasteful, tuneful and sentimental attempts to recapture the success of *Bitter-Sweet*. The first, embellished by Yvonne Printemps, second of Sacha Guitry's five wives, was set in Regency times; the second was a cliché-filled back-stage romance about a chorus girl. They yielded between them a couple of good waltzes, and one great satirical song which was really revue material—'The Stately Homes of England'.

The trouble was, perhaps, that others were judging the taste of the times more accurately. The big musicals of the Thirties came from two directions, Central Europe and America. From America, Kern's *Music In The Air*, and (in 1937) Rodgers and Hart's *On Your Toes*, the first musical comedy to contain a modern ballet, Balanchine's *Slaughter on Tenth Avenue*. With the wave of Viennese nostalgia came the wave of refugees from Hitler, bringing the genuine article with them. Even the un-genuine article, by 1935, was being provided, at Drury Lane, with less sophistication and more *schmaltz*, by Ivor Novello, in *Glamorous Night*, *Careless Rapture*, *Crest of the Wave* and *The Dancing Years*, which rescued the Lane from the financial doldrums.

Oswald Stoll's answer to the decline of music hall at the Coliseum and the Alhambra, and to the threat of the talkies, was lavish Continental-type productions like *White Horse Inn* and *Waltzes from Vienna*, using every available revolving stage, and in the case of *Wonder Bar* at the Savoy the audience were made to feel, by Basil Ionides' designs, that they were actually *in* the bar watching the cabaret. (True Anglo-Saxon cabaret was in the hands of such stars as Douglas

Dorothy Dickson and Ivor Novello in *Careless Rapture*, Drury Lane, 1936

Byng, who introduced Porter's 'Miss Otis Regrets' in *Hi-Diddle-Diddle*, 1934, and for many happy years treated more sophisticated late-night audiences to his own splendidly risqué songs, of which my own favourite was 'Doris the Goddess of Wind'.) From Germany in 1932 came *The Dubarry*, starring the tragic Anny Ahlers who killed herself soon afterwards at the age of twenty-six.

At Drury Lane, briefly in 1933, was Oscar Hammerstein's *Ball At The Savoy*, with Paul Abraham's music: very German, very waltzy, reminding people that two years before there had been an actual ball at London's Savoy Hotel, to the music of Johann Strauss, the Waltz King's nephew. There was also a "Viennese" band at the Hotel Splendide where the Prince of Wales, partnered by Lady Furness (Thelma Vanderbilt), was able to indulge his love of waltzes.

Whose was the voice of the Thirties? In America, possibly Ethel Merman's, who became a star overnight, singing 'I Got Rhythm' in Gershwin's *Girl Crazy* (1930) and holding a high C for sixteen bars; but in London probably Tauber's. Franz Lehár's operettas *Frederica* and *The Land of Smiles* had short runs, but the music was played everywhere, the records sold in thousands, and there was nobody who could not hum 'You Are My Heart's Delight'. The *falsetto pianissimo*, the sob and the whipped cream were brought under 'control when Tauber sang Mozart at Covent Garden in 1938. He knew he had the only instantly recognizable tenor voice since Caruso; and there were moments when it seemed the last link with a dying Europe.

What was the newest sound of the Thirties? It came, of course, from America; it was presented, of course, by C. B. Cochran. A nineteen-year-old youth who you must be joking, Mr. Cochran!—played a *mouth-organ*? Well, he called it a harmonica, which sounded better, and somehow he could give it a tone that lay between a viola and an oboe. Name of Larry Adler. "I think," said Cochran, "I'll take the Albert Hall for him." He could play Ravel's *Bolero*, and all the classics with the correct phrasing and a certain amount of harmony, and one day Vaughan Williams would write a concerto for him. But for the present, Cochran needed him for a showman's purpose. His 1934 revue *Streamline* was near the end of its run. He put Larry Adler into it, and it ran for another fifteen weeks.

# SOUNDS AND SWEET AIRS

The *radio* voice of the Thirties? In Britain there would be several contenders, and one of them would be Gracie Fields; but in America it could, among women, be narrowed down to two—Kate Smith and Ruth Etting. Vallee and Crosby might croon and boo-boo, but every American man had two mothers (his own and Kate Smith) and two mistresses (his own and Ruth Etting). In 'Ten Cents A Dance' and 'After You've Gone', Ruth was the voice of the Depression, yet the escape from the Depression. She had made her name as Columbia's top recording star, and as the "distaff star" of three different editions of Ziegfeld's Follies. She had sung with Eddie Cantor in *Whoopee*—songs which John Braine has found remarkable for their "self-assurance, innocence (and) lack of awareness of evil."

Competition on sponsored radio was acute, and for some years Ruth Etting outrated in popularity Irene Franklin, the Giersdorf Sisters, and even Bessie Smith (for radio had at last broken through the colour bar). She could displace Bessie Smith, but she was herself displaced by Kate Smith, the eighteen-stone blonde whose signature tune was 'When The Moon Comes Over the Mountain'. Thereafter Ruth Etting began a mysterious decline. You always felt that she was singing about her own life: "Love me or leave me or let me be lonely. . . ." Walter Winchell, the Broadway columnist, hinted that it had something to do with "a man named Smith," but even he had no more information than that. Today, aged seventy-nine, she is living as a recluse somewhere near Santa Monica, California.

There were, in 1935, thirty million radio sets in the United States, and more than six hundred broadcasting stations. Radio, sponsored as in America or monopolized as in Britain, was the most powerful medium of communication and propaganda the world had so far seen. Radio sets cost up to $135

Kate Smith

Ruth Etting

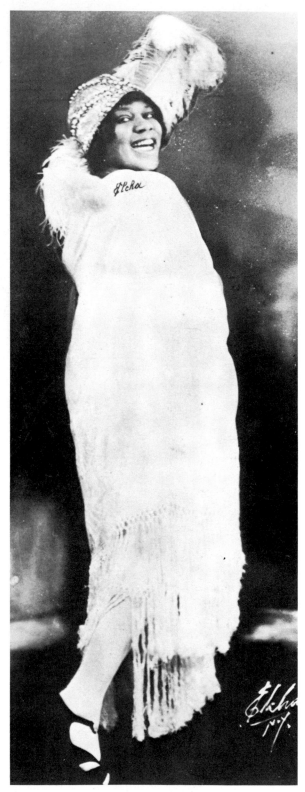

Bessie Smith

(£27), and with hire purchase there was hardly any Depression family that could not afford one. The unemployed, when not scavenging for food or looking for work, stayed home with the radio, listening to everything from Roosevelt's Fireside Chat to Amos 'n' Andy. NBC's Amos 'n' Andy, Freeman Gosden and Charles Correll, portrayed coloured folks as the northern States still imagined them to be, nice funny black men who said things like "dat's de propolition" and "I'se regusted wid you". They were imitated in Britain by a pair called Alexander and Mose, whose act, full of old minstrel jokes and riddles, always ended, in deference to the BBC's rules about the mention of alcohol, with "How's about a nice juicy sarsaparilla?"

Booming radio gave variety talent a new lease of life. The Chase and Sanborn Radio Hour gave American listeners Edgar Bergen and Charlie McCarthy, assisted by Mortimer Snerd. There were Fred Allen, George Burns and Gracie Allen, Bob Hope and Jerry Colonna, and that miracle of timing and understatement, Jack Benny, whose double-take pauses made sponsors groan at the thought of air time being wasted when it could have been selling something. There was room for the unknown too, in Major Bowes' Amateur Hour, forerunner of Carroll Levis and Hughie Green in Britain; and for splendid nonsense such as NBC's International Singing Mouse Contest. The young broke dates on Tuesday nights rather than miss Fibber McGee and Molly: the gimmick was a cupboard chock-full of everything, and you waited for the moment when it would be opened with a crash of stuff spilling out. In many American homes today there are still cupboards known as McGee closets.

The radio commentator grew powerful. He might be Lowell Thomas, Boake Carter, or H. V. Kaltenborn, bearer of bad tidings from a continent he called "Yirrup": while waiting for news of the Hitler-Chamberlain meeting at Munich in September 1938, he lived and slept in Studio 9 at CBS. Kaltenborn also gave the world's first running commentary on a war when he broadcast from Hendaye, just inside France, every day for five days: the Spanish Civil War, he saw fit to observe, was "like a football match". With Ed Murrow, who by 1937 had become European Director of CBS, he did the famous two-way broadcasts between America and Europe, "Calling Ed Murrow . . ."

*(right)* Ed Murrow
*(below)* Amos 'n' Andy—Freeman Gosden and Charles Correll
*(bottom)* Andrea Leeds and Charlie McCarthy

For several years Murrow had seen and exploited the popular educational role of radio. For CBS, in 1935, he had started *American School of the Air*. Radio's *March of Time* used the "living newspaper" idea of dramatising the news by employing actors to portray real people, speaking fictitious lines. None of this could have been done in Britain at the time. Moving over to NBC as Director of Talks, Murrow had secured speakers like Ramsay MacDonald, Norman Angell, Maynard Keynes, William Beveridge, John Masefield and H. G. Wells. He had G. K. Chesterton talking about Dickens on Christmas Day, as if to complement Lionel Barrymore's traditional reading of *A Christmas Carol* on Christmas Eve. He organized Bernard Shaw's notorious "little talk about Russia", addressed to "you dear old boobs in America". America heard the actual voices of Mussolini and Trotsky.

There was a running battle between CBS and NBC over coverage of the Abdication. CBS managed to report it from the House of Commons before Prime Minister Baldwin actually read out the Royal message, and gained a world scoop with the words: "The King has abdicated. Here is Sir Frederick Whyte to speak to you about this momentous event." And when Murrow covered the Coronation for NBC, American listeners heard what somebody called "the longest commercial for the British Empire on record." It included Herbert Hodge (the London cabby who wrote the Unity Theatre play), imported from London and talking to America from the Spread Eagle, the village pub at Little Bardfield, Essex, on a Saturday night, assisted by Professor Harold Laski of the London School of Economics (whose local it was) amid a great deal of unrehearsed singing and backchat from darts players.

Murrow was interpreting Britain to America as Alistair Cooke, whose transatlantic broadcasts began in 1938, was one day to interpret America to Britain. In his Savile Row suits he was, some Americans thought, too much a friend of Britain. Like many American journalists in London, his standing was higher than that of native pressmen: he could get Churchill direct on the telephone. Later, he did much to help America into the war by his affection for Britain, in his newscasts which began "This is . . . (dramatic pause) . . . London." That pause, we are told, was suggested by his old speech instructor at Washington State College, Ida Lou Anderson. It was

never used to better effect than on Saturday, August 26, 1939, a week before war was declared. "I have a feeling that Englishmen are a little proud of themselves tonight," he told America. "They believe . . . that the Lion has turned and that the retreat from Manchukuo, Abyssinia, Spain, Czechoslovakia and Austria, has stopped. . . . At the British Embassy in Berlin all the luggage of the personnel and staff has been piled up in the hall. It is remarked here that the most prominent article in the heavy luggage was a folded umbrella . . ." (An allusion to the emblem of appeasement carried on all diplomatic visits abroad by Neville Chamberlain, and the subject of a mocking little song by Flanagan and Allen.)

The greater freedom of American radio had its dangers. It enabled Father Coughlin, priest of Royal Oak, Michigan, to attack financiers (who to him were all Jews), Hoover, trade unions, Prohibition, the dollar, Roosevelt, Communists (i.e. everyone who wasn't isolationist). His warm, Irish voice had begun innocently enough in a Sunday children's hour on Station WJR, Detroit, which brought him fifty thousand letters a week, some of them enclosing money to finance his Radio League of the Little Flower or his God's Poor Society in Detroit. Soon his sermons, which he refused to let CBS censor, were on seventeen radio stations with an audience of over forty million. By 1936 he was on thirty-five stations, and was running a weekly paper, *Social Justice*, which even reprinted the discredited Protocols of the Elders of Zion; and a youth movement called Christian Front whose thuggish young members smashed Jewish property. If he had a hero, it was William Randolph Hearst.

Father Coughlin

Long before Britain, American radio discovered the kind of serial that, because of its original sponsorship, became known as soap opera. Sixty-five soap operas were said to be running simultaneously in the late 1930s. In January 1933 began *Lone Ranger*, an endless Western whose authors did not mind admitting that they had never been west of Michigan, and which, by 1939, was producing new instalments three times a week. Allegedly for children, *Buck Rogers*, beginning in 1932 by kind permission, one after another, of Kelloggs Corn Flakes, Cocomalt, Cream of Wheat and General Foods, featured mad scientists with disintegrator-ray guns. *Superman* (1938) took things a stage further by making the hero both omnipotent and indestructible, and involving him in interplanetary adventure. The trouble with Superman was that since he was all-powerful, the script writers could not dream up antagonists worthy of him.

A Mrs. Gertrude Berg invented, for Procter and Gamble, *The Goldbergs*, a study of Jewish family life, playing the part of Molly Goldberg herself. Paul Rhymer's *Vic and Sade*, one of the few humorous soap operas, began in 1932 and ran for fourteen years. Mrs. Elaine Carrington wrote *Pepper Young's Family* and made so much money that in the Radio Writers' Guild, which she helped to found, she was known as "the Member in Mink". Richest woman writer of all was Irma Phillips, turning out sixty thousand words a week for *Today's Children*. An advertising man named Frank Hummert, a Chicago *Daily News* reporter named Charles Robert Douglas Hardy Andrews (whose output at one time was over a hundred thousand words a week) and a journalist named Anne Ashenhurst joined forces to produce *Just Plain Bill*, in which the hero, a barber, was for once an ordinary citizen. This was followed by *Ma Perkins*, a children's series (based on a cartoon character) called *Skippy*, sponsored by Wheaties breakfast food, and a mystery, *Mr. Keen, Tracer of Lost Persons*, whose signature tune was Noël Coward's 'Someday I'll Find You'. There was one attempt, in Sandra Michael's *Against The Storm*, to upgrade the soap opera by having, as hero, a college professor trying to make his colleagues understand the danger of Fascism; but for most serials the official view was: "If it doesn't sell merchandise, something is wrong with the story."

Well, now: what had Britain to offer? Sir John Reith, dictatorially determined that the BBC should never depart from public responsibility for a revolutionary weapon of communication, left Broadcasting House in 1938 to become Chairman of Imperial Airways; but things didn't change very much. In the worst years of Depression (1929–33) the number of radio licences doubled, and by 1939 three-quarters of all British homes were listening every day to a medium that, during the coming War, would be the chief support of their morale. You could buy, cash down or easy payments, a 3-valve all-mains set for £15–£17 in 1931. By 1934 prices had come down so that a 4-valve Ekco superhet "with integral loud-speaker" cost only £8. 8s. The great one-up was to own a moving-coil loudspeaker with a huge baffle-board round it: it was the 1930s equivalent of stereo. Many people whose houses were still lighted with gas ran their radios by high-tension and low-tension batteries: the latter, being accumulators, took two days to recharge at the local garage.

In March 1930 the old 2LO London station closed down and new, high-power London Regional transmitters opened at Brookman's Park, Hertfordshire. The BBC, which had been muddling along for nearly ten years at Savoy Hill, built itself in 1931 a £350,000 temple in Portland Place like a great stone battleship, to be called Broadcasting House. There was a little trouble about Eric Gill's sculpture of Ariel with a flute (posed for by Leslie French who had played Ariel in *The Tempest*), a frontal nude which a Member of Parliament found "objectionable to public morals and decency". In the entrance hall was a Latin dedication: "This Temple of the Arts and Muses is dedicated to Almighty God by the first Governors of Broadcasting in the year 1931. . . . It is their prayer that good seed sown may bring forth good harvest."

Broadcasting could take a monarch's greeting to the other side of the Earth; it could also help him to announce his abdication. Both were to happen soon. One of the highest priorities was to establish an Empire Service; and on Christmas Day 1932, sitting at home at Sandringham, Norfolk, George V said gruffly: "Through one of the marvels of science I am enabled this Christmas Day to speak to all my peoples throughout the Empire . . . I speak now from my home and from my heart to you all, to men and women so cut off by the snows and deserts or the sea, that only voices out of the air can reach them." His voice was part of a programme that brought into every home, delaying the post-plum-pudding snoozes

Richard Murdoch and Arthur Askey in *Band Waggon*, 1938

microphone. It was not quite in the Ed Murrow class, but it was popular, introduced by the sounds of traffic in Piccadilly Circus, the Cockney voice of Vi Caley crying "luvly violets", and Eric Coates's 'Knightsbridge' march, which was such an instant hit that the BBC received twenty thousand letters the day after it was first played. In this year, too, the BBC experimented with its first woman announcer, whose name was Sheila Borrett. Many programmes were nostalgic, chief among them *Scrapbook*, devised by Charles Brewer and Leslie Baily: it chose a year—say 1911 or 1914—interviewed people who had done something newsworthy during that year (such as Claud Graham-White, who in 1910 had flown from London to Manchester, but had been beaten by a Frenchman, Louis Paulhan) and revived songs of the year; the whole building up into pieces of social history which relied increasingly on the BBC's own archives.

As war drew nearer, radio variety shows began to package themselves with permanent linkmen and regular features. One of the first was *Monday Night At Eight* (1937). 1938 saw the first edition of *Band Waggon* starring Arthur Askey and Richard ("Stinker") Murdoch, scripted by Vernon Harris and produced by Harry S. Pepper and Gordon Crier. It came on at 8.15 on Wednesday nights, and was the first really competitive radio show that had cinema managers seriously worried. One refused invitations in order to be at home for *Band Waggon*; and Arthur Askey's catchphrase *I theng yaw* (I thank you) entered everyone's lighter conversation. Sunday night serial plays (twelve instalments of *The Cloister and the Hearth* or *Les Misérables*) caused thousands to stay away from Evensong. *Send for Paul Temple*, Francis Durbridge's undying detective series whose hero is with us yet, also started in 1938. In 1939 came the great *ITMA* (It's That Man Again) scripted by Ted Kavanagh and starring Tommy Handley, the fastest show—faster than *Hellzapoppin*—radio had ever known. At last it was possible to make fun of the potential—who in a few weeks' time was to become the real—enemy, and also of Them, the authorities in Britain, whoever they were. Tommy Handley was the Minister of Aggravation who ran the Office of Twerps, Jack Train was Funf, the "spy with the feet of sauerkraut" . . . "it may be Funf for you, but it's not much funf for me . . ." oh, well, it seemed hysterically funny at the time, and the regular appearances of expected mad characters, each with his or her expected

of millions, the church bells of Bethlehem, the *Majestic* in mid-Atlantic, the *Empress of Britain* at Port Said, and thirteen other points round the world; and next day the New York *Times* headline was: DISTANT LANDS THRILL TO KING'S 'GOD BLESS YOU'. Queen Mary's voice was heard for a second or two in 1934 when, with a bottle of Australian wine, she launched the *Queen Mary*: it was noticed that, in the Edwardian upper-class way, she pronounced the operative word *lahnch*.

Henry Hall's newly formed BBC Dance Orchestra had replaced Jack Payne as leader of the BBC Dance Orchestra, and in 1934 he introduced *Henry Hall's Guest Night*: his first guests (unpaid) were Flanagan and Allan and Elsie and Doris Waters.

Programmes were as experimental as Reith allowed. For some reason the BBC broadcast, on May 13, 1930, the apes at the Zoo: we have no record of what they said. It was considered revolutionary when, on January 13, 1933, the BBC News, which never referred to crimes of violence, broadcast an SOS description of a man wanted for murder. In 1934 there was a brave attempt to introduce the 24-hour clock: why? nobody wanted it. In 1938 Spelling Bees, introduced from America, became a national entertainment. Closer to the news was *In Town Tonight*, beginning in 1933 with the voice of a large man named Brian Michie ordering London to STOP! so that new arrivals could be interviewed at the

catchphrase, such as a charlady named Mrs. Mopp ("Can I do yer now, Sir?") and Mona Lott ("It's being so cheerful as keeps me going") never failed to raise its expected laugh. This was the show that lasted all through the War.

Radio nurtured specialized talents such as that of Reginald Gardiner, stalwart supporter of many London revues and later Hollywood comedies, who imitated trains ("diddly-*dum*, diddly-*dum*", with the effeminate squeal of a French engine whistle entering the Simplon tunnel), and—"Good evening, England. This is Gillie Potter speaking to you in English." This master of polysyllabic pomp created a village called Hogsnorton where Lord and Lady Marshmallow lived in mounting insolvency, with Canon Fodder, General Maudlin-Tite and Potter's imaginary black-sheep brother, last heard of in "the Brazilian port of Cascara Sagrada".

Never neglecting its mission to educate, the BBC's schools programmes, run by Mary Somerville, were being received, in 1939, by ten thousand schools. For adults there were "Group Listening" Discussion Groups, talks by Dr. Malcolm Sargent in a Sunday lunchtime programme and a goodly selection of "serious" plays. The outside world was brought into everyone's sitting room by a device called the Blattnerphone, a cumbersome machine "like two Irish spinning wheels" which recorded open-air events on steel tape: it became mobile in 1935.

The BBC had always been criticized: by the masses for being too highbrow, by the upper classes for being too common—it was still fashionable, noted Minnie Hogg, the *Tatler* columnist in 1934, to say "I never listen to that dreadful wireless." Criticism reached a climax in 1936, when the Corporation's Charter was due for renewal, and its work was being reviewed by the Ullswater Committee. In 1935 Raymond Postgate had written a virulent pamphlet, *What To Do With the BBC* (published by Leonard Woolf's Hogarth Press), accusing it of financial scandals, overpaid officialdom, sinecures and much else. But the focus of popular discontent was the dullness of Sunday programmes. Not until 1935 was any programme allowed on Sunday morning: it was, of course, a church service. There was still no variety or dance music. Were people getting their licence money's worth?

Since 1930 there had been an alternative. If you switched on at breakfast time, you could hear this:

*Hurrah for Betox!*
*What a delightful smell!*

and

*We are the Ovaltineys,*
*Happy girls and boys!*

and Carroll Gibbons, George Formby, cabaret, crime serials, and—"this is your old friend the Happy Philosopher". For this was Radio Luxembourg, blasting away with all its 100 kilowatts, and Radio Normandie, and seventy-two other stations used by Captain Leonard Plugge's International Broadcasting Company, the first commercial radio Britain ever heard.

Television, everyone knew, would someday overtake radio. The 1933 Christmas number of *Punch* even foresaw the Christmas of the future, with families staring at a screen while tree, Santa, pantomime, pudding, were all done for them in the TV studio.

The first really practical system demonstrated in America transmitted pictures by radio relay between New York and Camden, New Jersey, analysed into 240 lines and sent at 24 pictures per second. The tiny screen showed everything happening in a blizzard of static. In 1934 the number of lines was 343 and the rate was 30. A crude colour TV broadcast was made as early as 1930. The BBC, still experimenting on the Baird system, had a 60-line picture in 1930. Catering for the only thirty people in the country who had TV sets, Lance Sieveking and Val Gielgud produced Britain's first television play, Pirandello's *The Man with the Flower in his Mouth*. Only one person at a time could be televised, and everybody, including the Paramount Astoria Girls who put on a cabaret at 11 p.m. in 1933, had to wear weird make-up (blue noses and black lips). The TV set-owners (called "televisors") saw greenish pictures on 9" × 4" screens.

By 1936, using the new Marconi E.M.I. system (405 lines), there were still only three hundred viewers (should they be called lookers, witnesses, glancers, visionists, teleseers, tele-observists? the Advisory Committee on Spoken English worried. The *Radio Times* settled the matter by printing the word *televiewer*). However, the BBC felt ready to launch a national television service, which it did in November 1936. There was a pre-release at Radiolympia on August 26 with Helen McKay singing 'Here's Looking At You', theme song and title of a programme produced by Cecil Madden, who also created *Picture Page*, a weekly television "magazine" introduced by Joan Gilbert. Immediately over a thousand girls applied for jobs as TV announcers: only two (Jasmine Bligh and Elizabeth Cowell) were successful, and made the most of their £25 a year dress allowance. They were soon joined by a beautiful young man named Leslie Mitchell. One of the earliest televiewers was Harold Nicolson, surprised to find that a show from as far away as Alexandra Palace could be seen at Sissinghurst in Kent. He stared at a flickering Mickey Mouse and an old Gaumont-British film, and then wrote in his diary: "As an invention it is tremendous and may alter the whole basis of democracy."

The Coronation procession of George VI was seen by two thousand televiewers (the number had risen sharply in a single year) by means of three static cameras at Hyde Park Corner; so was Wimbledon tennis; and in 1938 came the first television play ever broadcast live from a theatre—J. B. Priestley's *When We Are Married* at the St. Martin's. Television was in business; but not for a long time could it compete with eight million radio licences.

Radio could be used for propaganda, as we knew from Germany, Italy and Radio Luxembourg; and not a moment too soon, the BBC, during the Munich crisis, started news broadcasts to Europe in French, German and Italian, followed soon by Arabic, Spanish and Portuguese. What some suspected, but nobody yet knew for certain, was that it could also spread blind panic, as no other medium could.

One of the few CBS programmes which had no advertising sponsor, which indeed, being cultural, was thought to have "no listening audience at all" (especially since Charlie McCarthy was on the rival network), was a series of dramatized books called *Mercury Theatre of the Air*, produced by a precocious twenty-three-year-old named Orson Welles. On Sunday, October 30, 1938, exactly one month after the Munich agreement, the book happened to be H. G. Wells's *War Of The Worlds*. It began with a simulated news-flash in the middle of dance music: a professor at "Mount Jennings Observatory near Chicago" had seen explosions on the planet Mars. Over. The band went on playing 'Star Dust'. Fade down music: a Princeton scientist (fictitious) was interviewed on the Mars phenomenon. Then news bulletins: Martians had landed (at Princeton, of all

places), defeated the New Jersey militia and killed 1,500 people; now they were in other cities; New York was being evacuated; the Martians had death-ray guns.

Four times during the play there were announcements saying that it was all fiction, but people still telephoned newspapers, the Government, anyone, asking what to do. Surely it wasn't Martians, it must be Germans. People improvised gas masks with wet cloths, loaded cars with luggage; it was essential not to be wherever one was; what was a suitable poison in the bathroom cupboard to commit suicide with? What about the dog, the cat, the canary? Decent chaps from as far off as San Francisco telephoned offering themselves for national service. A few people rushed to church to pray, lest this should be the end of the world followed by Judgment Day. An unfortunate power-cut, blacking out a whole district of New York, increased the panic. An actor, imitating President Roosevelt's voice, told people to "evacuate New York City". Real Princeton science dons rushed out to find the "metal cylinder" or "meteor" in which the Martians had arrived. Meanwhile the CBS studio was filling up with police, unsure whether to stop the show.

Later, Princeton University saved its honour by a special Radio Project, financed by the Rockefeller Foundation, to analyse the panic. They interviewed hundreds of people, including a man in Massachusetts who said he'd spent $3.25 on a rail fare to get out of town, money he'd been saving up for new shoes, and would Princeton please send him one pair of black shoes, size 9–13.

Joseph Cotten, who was in the show, told Welles he was all washed up now: nobody would ever let him produce anything again. Welles told the press he was "deeply regretful" to learn that there had been "some apprehension". War Departments in all countries took note of what rumour and panic might do in a *real* war. The New York *Times* blamed the radio industry's lack of responsibility. Dr. Goebbels blamed the Jews. The Italian press blamed democracy. And Dorothy Thompson blamed "the failure of popular education". Could it be, after all, that John Reith was right about the dangers of radio?

*(opposite)* "Luvly violets". Flower seller, Piccadilly Circus, London, Easter 1936

# PLAYING THE GAME

"Well, Jack, you can have it! Now they'll all be after you," gasped Ellsworth Vines, when Australia's Jack Crawford beat him at Wimbledon in 1933. The strain of being champion was often analysed by Britain's Fred Perry, who was doing a certain amount of tennis journalism in the late 1930s. Why was Dorothy Round beaten at Wimbledon by Joan Hartigan, whom she had defeated easily several times in Australia? Was it the climate, or nerves, or what? Why, in February 1936, were three Davis Cup team members forced to stand down through illness? Why had America's Alice Marble had a complete breakdown in Paris two years before? Was there something about the game, or about the publicity it created, that was bad for one's health? Was a player finished at twenty-eight? Why could Dorothy Round, called by the American press "the English Sunday school teacher", beat Helen Jacobs, she of "the deceptive chop-strokes", in England but not in America? Perry thought it was all a question of relaxation and of ascetic physical fitness.

The Americans, despite that fearful will to win, were probably better at relaxing. Sometimes the men did it in the middle of the game, clowning for the crowd, like ginger-haired Donald Budge, apt to shout "Aw, Momma!" at every dropped shot, to whom a girl at my wife's finishing school in Paris wrote an ode which began:

*Thanks for the memory. . . .*
*Of your profile like a cod,*
*Your breathless cry of 'God!'*

Budge was the up-and-coming challenger to Fred Perry and the British team (Lee, Bunny Austin and G. P. Hughes). The British, when 32 countries challenged France for the Davis Cup in 1933, had won it for the first time in twenty years. Perry won three successive men's singles championships at

*(opposite)* 'Jockeys', 1934, by William Roberts

*(above)* Jack Crawford (left) and Ellsworth Vines after their match at Wimbledon in 1933

*(below)* Dorothy Round (left) and Helen Jacobs at Wimbledon in 1933

Fred Perry at Wimbledon in 1936

Wimbledon (1934–36) and three at Forest Hills: in 1936 Britain won the Davis Cup for the fourth consecutive year.

A particularly satisfying year for Britain was 1934, when Perry and Dorothy Round both won at Wimbledon. Was Dorothy Round's victory helped by her shorts? After beating Helen Jacobs she said: "I bought a pair of pleated shorts the morning of my final against Helen and wore them in the afternoon. I must have been mad not to try them before." Helen Jacobs claimed to be the "first woman player to wear shorts in a major tournament—the United States Championship at Forest Hills in 1933." Was she? Some say that Eileen Bennett of Britain was. The matter became academic as both skirts and shorts for tennis got shorter and shorter until in 1939 *Punch* said of Alice Marble: "Her shorts will keep her memory long."

Budge set a new record in 1938 by winning the four major singles championships of the world—Australia, France, Britain and America. His victory over Germany's Baron Gottfried von Cramm at Wimbledon in 1937 was described by Bill Tilden as "one of the finest matches I ever saw"—and he did it again at Forest Hills. The Davis Cup went to Australia in 1939 when America's Bobby Riggs and Frank Parker, the two "boy wonders", lost at Haverford, Pa.

Von Cramm, rumoured to be both homosexual and a convert to Buchmanism, was regarded as a great German gentleman, an apologist for his country. He needed to be after the 1936 Olympic Games. In 1935 a book by Bruno Malitz, sports director of the Storm Troops, had had wide publicity, resulting mostly from one sentence: "We can never forget that our sporting activity is based on hatred." Competitors, therefore, were enemies of the Fatherland. It was known that at all gates of the Olympic village at Berlin there would be notices saying "entrance forbidden to Jews." Many British and American athletes voted against participation in this Nazified affair which was clearly of great propaganda significance to Germany.

The first Olympic Village at Los Angeles, four years before, had realized the classical ideal of Baron Pierre de Coubertin, who had founded the Games—the brotherhood and sisterhood of all nations united by a love of sport. Lake Placid and Garmisch-Partenkirchen had been the scenes of the first Winter Games. In 1932, 37 nations and 1,408 athletes had taken part: now there were 49 nations and over 4,000 participants. It was known in Germany that many of America's best athletes were Negroes: could anything be done to stop them coming?

The master race took a humiliating beating. The picture that flashes into everyone's mind at the mention of the XIth Olympiad is of Jesse Owens, star of the 100 metres, 200 metres, and long jump, who won a total of four gold medals, set two records, tied for a third and ran in a relay team which set another world record. There were six other Negro gold medallists, among them Archie Williams (400 metres), John Woodruff (800 metres), Cornelius Johnson (high jump) and Ralphe Metcalfe, who ran with Owens in the relay team. There were Nazi sneers at the British performance, which, unless we claimed Jack Lovelock of New Zealand (1,500 metres) as one of us, was confined mainly to walking, water polo and sculling, with one glorious exception: in the Winter Games the British ice-hockey team beat Canada, champions since 1920, at their own game. The Herrenvolk won mainly weight events—shots, hammers and other ponderous objects.

The great figure in boxing, by 1937, was a Negro—Joe Louis from Alabama, then twenty-three, about to gain the world title and to hold it for a record twelve years. "The best weapons in his armoury," said *Vanity Fair*, "are a supply of short, swift punches which he deals with either hand. He seldom scowls or smiles, and he reads the Bible often." The typical heavyweight American boxer was no longer an Italian, Latin American, Irishman or Jew, but Negro. Managers like Tex Rickard used to exploit race prejudice by setting white to fight black. No longer. In 1935 Mike Jacobs signed Louis to a contract, and started a new boxing boom. The money was no longer so good in these Depression days, yet the Brown Bomber, the biggest box-office draw since Dempsey, had made $600,000 by the time he had fought ("quarrelled with" was a favourite expression among sportswriters) Max Baer (1935) and Max Schmeling (1938).

*(above)* Joe Louis in the ring
*(left)* Max Baer

Schmeling, a German national hero who somehow managed to avoid joining the Nazi party and married (and stayed married to) Anny Ondra the film-star, had become world heavyweight champion in 1930—on a foul, because Jack Sharkey had punched him in the groin. Sharkey took the title away from him two years later. The ex-sailor from Boston, who sometimes threw tantrums in the ring, lost in 1933 to Primo Carnera from Italy. Carnera, a simple giant with outsize feet whom Sharkey called a deadhead, lost to Max Baer in 1934, and Baer to James Braddock the following year. For Braddock, slow, wiry "Cinderella Man of boxing", this was a triumph over a run of bad luck, a difficult weight (180 lb., a good 40 lb. less than many heavyweights) and a tendency to break his hand. Then came Joe Louis, and retirement—but not before he had beaten Britain's Tommy Farr. Britain had no great heavyweight, but was fond of a small, courageous Cockney named Kid Berg.

Hungry Lou Gehrig

Baseball's hundredth birthday was coming up. In America more people than ever were watching it—because they could now do so by night on weekdays at floodlit stadiums, though the Chicago Cubs still played their home games by daylight only. There were new All-Star games, played for charity, beginning at Comiskey Park, home of the White Sox, as part of the Chicago Century of Progress World Fair in 1933. Babe Ruth was now helping to manage the Boston Braves, and the new star was Hungry Lou Gehrig, sometimes known, for certain amplitudes, as "Biscuit Pants". He earned the highest salary in the American League, but could not equal Ruth's total earnings, over a quarter of a century, of nearly $1,100,000. Gehrig died young of sclerosis.

Talent spotters in 1934 were observing an eighteen-year-old named Tom Henrich, born in Massillon, Ohio, and now playing for the Zanesville team: four years later he was playing in his first World Series. One day, no doubt, he would qualify for the new National Baseball Hall of Fame, dedicated at Cooperstown, New York, where the game had started, in June 1939; its first occupants were Ty Cobb, Babe Ruth, Walter Johnson, Honus Wagner and Christy Mathewson. A performance which I can hardly believe was that of Joe Sprinx, of Cleveland Indians, who in 1931 caught a baseball dropped from an airship 800 feet above him: unfortunately it hit his jaw first, breaking it.

Tom Henrich

Britain's national game, Soccer, drew bigger crowds than ever: crowds on the whole were well-behaved, shouted abuse at any "dirty" play, and envied the salaried professional who could make a living at the game. Train-loads of supporters from the North came "oop for t'Coop", the F.A. Cup Final whose hero in 1933 was Dixie Dean, he of the 379 goals, when Everton defeated Manchester City. Memory's most enduring image is that of Alex James in droopy drawers as if the elastic had broken: transferred to Arsenal for a record £9,000, he became (in John Arlott's words) "the most successful goal-maker in the history of English football". The World Cup had existed since 1930, and Latin countries like Uruguay and Italy were winning it, but Britain did not compete.

"Give 'em plenty of beer and racing," was one statesman's recipe for coping with the unemployed. In the early 1900s it might have been true to say that "in England racing is a sport, in France an entertainment, in America a business," but by now it was all three everywhere. For one thing, it now had to compete for the mass market with greyhound racing. Betting had been partly mechanized by the Totalizator, or "Tote", which discouraged the welshing bookie. The great jockey, replacing Steve Donoghue, was now Gordon Richards, who in 1933 had twelve consecutive wins. The Aga Khan (for a long time I was uncertain whether he was an owner, a jockey or a horse) had three Derby winners, Blenheim (1930), Bahram (1935) and Mahmoud (1936). From the mists of memory come the names of Reynoldstown,

Dunn, the Everton forward, crowded out by Manchester City backs during the F.A. Cup Final, 1933

(above) The Aga Khan leads in the Derby winner 'Blenheim' with H. Wragg up, 1930

who won the Grand National two years running (1935 and 1936) and Golden Miller, who won it in 1934, the same year that Windsor had won the St. Leger. But Golden Miller, favourite in the 1937 Grand National, refused a fence, and Royal Mail won instead.

To see the horses you had to go out of town to a race-course in the far suburbs, if not in the deep country. To see the greyhounds, you only had to take a bus to somewhere like Clapton Stadium or the White City. Mechanized by the electric hare, "greycing" always contained an element of chance in the absence of a rider, and dogs bumping each other on a turn could make nonsense of "form". Yet form there was: how else to explain the nineteen con-

(left) Gordon Richards (left) with Fred Fox, 1930

secutive wins in 1930 of brindled Mick the Miller? He
was the favourite who, often last at the first bend,
seeming to know how to conserve his energy, reached
third place at the last bend and (I quote a witness)
"overtook on the outside and . . . got up on the line to
win by a nose." Bred by Father Brophy, an Irish
priest, and owned by Mr. Sidney Orton, Mick went
on the variety bill at the Palladium before he retired.
He died in 1939, aged thirteen, and, now stuffed, may
be seen in London's Natural History Museum.

The 1932 Olympic Winter Games at Lake Placid
had not only started Sonja Henie on her rise to skating
fame: they made America want to ski. Some of the
European ski teams stayed in America to start ski
schools, and at Macy's store in New York (sports
section) a twenty-foot hill, covered with borax to
imitate snow, was built and an hour's free instruction
was offered to anyone who bought a pair of skis.
Pretty soon, promoters realized that snow could be
sold to the travel industry. Speed and comfort were
the new developments: by using chair- and gondola-
lifts or (in America and Canada) rope tows instead of
funicular railway or laborious climbing, you could
squeeze at least four times as much downhill ski-ing
into a day, much of it 60 m.p.h. stuff, following new
Alpine techniques. Due largely to the advocacy of Sir
Arnold Lunn, inventor of the zig-zag slalom, downhill ski championships were now the regular scene in
Switzerland. And in Sun Valley, Idaho, a fashionable
new ski resort was designed and built by Felix
Schaffgotsch, an Austrian, with finance from Averell
Harriman, and it became for some time Hollywood's
favourite winter holiday spot.

*Punch* drawings, in the early 1930s still showed golf
caddies as dirty, ragged, often wearing cast-off tail
coats much too big for them. But already some of the
caddies were playing better than members, some
were even becoming pro's, as golf slowly de-
mocratized itself. Other things were changing
including equipment. The rubber "balloon ball",
pioneered in America in 1930, lasted no time at all: it
was too light, and even a breeze would carry it into
the rough. Seamless, stainless steel clubs were
replacing the old hickory shafts. Gene Sarazen
experimented with a straight-edged "sand wedge"
for bunkers (or traps) and used it to help win the
British and American Opens in 1932. Nomenclature
was confused, for manufacturers were flooding the
market with new kinds of club, until the authorities

Mick the Miller

Sonja Henie

on both sides of the Atlantic limited the total number of clubs to 14.

For the hall of fame we may pick out, for America, Mrs. Glenna Collett Vare, champion woman golfer in 1930 and 1935, with Betty Jameson and Virginia Van Wie in support; W. Lawson Little, Jr., who in 1934, and again in 1935, won both the United States and the British amateur titles before turning professional; Tony Manero, who won the United States Open with a score of only 282; and Britain's well-loved Henry Cotton, winner of the British Open Championship in both 1934 and 1937. In the Walker Cup series, Britain was monotonously beaten by America—except once, in 1938 at St. Andrews, when Britain won by 7½ matches to 4½.

In Britain, cricket was still important enough to make an old joke come true: there actually were newsbills in September 1938, while Neville Chamberlain was at Berchtesgaden, which said ENGLAND IN DANGER, referring to the Test Match against New Zealand. Cricket was important even in Hollywood, where Englishness was fashionable, and C. Aubrey Smith's Hollywood Cricket Club (one of about twenty cricket clubs in California) played on the football ground at Los Angeles University. Aubrey Smith, himself a county cricketer, gathered around him Nigel Bruce, Basil Rathbone, Eric Blore (plump, condescending butler in dozens of comedies) and David Niven. It was a lot more fun than Darryl Zanuck's polo team.

County cricketer.... It meant something: it helped an otherwise ordinary Englishman to get a job in a bank, on Lloyds, or as a headmaster. Any schoolboy could argue North v. South. The northern counties always beat the southern counties: they had more professionals. Their bowling was formidable—Verity's left-hand spinners, Bowes's "deceptive leisureliness". Holmes and Sutcliffe, of Yorkshire, piling up 555 runs between them at Leyton in 1932; and the appearance of twenty-two-year-old Len Hutton, who made 364 against Australia in the fifth Test at the Oval. Would he equal or even pass the 61,221 runs made during his career by Sir Jack Hobbs who had now retired? From Middlesex came Hearne the all-rounder, and Patsy Hendren with his 170 centuries; from Kent, Frank Woolley, another all-rounder, Ames, who never made less than 2,000 runs in a season, and "Tich" Freeman the "googly" bowler....

Henry Cotton, 1934

Len Hutton

Patsy Hendren

There was this man Don Bradman of Australia, whom everyone had been watching since the summer of 1930—Bradman's debut in England, and Wilfred Rhodes's retirement—Rhodes, who had taken 4,188 wickets and made 39,797 runs since *his* debut in 1898. Some purists of cricket said Bradman was "a technician rather than a artist". Well, we would see what could be done about him.

Cricket, it was well known, held the Commonwealth together. We were about to see how cricket could help to loosen the bonds of Empire, and precipitate something akin to war. Was it cricket, anyway, by the standards we all learnt at school, Poms and Diggers alike, bearing in mind that the game is played with a hard ball and the pads give only partial protection? We called it leg-theory, they called it body-line bowling. Douglas Jardine, the England captain, plainly thought that only by some new tactic could we do something about the Australian line-up of Bradman, Woodfull, McCabe, Ponsford and the others. To deliver his secret weapon he chose Harold Larwood, an ex-miner who could hurl a ball at 93 m.p.h. This was what he was doing at Adelaide in January, 1933.

The two captains, Douglas Jardine (left) and W. M. Woodfull, toss up before the start of the Third Test Match in Adelaide, 1932

The result was that Australian batsmen were forced to use their bats in an undignified way to protect their persons. If they hit the ball, they were almost certain to be caught out by fielders grouped abnormally around the leg stump. Woodfull retired with a blow over the heart, Oldfield took a ball on the head and was knocked unconscious; McCabe, Fingleton and even Bradman were all out for only 34 runs. The crowd roared abuse, but Larwood ("as inoffensive a chap as I ever met," said an observer—British, of course) went on stolidly obeying orders. Plum Warner, the veteran captain, went to the Australian dressing room to inspect the injured, and was told by Woodfull: "I don't want to speak to you, Mr. Warner. There are two teams out there and one is playing cricket. Good afternoon."

The Australian Cricket Board of Control cabled the M.C.C. in London: "Unless it (body-line) is stopped at once it is likely to upset the friendly relations existing between Australia and England;" 51,000 people had watched the first and second day's play, but 15,000 of them stayed away on the third. Maddeningly, Larwood suddenly stopped leg-theory and got Fingleton and Ponsford out by conventional means. The London *Times* said there was nothing new about Larwood's bowling, the fault probably lay with the batsmen who adopted the modern stance of covering the wicket with their legs. In Australia a Mr. Boyce, of the New South Wales Cricket Committee, said that "England's victory was won at the price of cricket." The President of the Victoria Cricket Association wanted to cancel the two remaining Tests: "Let England take the Ashes for what they're worth." And Sir Arthur Robinson, a former Attorney-General of Victoria, said: "We face the importation of a principle utterly foreign to cricket—the threat of bodily harm as a means of winning the game." The row went on and on, monopolizing headlines, and there must have been many readers who failed to notice that someone called Hitler had become Chancellor of Germany.

The Australian press was astonishingly restrained. The *Sydney Sun* thought the Board of Control ought to pack its head in ice. The *Melbourne Herald* thought that "if the English captain considers that body-line bowling is the right tactics at Brisbane and Sydney, then our batsmen will have to do their best to stand up to it." The M.C.C. had suggested, with great dignity, that if good relations between Britain and Australia were in jeopardy, perhaps the remaining tests should be cancelled. This made the Board of Control look rather silly, many Australians thought; yet the Board replied with equal dignity that, although it did not want the remaining matches to be cancelled, it had appointed a committee on body-line bowling, and its recommendations would be forwarded to London in due course. The M.C.C. replied that when the recommendations arrived they would be pleased to put them before the Imperial Cricket Conference. . . . It was not now a question of cricket, but of Anglo-Australian relations: there were agitated meetings between the M.C.C. and J. H. (Jimmy) Thomas, Dominions Secretary, who in after years used to say that nothing in Commonwealth politics ever gave him so much trouble as body-line bowling.

In the Fourth Test Larwood again did his stuff; but suddenly the Australian batsmen began to make nonsense of it: they had found ways of dealing with it: the new weapon, as always in war, had produced a counter-weapon. Nevertheless England won by six wickets and got the Ashes back.

Of course, it couldn't happen today. Today the whole issue would have exploded in a series of slanging matches in front of television cameras in London and Sydney simultaneously. A recent analysis of what happened has blamed the "Gentlemen v. Players" tradition, the imperial majesty of the M.C.C., and the fact that the captaincy of the England side always went to someone who wasn't necessarily playing in the match. This of course was the opposite of the Australian tradition. And there was the personality of Jardine himself. In 1934 William Pollock, cricket correspondent of the *Daily Express*, wrote him an open letter: "You are the Gibraltar of cricket, firm, aloof, and—so far—untouchable, and just about as romantic. There is precious little about you except your unyielding pertinacity, your Douglas Haig-like backs-to-the-wallishness that one can lay hold of. You are a hero made of the stuff of which popular heroes are *not* made. And I should say that you don't care a damn if you are."

The fall guy was Larwood. When the Australians came to England again, he was not included in the England side. He retired, aged only thirty-three, in 1937, and for years would have nothing to do with cricket. Today he lives, not in his native Nottinghamshire, but—in Sydney, New South Wales.

# KINGS AND QUEENS

The British Royal Family, alone among royal families, had a consistent news value in America. The others only became news when they were assassinated or involved in a scandal. In 1933 Louis Adamic, who had come to America from Yugoslavia, was trying to sell an article on King Alexander. Why, editors asked, was Alexander news? Because he *might* be assassinated. So what? Would that prevent banks from crashing or shorten the soup queues? Eight editors turned the article down. So did the ninth, but he had the grace to explain: "But who *cares* about your King? Yugoslavia—Syria—they're all the same. Has Syria a King? *I* don't know." Next year Alexander of Yugoslavia *was* assassinated, with M. Barthou the French foreign minister, at Marseilles while on a visit to France. He was succeeded by his son Peter, aged twelve. The assassin, Georgiev, did not live to realize his greatest ambition—to blow up the League of Nations building at Geneva.

There were, at this time, a round dozen of

The assassination of King Alexander of Yugoslavia and M. Barthou, 1934

monarchies in Europe; or fourteen, if you included the Princes of Monaco and Liechtenstein: they ranged from the elderly Gustav of Sweden, playing energetic tennis in a Panama hat, to the improbable Zog of Albania, who had married Geraldine Apponyi, one of those plentiful impoverished Hungarian countesses with several equally beautiful sisters. Some of their thrones were rocky. That royalty had human desires, that it might not want to rule, had been suspected since the tragedy of Mayerling in 1889, the suicide pact of a Crown Prince and his mistress. Could such Balkanization ever happen to the British monarchy? Unthinkable that there could ever be a British Elena Lupescu (always called Magda by the press), for whom the King of Romania, the same age as his second cousin the Prince of Wales, had sacrificed his throne, regaining it in 1930 and ruling with his mistress as a sort of unofficial Prime Minister.

Magda's father, described by different authorities as an apothecary, a junk-dealer and an automobile accessories merchant, was a Jew named Wolff (Lupescu is Romanian for wolf). The story goes that Magda met King Carol by a trick. Returning from dinner at his summer residence in Sinaia, by car along a lonely mountain road, he saw, in the glare of his headlamps, a girl with half her clothes torn off, apparently in distress, and "rescued" her. He had married first an unsuitable commoner, then a suitable princess. He never married Magda until she was dangerously ill in 1947. When, after five years' exile with Magda, he took the crown from his young son Michael, she became the "Du Barry of Bucharest", consulted about everything and even, it was said, running her own secret service. She lived in a modest villa on the outskirts of the capital, and was always to be seen at Sinaia, where the Carol entourage spent a great deal of time shooting and playing roulette. When she arrived at night, a certain tune was played on the gramophone: this was the signal for guests to say goodnight and go.

From 1934 Magda was threatened by the Iron Guard, a fascist organization dedicated to "cleaning up Romania" and exterminating Jews. Magda was half Jewish. The "Sinaia set" were a national scandal, carousing while the peasants starved; yet there were many who regarded Magda as a moderating influence. Foreign Minister Nicholas Titulescu managed to break up the "Sinaia set", but never

Princess Marina of Greece and the Duke of Kent with their parents at the time of their engagement, 1934

succeeded in getting rid of Magda. In April 1934 thirty Army officers were arrested for plotting to murder Carol, Magda and the whole royal family at the Easter service in Bucharest cathedral. She followed Carol into exile again in 1940.

Even in this Ruritanian atmosphere, royalty was performing one of its most important functions: providing an escape from the Depression for millions of people who might not know about the agrarian problem but could certainly have told you the colour of the wallpaper in Mme. Lupescu's bedroom, for this was the extent of the coverage of foreign news in most of the popular papers. So that when, in September 1934, it was announced that Prince George was to marry Princess Marina of Greece, and soon afterwards that they would be known in future as the Duke and Duchess of Kent, a wave of romance rippled through the country, and cheerfulness broke in. The wedding in November had the full treatment, no expense spared; newspapers and magazines published special gilt-edged souvenir editions; at the wedding two children, Prince Philip of Greece and Princess Elizabeth, thirteen and eight, met for the first time; and the procession was broadcast by the BBC, whose commentator described Princess Marina as "a vision of loveliness in white and silver; smiling and bowing, she drove slowly by, in a swirl of scarlet jackets, dancing white plumes, and flashing swords." The Duke was nearly late for the ceremony at Westminster Abbey because, feeling that he could not start his honeymoon at Himley Hall in Staffordshire, followed by a West Indian cruise, with only a few shillings in his pocket, he had rushed out to the bank to cash a cheque.

Those who met Marina, such as the gossip-writer of the *Tatler*, praised her "immense brown eyes, oval face and tiny well-set head." She was known to be "a good horsewoman", so that was all right. And, noting that her style was many times more sophisticated than that of the Queen, the fashion trade looked forward to the Marina touch in everything. There was a special family warmth in the King's Christmas broadcast that year; and also a rumour that the Kents might one day become King and Queen of Greece.

George V was in some doubt about how far the twenty-fifth anniversary of his accession should be celebrated. Everybody except the unemployed now regarded the worst of the Depression as over, and local Jubilee committees took over with such en-

thusiasm that only the King's death could have stopped them. There were Jubilee china mugs, Jubilee flags, banquets, concerts; a special issue of Jubilee stamps; Jubilee garden fêtes, floodlit buildings, flowers everywhere; trees were planted; a monkey born in the Zoo was christened Jubilee; so was a new kind of chocolate bar. In the East End where unemployed families had saved a penny a week to buy flags and decorations, someone put up a banner which read "Lousy but Loyal", and when the King and Queen visited the slums there, people sang "For they are jolly good fellows". The London and North-Eastern Railway launched a new streamlined non-stop train with a corridor connection to the engine so that a relief crew could take over: it touched 112 miles per hour, and was named *Silver Jubilee*.

On the great day, May 6, the King, never able to understand his own popularity, wrote in his diary: "It was a glorious summer's day, 75 degrees in the shade. The greatest number of people in the street that I have ever seen in my life, the enthusiasm was indeed most touching. May and I drove alone with six greys." The Thanksgiving Service at St. Paul's Cathedral was "very fine—4,406 people present. . . . By only one post in the morning I received 610 letters." It was all rather like the first night of *Cavalcade*—we had all come through a difficult time, and from now on (despite a Home Office leaflet, posted to every home in the country, explaining air raid precautions and showing a child in a gas-mask) things were going to be, must be, better. Several thousand people gathered in Trafalgar Square and sang, not jolly songs of music-hall and film, but old, sad, wartime songs like 'Take Me Back to Dear Old Blighty' and 'Tipperary'. Others, in full evening dress, crammed into open taxis and careered about the West End as if it were Boat Race Night or we had just won a war.

The King had a little over eight months to live. When he died at five minutes to midnight on January 20, 1936, it was the first Royal death ever managed by the BBC. All programmes stopped, the silence broken only by a ticking clock, horribly like a beating heart, and the voice of Stuart Hibberd the chief announcer saying every hour: "The King's life is drawing peacefully to a close." All restaurants, nightclubs, theatres and cinemas shut for a day. The King's body lay in state in Westminster Hall, recorded in Wilbur Davis's famous photograph; the

*(above left)* Members of the Royal Family in procession at the
funeral of King George V, January 1936
*(above)* King George V lying-in-state in Westminster Hall

new King and his brothers mounting guard for half an hour on the night before the funeral. The coffin had been made by the village carpenter at Sandringham. Six Kings marched in the funeral procession, with General Goering representing Hitler. The streets were lined with the densest crowds ever seen in London: seven thousand people received first-aid for injuries or fainting. It was reported all over the world, and officially denied, that a little man in a white coat skipping along behind King Carol of Romania was his masseur, a Mr. Stoebs, who had been trying to make his master fit enough to stand the strain: the story was traced to Frank Pitcairn of the *Daily Worker*, alias Claud Cockburn of *The Week*. The strain was certainly too much for Lord Beatty of the Royal entourage, who died soon afterwards. Another famous story, reported first in the American press, was that "as the gun-carriage bearing the coffin crossed the tramlines at the corner of Theobald's Road, the ball of diamonds topped by a sapphire cross, fell from the Imperial Crown and rolled from the coffin to the roadway". There are several versions of this story: Harold Nicolson says that the cross was already missing at the lying-in-state, and that it was a golden cross; another witness says that it happened in Palace Yard, and that the cross was picked up and pocketed by a Grenadier sergeant-major. No matter: it was regarded as an omen of the reign to come.

The new King, Edward VIII—it was almost impossible not to go on thinking of him as the Prince of Wales—did not go to church on the Sunday after his father's funeral, but did some gardening at Fort Belvedere. There were many other symptoms of change. At his first investiture he made Christabel Pankhurst, a suffragette, a Dame of the British Empire. He used a private aeroplane at public expense. He seldom wore a hat. He was unable to conceal his boredom at Royal Garden Parties and Presentations. For some of his subjects, these impatient brusquenesses merely increased his enormous popularity: he would "stand no nonsense", he would bring the Monarchy into the twentieth century, he would get things done. He disliked the elderly men who were his ministers, and who wanted no more of him than to "do his red boxes", approve of their advice, and make the suitable speeches that were written for him. And still a bachelor at forty-one. . . .

The few people who were close to Edward VIII and saw behind the "Prince Charming" façade were baffled by the contradictions of his character: democratic yet high-handed, intensely selfish yet public-spirited, promiscuous yet monogamous, touchy yet insensitive, and sometimes ill-mannered. His biographers blame his upbringing, the bad relationship with his father, his lack of education, and, more recently, "character defects", an expression which even psycho-analysts are now using. And then those reports, never mentioned in the British press except by implication in the Court Circular, about Mrs. Simpson. Of course it was always married women—well, the old Edwardian reason for that was that you could rely on Society's discretion, but wasn't there something else? Some abnormality, physical or mental?

The Prince of Wales with Mrs. Simpson at Ascot, June 1935

The Duke and Duchess of Windsor after their wedding at the Château de Candé, Tours, France, June 1937
(*opposite*) Projected stamp issues of King Edward VIII

Thelma, Lady Furness, his dining and dancing partner when he was Prince of Wales, could not remember whether it was in 1930 or 1931 that she gave a party at which she introduced "David" to Ernest and Wallis Simpson. Wallis had been married before, but this did not apparently disqualify her from being presented at Court soon afterwards, despite Nancy Astor's opinion that only the best Virginian families should be received at Court; to which Wallis Simpson might have replied that her family, the Warfields, had been settled in Maryland since 1662, a good fifty years before the House of Hanover came to England.

Thereafter David and the Simpsons went about as a threesome, and there were those who drew a parallel between this situation and that of Edward VII and the Keppels. Mrs. Simpson became a leading London hostess, famous for her Southern dishes, her knowledge of antiques, her wit, her style. Who was the smarter, Princess Marina (dressed by Molyneux) or Wallis Simpson (dressed by Mainbocher)? The Prince of Wales was now in the Anglo-American International Set which was to be found variously in London, the Riviera, Venice, Vienna, Paris, the Adriatic.

These were probably the happiest years of his life. He could live like this; but he could also feel guilty shock when talking to a man who had been unemployed for five years: "Manifestly he expected me, the King's son," he said in his ghosted autobiography, "to offer him some hope." It was the same at the steelworks at Dowlais, only a few weeks before his Abdication, when the *News Chronicle* reporter wrote: "The King's arrival at the great silent steelworks, which has been lying derelict for over six years, was the most moving event ever seen by South Wales in living memory. When the people broke spontaneously into the National Anthem I thought for a moment the King was going to break down." It was then that Edward VIII uttered the dangerous words: "Something ought to be done," variously reported as "must be done" and "will be done."

The Adriatic was the principal background to the pictures nobody ever forgot, with Mrs. Simpson, the Duff Coopers and others on the yacht *Nahlin* in August and September 1936. By now the American press were following the King everywhere. The Foreign Office were practically ordering him to meet political leaders wherever he went, so as to justify

what the King had already clearly planned as a pure holiday. The press photographers concentrated on Mrs. Simpson and the King, who was the first British monarch ever to allow himself to be seen in public naked but for a pair of shorts.

In October Prime Minister Baldwin told the King of the Cabinet's anxiety about Mrs. Simpson, whose divorce from Mr. Simpson was expected to go through on October 27 at Ipswich, where it was hoped that it would not attract attention. In November Baldwin told the King bluntly that the country would not tolerate his marrying a divorcee, and received the famous answer "I am prepared to go." Meanwhile Ellen Wilkinson, trying to break the conspiracy of silence in the British press, asked in the House of Commons why American news magazines were being sold in England with pages and paragraphs cut out, and Bishop Blunt of Bradford, addressing his Diocesan Conference on the subject of the religious significance of the forthcoming Coronation, used cryptic words in which he hoped that "His Majesty was aware of his need for God's grace," and so sparked off editorials all over the country.

In all this drama there was a conflict between American and British ideas on divorce. The King was supposed to be head of the Established church which would not allow divorce but might have tolerated a morganatic marriage. Mrs. Simpson, in A. J. P. Taylor's words, "knew only the American code, in which marriage was essential and divorce a harmless formality." It didn't matter that Mrs. Simpson was a "commoner": come to that, both Lord Lascelles, married to the Princess Royal, and the Duchess of York, although she could trace her descent from kings, were "commoners". And an Anglo-American Royal marriage could have been extremely popular, and rather useful in the coming war. The only solution might have been to disestablish the Church. Winston Churchill, and the two press barons Rothermere and Beaverbrook, favoured a morganatic marriage; they were resolutely opposed by the Prime Minister, the Archbishop of Canterbury, Geoffrey Dawson, editor of *The Times*, and, on a quick whip-round of opinion, the Dominions. Public opinion was never consulted, and there is little doubt that the mass of people (who knew little about the King) would have let him marry "the woman I love". Others relieved their feelings by throwing stones at Mrs. Simpson's house in Cumberland Terrace.

Many and agitated were the comings and goings between Buckingham Palace and Fort Belvedere, where the King still preferred to live. On Sunday evening November 29 the King's brother, Bertie, Duke of York, went to Edinburgh in his place to be installed as Grand Master Mason of Scotland. Back in London two days later, he telephoned Fort Belvedere incessantly to hear the King's decision, which did not come until December 7. There followed a dinner party at Fort Belvedere with both Prime Minister Baldwin and the King's friend and legal adviser Sir Walter Monckton present. "My brother" Bertie noted in his diary "was the life and soul of the party, telling the P.M. things I am sure he had never heard before about unemployed centres etc. I whispered to Walter Monckton: 'And this is the man we are going to lose!'"

There had been rumours that the Duke of York, who was nervous and stuttered, would refuse the throne in favour of Princess Elizabeth, who was only ten; but Bertie had a wife who held his hand tightly while he made a speech, and the discipline of duty.

When Bertie went to tell Queen Mary, it was he, not she, who burst into tears. He witnessed the Instrument of Abdication, and then went home and "found a large crowd outside my house cheering madly.... I then went to the Fort as King with Harry (Duke of Gloucester) arriving at 7 p.m. All David's servants called me Your Majesty.... When David and I said goodbye we kissed, parted as Freemasons, and he bowed to me as his King."

The Archbishop of Canterbury, Dr. Cosmo Gordon Lang, permitted himself a tactless Sunday night broadcast two days later in which he attacked the ex-King for "craving private happiness." This drew from Gerald Bullett a verse which was passed on by word of mouth, but not published for more than twenty years:

*My Lord Archbishop, what a scold you are!*
*And when your man is down how bold you are!*
*Of charity how oddly scant you are!*
*How Lang, O Lord, how full of Cantuar!*

George VI's first act as King was to prevent Sir John Reith from announcing David as "Mr. E. Windsor", substituting "His Royal Highness Prince Edward". The historic broadcast, the H.M.S. *Fury* at Portsmouth, the hospitality of Baron Rothschild in Vienna; the speed with which all but a few of David's

*(opposite)* 'Flask Walk, Hampstead, on Coronation Day', 1937, by Charles Ginner

The King and Queen in Coronation robes and crowns with their daughters, Princess Elizabeth (right) and Princess Margaret Rose, May 1937

friendships, the visit to Hitler at Berchtesgaden; then temporary oblivion until the War—and the Windsor literary industry—began. So ended the "year of the three Kings", and what H. L. Mencken chose to call "the greatest news-story since the Resurrection", and Margaret Case Harriman, hardly less temperately, "the last really great romance likely to be known in a world that loves romance and loves Kings too, and has efficiently been deprived of both. If ever two lovers had to *stay* in love, or else get the whole world mad at them, the Windsors were those two."

So David's Coronation became Bertie's Coronation. The Jubilee Committees became the nuclei of the Coronation Committees. The Coronation, a much grander affair, lent itself to military parades, and there were pacifist objections, especially to Edward Wadsworth's Underground posters advertising the procession, which showed too many weapons of war. Coronation ale, brewed locally in some villages, proved too strong for some. Village celebrations, since Coronation Day was May 12, often got mixed up with May Day customs. Stands of seats along the procession route were sold at high prices, and special trains brought hundreds of people to London. There were a million seats, and twenty million people wanted them. Selfridge's decorations so impressed an Indian prince that he bought them to take home. Many peers and peeresses had to hire their robes for Westminster Abbey, and there were hardly enough to go round: the Countess of Dudley, who had once been an actress, telephoned Nathan's, the theatrical costumiers, and was told there were none left. "You surely won't let Gertie Millar down?" she pleaded, using her stage name. "Oh, it's you, Miss Millar! Why didn't you say so before? We'll fix you up!"

Inside the Abbey there were the usual human difficulties, sometimes due to the shortage of lavatory accommodation, sometimes to hunger—sandwiches fell out of coronets when they were put on, one peer's hip-flask of brandy burst in the middle of prayers. It had taken six hours to get everyone into the Abbey. The BBC had thirty-eight microphones in position. A Mr. Neil Vanderbilt from America appeared to be praying excessively: he was actually scooping the BBC by broadcasting a running commentary which was picked up in a van outside the Abbey and relayed direct to New York. René MacColl, reporting for the *Daily Telegraph* in an unaccustomed morning coat

friends melted away, the swing of public opinion from sympathy to censure; the wedding by the Durham parson at Candé, the photographs by Cecil Beaton (whose brother-in-law Sir Hugh Smiley's aunt's brother was Ernest Simpson), the unwise Nazi

and top hat, dropped a sheaf of notes on the ceremony, based on what had happened in 1911 at George V's Coronation, from the Triforium gallery, and had to retrieve it from a ledge by means of an open umbrella and a malacca cane.

When the great day was over, and thousands of people had to walk home because there was a bus strike, the King made his first broadcast to the nation: why, his stammer wasn't nearly so bad as everyone had feared! He was going to be *all right*! Two weeks later he reviewed the Fleet and eighteen warships at Spithead, and gave the order "splice the mainbrace". The BBC commentator, Commander Thomas Woodruff, had taken the order so seriously that, in describing the scene to millions of listeners, he lost his thread and repeated "The fleet's . . . lit up" several times, and when the fairy lights went out, he seemed not to understand what had happened, and said "The whole ruddy Fleet has gone—nothing but shea and shky . . ." A quick fade-out: "technical fault". Never mind: he had made radio and linguistic history, and ever afterwards "lit up" meant "drunk". Next year *The Fleet's Lit Up* was the title of "a musical frolic" at the London Hippodrome.

The new King, his smiling wife and the two little Princesses were soon known to all their subjects. Ordinary families could identify with them. There was a famous newsreel showing them at Southwold camp ("the Duke of York's Camp for Boys") singing and miming 'Under the Spreading Chestnut Tree' with an extraordinary defenceless innocence. It was now seen that the gossip about little Princess Margaret Rose being deaf and dumb was false. They had been given a doll's tea set in real Sèvres by the wife of the French President, and a toy nightingale that really sang, and a model loom with which they had woven table napkins embodying a Royal Crown design.

In 1937 the American ambassador, Robert Bingham, a sick man, was replaced by Joe Kennedy. It was soon learnt that he had holed out in one at Stoke Poges, rode regularly in Rotten Row and, like Brigadier Dawes, his predecessor in 1929, refused to wear Court dress. His wife Rose had tea with the Queen, and their son Jack, during vacations from Harvard, was visiting trouble spots in Europe and collecting material for an undergraduate thesis on British foreign policy which would eventually be published as *While England Slept*, a best-seller in

Joe Kennedy with two of his sons—
John F. (left) and Joe, junior

America, while his father reported to President Roosevelt that "democracy is finished in England." Jack's own view of political systems at that time, after a summer course at the London School of Economics under Professor Harold Laski, was: "Have come to the decision that Fascism is the thing for Germany and Italy, Communism for Russia, and Democracy for America and Britain."

His father's tendency to say worrying things like (in a speech at Aberdeen) "I can't for the life of me understand why anyone would want to go to war to save the Czechs" did not hinder the Kennedys from getting on well with the King and Queen, and also with the Chamberlains. The Court was now fashionable for Americans, and there was a racket by which some of them paid fees of up to $5,000 to British aristocrats for arranging Presentations. Rose Kennedy greatly admired the Queen's "Winterhalter style" (rose-pink gown with opalescent trimming, double necklace and diamond tiara, and the blue ribbon of the Order of the Garter), designed by Norman Hartnell, who had been dressing the women of the Royal Family since 1935, when he had suddenly become famous after designing a wedding-dress for Lady Alice Montagu-Douglas-Scott, when she married the Duke of Gloucester.

The Kennedys were invited to Windsor Castle, where they stayed in the Lancaster Tower, and Rose wrote home to the children on Windsor Castle stationery. They returned hospitality by inviting the King and Queen to the Embassy (then in Princes Gate) for an all-American dinner of mushroom soup, Baltimore shad roe, mousse of Virginia ham with Georgia peaches, roast young chickens, peas, potatoes, asparagus with Hollandaise sauce, American coffee—and, which the Royal guests enjoyed above all else, strawberry shortcake.

King George VI and Queen Elizabeth
at the World's Fair, New York, 1939

As war drew nearer, George and Elizabeth visited countries likely to be our allies. A week's State visit to Paris in 1938 was praised by the press as another Entente Cordiale. I was there at the time, and saw posters in the Place de la Madeleine saying: "The people of Paris are requested to show the utmost politeness towards English visitors"; and a woman in a bar said to me: "You send your nice simple King over here, and meanwhile you close one eye at Hitler and Henlein." Certain Paris cinemas revived a hilarious film called *Le Roi S'Amuse* in which Victor Francen played a King trying to "improve relations between France and Cerdagne"; and the *chansonniers* had a wonderful time imitating George VI's stutter. Diplomatically the visit achieved little; and it was the Hartnell-dressed Queen who stole the show.

In May 1939 George and Elizabeth toured Canada for six weeks: "this country gives me strength," said the Queen. There were rumours that a Royal refuge was being prepared in Canada in case Britain should be invaded. They were the first British King and Queen ever to visit the New World while in office. The Queen inspected the Dionne Quintuplets and delighted everyone by singing 'Alouette' to them. They went on to Washington, the King sweating in his admiral's uniform. At the Capitol a Senator wrung the King's hand and said: "My, you're a great Queen-picker!" Ten "Flying Fortresses" flew above the procession to the White House, and sixty small tanks led the motorcade. After dinner in the White House, there was a concert in their honour, with negro spirituals, cowboy songs, square dancing, Marian Anderson and Lawrence Tibbett singing operatic arias, and radio's very own Kate Smith singing 'When The Moon Comes Over the Mountain'. In New York they visited the World's Fair, where they were greeted with 'Land of Hope and Glory;' and the Royal love of picnics was taken care of by a hot dog and beer meal in the garden of Hyde Park, Roosevelt's retreat on the Hudson River. When the King and Queen left, Franklin Roosevelt led the crowd in singing 'For He's a Jolly Good Fellow'. The only mishap at Hyde Park was when the butler dropped a tray of drinks; and readers of Eleanor's *My Day* column were told all about it a week later. George and Elizabeth had not expected such an ovation in a republican ex-colony, and for years afterwards Elizabeth said: "That tour *made* us."

# SCANDAL

Scandal is what happens when we are found out. Even more is it the excitement we feel when someone else is found out. Forty years ago Society could still, in certain cases, close its ranks and by the skin of its teeth hush something up. "Clarence Hatry broke the code, you know," an old stockbroker once told me, implying that there was a code for bad behaviour as well as good; "he should have gone bankrupt like an honest man." Mrs. Simpson was a scandal until she became Duchess of Windsor. We know that clergymen have the same desires as other men, but when one goes around Soho reforming fallen women, as Mr. Gladstone tried to do a hundred years ago, we instantly suspect the worst, for scandal condemns him who, but for the grace of God, might have been you or me. When a Cabinet minister is caught in bed with a call-girl, our moral indignation may even be tempered with envy. It was no doubt a scandal that clever men went on building airships with one known fatal fault—they were borne aloft by an inflammable gas. It was a scandal that Geneva, headquarters of the League of Nations, whose tasks included control of the drug traffic and white slavery, was also a major distribution centre for both; or that Bishop James Cannon of the Methodist Episcopal Church, the great Prohibitionist, should have speculated in stocks and shares; or that a Mr. Garabed Bischirgian, an Armenian commodity broker, should have attempted, in 1936, to corner all the pepper in Britain. The Spanish Civil War was a scandal to anyone with left-wing opinions (and in the Thirties we were many of us "left", including Lady Louis Mountbatten, because there was nothing else to be). It was a politico-economic age, and so its worst scandals were seldom sexual, more often financial. Depression times tend to uncover the crooked businessman because he panics or overreaches himself. In boom times he has to be very stupid to get found out.

None of this, however, applied to the Rev. Harold Davidson, Rector of Stiffkey (pronounced Stewkey) in Norfolk. Aged fifty-seven, with five children, he was in the habit of catching the early train to London on Monday mornings, and the last train back to Stiffkey on Saturday night, just in time to take Sunday services. Sometimes he didn't even return for Sundays and sent messages asking other neighbouring vicars to stand in for him, of such supreme importance was his missionary work in London. By his own account, he was bridging the gap between the passive, trivial work of a parish priest in a middle-class village and the dynamic work of a missionary. Girls, to him, especially in Soho (prostitutes, real or potential) and West End and City teashops (waitresses at Express Dairies, A.B.C.'s and Lyons, where, by a prolonged advertising campaign, they were known as Nippies), were surrounded by temptation. Sooner or later they would fall, and then—only then, by his curious reasoning—could they be saved. It might even be necessary to help them to fall, so that salvation could be completed. And he loved them all: who shall blame him if he confused Christian with carnal love?

This had been going on for at least ten years, which was the time he had known the girl Rose Ellis, his oldest "bad girl" who was now, in 1932, thirty. What neither Rose nor Mr. Davidson knew was that she had been followed everywhere for the past few months by a private eye who one day made her rather tight on eight glasses of port so that she talked for publication. Afterwards, in sobriety, she took back what she had said; but it was too late—Fleet Street was on to the story. In the *Empire News* Mr. Davidson wrote an article, followed by others. He preached about love, and the need to save girls, in the pulpit at Stiffkey to a hugely increased congregation, some of them arriving by charabanc from Bournemouth, 230 miles away.

The Rev. Harold Davidson, Rector of Stiffkey

The Bishop of Norwich then did something that had never been done before in quite the same way. He had received a letter from an eighteen-year-old girl named Barbara Harris containing sensational allegations about Mr. Davidson's behaviour in London. Instead of minimizing publicity, he now sought it by prosecuting not only Mr. Davidson, but the two national newspapers that had featured the case most prominently. The situation was complicated, both in the Davidson family and in Fleet Street, by the fact that Mr. Davidson's son-in-law was one of the reporters. The Rector was to be tried by the Norwich Consistory Court, not in Norwich, but at Church House, Westminster. The charge was immoral conduct, naming Rose Ellis and certain other girls, some waitresses, whom he was vaguely accused of "kissing", presumably in the sense of the French *baiser*.

The Rector denied all the charges. He seemed to be enjoying the spectacle of watching church and law striving to ascertain, not whether he was a good parson or not, or whether his work in London was relevant to his parish duties, but whether his association with all those girls was or was not "innocent". He even sometimes burst out laughing, and had to be disciplined. The evidence proceeded. He had taken the girls to films, theatres, restaurants—how could he possibly afford it, since (it was now revealed) he was an undischarged bankrupt? Well, he took in paying guests at the crowded rectory, and, it seemed, brought some of his girls down from London to lend a hand with the housework. Two girls so treated had been Rose Ellis and Barbara Harris.

It was Barbara who had written the fatal letter to the Bishop—why, we do not precisely know; but she was the only one of very many girls for whom he had not only bought clothes—a highly compromising circumstance—but had actually promised to marry, undertaking to divorce his wife in order to do so. He had told her that God was not too fussy about sins of the body. Barbara specialized in Indian boys and lived with one of them, at least when she wasn't living with a theatre-queue busker known as the Strong Man. To both of them she posed as the Rector's niece. In her evidence she alleged that the Rector had advised her to work in a brothel. A landlady testified that she had heard the Rector call Barbara "Queen of my heart". There was an actress whom the Rector had asked to stay at Stiffkey, apparently to prevent her from becoming a Roman Catholic. There was a duchess to whom the Rector had written a begging letter, saying that his family was starving and they could not afford coal. . . . The defence sought to prove that the Rector only kissed people in a Biblical way, and supported his plea for understanding of what he meant by "spiritual innocence". In vain. He was found guilty on all counts. All through the trial he had continued to take services at the church of St. John with Mary at Stiffkey before the biggest congregation of any parish church in the land.

He now needed money for appealing against the Court's verdict, so he sat in a barrel at Blackpool, next to a flea-circus, but was fined for attempted suicide by starvation: he brought an action against Blackpool Corporation and got £382 damages.

His unfrocking at Norwich Cathedral, for which he

arrived late, was constantly interrupted by his furious shouts. He was now not only bankrupt but without a stipend. Before his ordination he had been an actor, earning enough on the stage to pay for a university education. He now returned to show-business, appearing at cinemas (in between the second feature and the big picture) in evening dress to make a short speech about his persecution, followed by a "humorous recitation". He was exhibited at a Bank Holiday fair on Hampstead Heath next to a dead whale. And he died courageously at Skegness Amusement Park in 1937, in an act which required him to enter a lion's cage. He had been told that the cage would contain only one lion, but when he went into it he saw that there were two, male and female. It was the show of a lifetime, for the male lion killed him.

Somewhere in this story there is a parable which makes the Rev. Harold Davidson one of the truly innocent men of the age. Inevitable that the press, reporting his end, should write about Christians being thrown to the lions. I think of him tenderly.

Back to finance. In 1931 Lord Kylsant went to prison for six months for "drawing up and circulating a prospectus, the contents of which he knew to be false in an important particular." At sixty-eight he controlled the biggest shipping company (Royal Mail Packet plus Elder-Dempster plus Union Castle, White Star and others) in the world. Was he the "fall guy" who hadn't read the small print? No matter: under company law he, as director, was responsible for every statement in the prospectus. In America he would have got off. The next year saw the suicide of Ivar Kreuger, the Swedish Match King, who shot himself in his Paris flat. He had been a friend of Herbert Hoover and of Maynard Keynes, who called him "the greatest financial intelligence of his time". The shares of Kreuger and Toll were practically gilt-edged. It now appeared that he had counterfeited $142 million worth of Italian Government securities, forging the signatures himself and spelling them wrong. His book-keeping was found to be childish. He had been bribing, blackmailing and rigging markets for the past twenty years.

A stockbroker named Blennerhassett brought an action against the London *Evening Standard* because it had published a humorous advertisement for the yo-yo, featuring an imaginary stockbroker named Blennerhassett who had had to be taken to an asylum because of his obsession with the yo-yo craze: the

Lord Kylsant

judge, rocking with laughter, dismissed the case with costs. In America in 1932 a Senate Committee, investigating the New York Stock Exchange, went out of its way to pay tribute to Richard Whitney, Acting President of the Exchange's Governing Committee, for his "efficient and conscientious" work to expose malpractices. He had made a celebrated speech to the St. Louis Chamber of Commerce saying that he looked forward to the day when supervision of members would be so strict that "failure will be next to impossible." The impossible happened: six years later Mr. Whitney was arrested for grand larceny: the man who in the 1929 crash had patriotically bought steel to stave off collapse was now shown to have misappropriated trust funds to stave off his own bankruptcy in the Recession of 1938. Mayor Jimmy Walker resigned and went to live in the South of France after being tried for misconduct in office: sad end to the Jazz Mayor of New York, the Tammany Troubadour (he wrote terrible sentimental songs), the unpunctual (late for his own wedding), inefficient, orating, sharp-dressing ("neat *and* gaudy", said his tailor), much-loved "small little man".

Huey Long

Was Huey Long a scandal or a criminal or both? He was America's own dictator in his state of Louisiana, using his own private army and secret police, going everywhere with a bodyguard. A lawyer by training (if you can call an eight-month course at Tulane University a training), he was Governor of Louisiana and junior Senator at Washington. Ostensibly a Democrat, "Kingfish" (the nickname came from a character in the radio serial *Amos 'n' Andy*) abandoned the New Deal in favour of his own corrupt "Share Our Wealth" programme, a system of clubs directed by one Gerald L. K. Smith. He faked elections. He ran his own newspaper, *Louisiana Progress*: editors of other papers were controlled by threatening telephone calls, and found it prudent to carry guns. "A wise statesman in Louisiana," it used to be said, "steered a safe course between the Scylla of Standard Oil and the Charybdis of the poor man's yearnings," and there were people who saw Long as people's champion versus ruthless corporations. He gave Louisiana modern highways, hospitals, a bridge over the Mississippi and many other things, but he did it with machine-guns. He badly wanted to be President, and indicated his disrespect for Roosevelt by keeping his famous straw hat on while talking to him. "Anybody working for Huey is not working for us," Roosevelt told his entourage.

Huey's bad dream was that he would one day meet "one man, one gun, one bullet". It happened on September 8, 1935, when a "quiet young doctor in a white suit," Carl Austin Weiss Jr., the son of one of his political enemies, shot him dead, and was himself instantly the recipient of sixty-one bullets from Huey's bodyguard. "His body shall never rest," wrote Gerald Smith, "as long as hungry bodies cry for food, as long as lean human frames stand naked, as long as homeless wretches haunt this land of plenty." He had done America a service: now everybody knew something of what it was like to be ruled by a dictator.

Martin Coles Harman was the dictator of the $1\frac{1}{2}$ square miles of Lundy Island, inhabited mainly by puffins, off the north coast of Devon. In 1930 he had been summoned for illegally issuing his own local coinage: Lundy, he had maintained, was a self-governing Dominion. Nobody minded him much until, betrayed by the Depression, he went bankrupt for £500,000 blaming Wall Street and the Hatry Crash for the fact that he had, as financial adviser to a firm of wholesale grocers in Liverpool, sold their Gilts and reinvested the money in his own speculative or fraudulent companies, including the notorious Lena Goldfields in Russia. He went to prison for eighteen months, and afterwards became a familiar writer of letters to *The Times*, usually on sea-birds and their habits.

Amid a wave of embezzlements, there were Samuel Insull, who had been Edison's secretary and eventually manager of his company, tried three times in 1934 for what have been called his "mistakes in utility financing," and three times acquitted; and Donald Coster, head of McKesson and Robbins, the ethical drug manufacturers, who turned out to be an ex-convict named Philip Musica; he had extracted millions of dollars from the company by tampering with the books. Well, that was the state of accountancy in some companies in 1938. Mr. Musica committed suicide at his charming Connecticut home.

Popular, 'aitchless' Jimmy Thomas, old Socialist and Lord Privy Seal in the National Government, was found to have been the cause of speculation in insurance against the increases in tea-tax and income tax in the 1936 Budget. He had let slip these facts to his friend Sir Alfred Butt, M.P., the theatre-owner. There was a slight suggestion of bribery in the fact that Sir Alfred's friend Mr. Bates, owner of the *Leader* magazine, had given Mr. Thomas an advance of £20,000 for his—as yet—unwritten autobiography. Both Butt and Thomas had to resign their seats: poor Jimmy became a director of the Crystal Palace for a few months before it was burnt down in November 1936.

It was a scandal, no doubt, that Stanley Baldwin should have promised to avoid rearmament in the 1935 Election, concealing the true weakness of the country's defences because the truth would have lost the election. There was a spy-plus-sex scandal in Lieutenant Norman Baillie Stewart's sale of military information to Germany through a girl named Marie-Louise for a mere £90. He was imprisoned as a traitor in the Tower of London. And the forger of the age, and in bibliography of all time, was Thomas J. Wise, who had been the great source of rare first editions for some forty years, and indeed the greatest collector of modern books and manuscripts. In 1934 John Carter and Graham Pollard published *An Enquiry into the Nature of Certain 19th Century Pamphlets*. Using scientific tests of paper and type they had established twenty-two forgeries. Mr. Wise, interviewed by reporters, said that

Martin Coles Harman

he had got them from another bibliophile, Mr Buxton Forman, deceased. The *London Mercury* cautiously concluded that "the person who seems most likely to be able to discover the identity of the forger is Mr. T. J. Wise." Because, of course, the forger *was* Mr. Wise.

Over to Hollywood, where, in the summer of 1936, attention was concentrated on the divorce of Mary Astor, during which her diary was produced in evidence. In it she had recorded, day by day, not to say minute by minute, her affair with George S. Kaufman, author of innumerable comedy hits on Broadway and in Hollywood. His friends recall Mr. Kaufman at that time as short-sighted, gangling, desperately shy, and forty-six. She described "thrilling ecstasy . . . many exquisite moments . . . twenty, count them, diary, twenty . . . I don't see how he does it." The story goes that to escape prosecution in California, Kaufman was carried aboard a train to New York as a stretcher-case. One newspaper explained to its readers that the figure twenty referred to the number of nightspots Kaufman and Miss Astor had visited in a single night, but no-one believed it.

There was one scandal that had everything: embezzlement, corruption, sex, politics, perhaps espionage too: Stavisky. Living on women and selling their jewellery, running clip-joints, winning at baccarat on the Riviera with marked cards, rum-running during Prohibition, forged cheques, a bodyguard named Jojo le Térreur, selling worthless Hungarian Reparation Bonds, over-issuing shares in municipal pawnshops—even Capone was less versatile. In the France of the 1930s, believed by other countries to be the most corrupt in Europe, where a Cabinet Minister was said to own brothels, anything seemed possible; so that the death of Alexandre (Sacha) Stavisky, shot in a Chamonix villa on January 8, 1934 (by himself? impossible—there were *two* bullets in his head; by the police? by a friend—"of course! what are friends for?" asked Janet Flanner) brought down two French governments, caused the police to fire on rioting mobs outside the National Assembly, and was linked with the unexplained decapitation of Judge Albert Prince, who had been investigating the Stavisky affair, on the railway near Dijon.

Why had adverse reports by two police inspectors on the Crédit Municipal at Bayonne, near Biarritz, been suppressed? It was approved by the Government, wasn't it? Anyway the Minister of Labour's name had appeared on certain documents. Thousands of small investors, and some large companies, had bought bonds. The Mayor of Bayonne, who was also a Deputy, approved. Nobody in any Government department supervised the scheme; nobody showed the faintest curiosity until, in December 1933, an anonymous investor (possibly from an insurance company) demanded to see the list of securities held against the bonds. There was no list, not even a forged one. Moreover pawned jewels were being replaced with paste. The Director, Gustave Tissier, panicked and told the police everything. There was a warrant out for Stavisky's arrest. So why was he escaping, with a police card made out in the name of "M. Alexandre"? Newspapers said openly that he had been *allowed* to escape. Premier Chautemps cut short his Christmas holiday and promised drastic action: no-one in the Government should be spared, not even

his brother-in-law M. Pressard, Director of Public Prosecutions.

Exit Chautemps, enter Daladier, who dismissed Jean Chiappe, the Corsican Prefect of Police, and transferred the Head of the Deuxième Bureau to the Directorship of the Comédie Française, a *coup de théâtre* seldom equalled in politics. More, bigger, worse demonstrations, culminating in "Bloody Tuesday" (February 6, 1934) when 50,000 unarmed people were fired on by the police: 18 killed, over 2,000 injured. Exit Daladier, enter Doumergue, recalled from retirement: he promised a commission of inquiry. Judge Prince, killed on the Dijon railway, was said to have been able to name *all* Stavisky's accomplices. Nineteen of them were identified, and it took eighteen months to set up their trial. Meanwhile Ministers had resigned, more police officers had been sacked, a civil servant (said to have accepted a 225,000 franc bribe) had committed suicide, and two barristers had gone into mental hospitals. Among many books about Stavisky was one by a M. Bardanne in 1935 saying that he was, added to everything else, a German spy.

Among the accused were Mme. Arlette Stavisky, Gilbert Romagnino (Stavisky's secretary/muscle man), the Mayor of Bayonne, and a cashiered General Bardi de Fourtu, who dragged in the name of Pierre Laval as a "delayer of proceedings against Stavisky". Romagnino named twenty-two Ministers, Senators, Deputies and senior civil servants. The jury, halfway through the trial, went on strike for more pay (50 francs a day instead of 12½). They romantically acquitted the beautiful Arlette, an ex-Chanel model—"her only crime", said her defence counsel, "was to have thrown herself on the dead body of the man she loved." She had offers of marriage from all over the world. In 1936 she went to New York. Two weeks later *Paris-Soir* reported that she was "displaying Paris dresses" in a Casino revue, and the London *Daily Express* that she was one of "50 French Nudies" in a nightclub show. During World War II she married a soldier from the Middle West and became Mrs. Russell Cook.

# CHAPTER
## XV

# THE FACES OF VIOLENCE

The cases of Kreuger and Stavisky showed how near to each other, even interconnected, big business and crime could be. There were all kinds of theories about crime. That a hot climate was more conducive to homicide than a cold one. That crimes of violence were attributable to "moral insanity", a very difficult term to define in a court of law, but at least an improvement on Signor Lombroso's theories about head-bumps, pointed ears and eyebrows that met in the middle. In the Thirties it was fashionably Marxist to say that John Dillinger, Bruno Hauptmann and, for that matter, Mae West were all undesirable products of capitalism.

If it is at all true that each age produces its own special kind of crime, then we have little difficulty in selecting crimes of the Thirties. We begin in America, where it was being found that when organized crime becomes bigger and more efficient than big business, it has to be suppressed with the same violence that it uses itself. In the last years of his presidency Herbert Hoover was determined that he would get Capone, who, as virtual dictator of Chicago, had escaped the law for so long. Mayor Cermak of Chicago was equally determined to clean up his city after Big Bill Thompson, and, after Cermak stopped the bullet intended for Roosevelt in Miami in 1933, his successor Mayor Kelly was of the same mind.

Hoover directed Elmer J. Irey, of the Treasury Enforcement Branch, to do this. If you couldn't get a criminal for anything else, it had to be either tax evasion or parking over a fire hydrant. They began with Al Capone's brother Bottles, his A.D.C., Frank Nitti, and Jack Guzik, finance head of the vice and other syndicates. They tried a vagrancy charge, but it wouldn't stick. Capone blandly approached the Department of Internal Revenue saying he was only too willing to pay anything he owed. He may or may not have been aware, at that point, that a man known

Al Capone being led from the Chicago Federal Court after receiving sentence for income-tax evasion, 1931

to him as Michael Lepito, and to others as O'Rourke, who had joined the Capone mob as a gunman from Philadelphia, was in fact a Secret Service agent who had been planted to go through his books and accounts.

Capone, fearing revenge for the St. Valentine's Day massacre in 1929, managed to get himself arrested in Philadelphia for illegal possession of firearms, and spent a peaceful year in jail, reading *Country Life*, directing his vice empire by telephone from the prison governor's office, and writing about his life ("you fear death every moment. . ."). In the end he went down on the income-tax rap for eleven years, first at Atlanta and eventually at Alcatraz. He was released in 1939, his syphilitic body sick, his brain gone.

In New York the new names, mostly linked by the Mafia, were Lucky Luciano, Salvatore Maranzano, Joe Masseria, Joe Adonis, Albert Anastasia, Bugsy Siegel: the first shot the second and third, thought he had Roosevelt in his pocket, found he hadn't.

The Bureau of Investigation (not until 1935 called the F.B.I.), headed by J. Edgar Hoover ("a sledge-hammer in search of an anvil"), moved in with greatly enhanced powers to deal with crimes of the times. When Prohibition was repealed bootlegging lost much (but not all) of its profitability: the typical gang crimes or "rackets" were now bank robbery and kidnapping. In the Depression you needed money quicker, so you got it by the most direct means, without all the trouble of organizing speakeasies, shipments, brothels, blackmail—in modern business terminology they were all too "labour intensive".

What we are about to watch is a curious public relations operation by which the glamour once attached to gang leaders is transferred to the new soldiers of law and order, known as G-Men. They are the heroes of Hollywood films and of an almost endless radio series called *Gangbusters*. Gangsters are now labelled Public Enemies Nos. 1, 2, 3 and so on: the element of star billing preserves some of their glamour. So, cops and robbers it is, and "death while resisting arrest" the normal epitaph, as John Dillinger is shot by Department of Justice agent Melvin Purvis in Lincoln Avenue, Chicago, followed soon by Charles Arthur ("Pretty Boy") Floyd and Lester Gillis, better known as "Baby Face Nelson" (all three in 1934). Then Russell Gibson, Kate and Fred Barker, Alvin Karpis and Alfred James Brady (even the names are getting more business-like).

(*above*) John Dillinger
(*below*) Bonnie Parker

Dillinger, who saw himself as a Robin Hood and couldn't even break jail without liberating other even dumber hoodlums just to show what a nice guy he was, probably represented the turning point: rather an amateur as bank robbers go, blasting his way in and retreating to the sound of machine-gun fire ("Chicago typewriters"), pooping off in bars so that everyone should know they had had the privilege of

Clyde Barrow

fullness of time, Hollywood did. So, long after, were Bonnie Parker and Clyde Barrow, untidily shooting people in three States, raised to an undeserved stature.

The F.B.I. owed much to a young Federal attorney, Thomas E. Dewey, thirty-three, who in 1935 was appointed by Governor Herbert Lehman of New York county to investigate rackets, especially the protection racket. So Lucky Luciano was convicted for intimidating call-girls and other crimes, and Tom Dewey became D.A. of New York. The hero of the Luciano conviction was Frank S. Hogan, one of the original eight racket-busters hired by Dewey in 1935. If the Rev. Harold Davidson was the Prostitutes' Padre in England, Frank Hogan was something of the kind to Nancy Presser, Cokey Flo Brown, Mildred Harris and other girls who were persuaded to turn State's evidence and testify against Luciano. They called their new friend Father Hogan.

Crime in Britain during the years just before World War II followed no pattern which a sociologist could seize upon. Greed, lust, fear—few of them made world headlines: you could even say that British crime was *out of date*. Salesmanship in the United States is the matter of heroic tragedy: no other country could have produced *Death of a Salesman*. In Britain, commercial travellers have traditionally been a have-you-heard-the-one-about joke. Men like Alfred Arthur Rouse, thirty-six, traveller in braces, garters and woollen goods, earning £10 a week (an excellent salary for 1930) with a Morris Minor car on the firm. Dapper, glib, popular, posing as a public school and university man, he could always be relied on for a stylish baritone rendering of the Cobbler's Song from *Chu-Chin-Chow* at parish hall concerts in Finchley, North London, where he lived. However, he spent little time in Finchley; much more on the road, where, it was afterwards revealed, he had had affairs with some eighty women and had illegitimate children by some of them, including a five-year-old boy Arthur born to a housemaid, Helen Campbell, whom he had bigamously married in 1924.

With Ivy Jenkins, of Gelliager, Glamorganshire, his inventive web of lies had gone too far: she was pregnant by him, and he had promised, not only to marry her, but to take her to a beautiful £1,250 house at Kingston-on-Thames. So, adopting a plan that had already been used in Germany by Kurt Tetzner and would be imitated two years later by Samuel Furnace, he decided to "disappear". First he insured

meeting him, it was still possible to regard him as a "victim of capitalism", a "hero of the dispossessed"; and to people who had lost almost everything in the Depression a bank being robbed was no worse than a bank going bust. That he was disguised by a face-lift, dyed hair, false moustache and gold-rimmed spectacles when he was shot was like a challenge to Hollywood to make a movie of his life, which, in the

his life, so that his wife would be provided for. He then chose Guy Fawkes' Night, November 5, when the country would be full of bonfires, to give a lift near St. Albans to a complete stranger whom he met in a pub, bash his head in and set fire to the car with his victim inside. He might well have got away with it if he had not been seen walking away from the blazing car, if he had not told Ivy his real name, if. . . . In the witness box his stupidity astonished the court: each fresh lie was prefaced by "Frankly . . . candidly . . . to be perfectly honest with you." And the trial was remarkable for the discrediting of an expert witness by Norman Birkett (prosecuting counsel). Had Rouse loosened the petrol union joint to make a bigger blaze? Or was the leakage due to the expansion of the pipe under heat? "What," Birkett asked the expert, "is the coefficient of expansion of brass?" Brass being a variable alloy, there is no standard answer to this question; but the expert seemed confused, and his confusion undid him.

Rouse had suffered a head-wound in the War; it was suggested that this caused his sex-mania, his lies, his lapses of memory. Maybe; but the mass of irrelevant evidence about his "harem" (his own insensitive word) had prejudiced a righteous jury, and he swung.

Crime in Society has always fascinated the British. Mrs. Elvira Barney had no title, but she was the daughter of Sir John Mullens the Government Broker and her sister was Princess George Imeretinsky. At twenty-seven, coarsened by drink and nightlife, she had taken a lover of twenty-four, Scott Stephen, whom she appeared to be keeping. There was a Mr. Barney somewhere, but not at 21, William Mews, where she lived in what the press called a "luxury" flat, just as they never failed to call Mrs. Barney "beautiful", which she no longer was. The term "mews flat" was still, in 1932, redolent of sin, and Mrs. Barney, oscillating between the Café de Paris and the Blue Angel Club in Dean Street, was headlined as a sort of Michael Arlen heroine left over from the Twenties.

She was a noisy woman: her parties made sleep in William Mews almost impossible, and her rows with Scott Stephen were audible round the corner in Lowndes Square. The police had been sent for several times. Neighbours said she had once fired a pistol at Stephen out of the window as he was leaving, presumably to visit a less troublesome girl. She had

also threatened dramatically to shoot herself. When, therefore, doctor and police, summoned by a telephone call from her, found Stephen dead, shot through the lung, nobody was surprised.

Her story, which she stuck to all through the trial, was that she had tried to shoot herself, he had struggled with her for the weapon, and it had "gone off". Could she have managed the very stiff trigger? Was she left-handed, as one witness had said? The great Sir Bernard Spilsbury found her story consistent; so did Robert Churchill the gunsmith; and Sir Patrick Hastings, defending, brought off one of his dramatic *coups* by suddenly shouting: "Pick up that revolver, Mrs. Barney!" She did—with her *right* hand. Verdict: 'Not Guilty'; and as she left the Old Bailey Mrs. Barney was wildly cheered by a crowd. Public curiosity about a persistent rumour that a member of the Royal Family had been present at the party just before the shooting was never satisfied. Mrs. Barney left for Paris, where she lived exactly as she had lived in London, and died a few years later.

Crime in Society, and in that fictional district of Mayfair; but a new kind of crime for London—crime for kicks, committed by young men who did not need the money. One was the son of a Peer, and all were public school men in their early twenties. They haunted the bars of West End hotels, and so earned the press label of "Mayfair Men". In one hotel they beat up and robbed an elderly jeweller. The effect was one of inexpressible horror: it happened at a time of national loss of face; it seemed to show the decay of public schools and the decadence of society, with or without a capital S. The fact that all the youths were sentenced to flogging with the "cat o'nine tails" followed by stiff prison sentences produced a first public reaction of "quite right too", and a second one of wondering whether this barbarous revenge of society was not more savage than the crime itself. Would it have done the slightest good, had they been a few years younger, to send well-heeled delinquents to one of the new Approved Schools? No: better was expected of the ruling class. Every newspaper carried gruesome pictures of the "cat" and what it did to both the recipient and the administrator: was it really a deterrent? Anyway, the Home Secretary abolished it soon afterwards; and one of the Mayfair Men became popular at parties where he took off his shirt to show the scars which would be there for life.

In the Graham-Greeneland of Brighton, in 1934,

Tony Mancini (whose real name was Cecil England), a waiter in the Skylark Café, with a long record of petty theft, was found not guilty of murdering a dancer-turned-prostitute, Violette Kaye, whom he said he had found dead in bed, and whose body he had chopped up and put in a trunk which he took to his new lodgings. Tony Mancini became a rich man's chauffeur, the first steady job he had ever had.

In leafy Bournemouth Mrs. Alma Rattenbury, thirty-seven, married to a man twenty-five years her senior who seemed to be married to his whisky bottle, took as her lover George Stoner, the odd-job boy, half her age, who "lived in" at the Rattenburys' house, Villa Madeira. The boy borrowed a mallet from his grandmother and killed Mr. Rattenbury. Mrs. Rattenbury, a romantic mixture of Elvira Barney and Edith Thompson, who had once earned her living writing song-lyrics, swore to the police that she had done it. She and Stoner were tried together, like Bywaters and Thompson; she was discharged, he confessed and was condemned to life imprisonment; but she never heard the verdict, because she had killed herself, believing that he would be hanged.

So to the black comedy of Bikhtyar Rustomji Ratanji Hakim, a Parsee living at Lancaster who preferred to be known as Dr. Buck Ruxton, the "Buck" being part of his fantasy-life as an English gentleman. (He had formerly called himself "Captain Hakim"). He was tried at Manchester for the murder of his Scottish "wife" Bella, whom he had accused of having an affair with a clerk at Lancaster Town Hall, and her maid Mary Rogerson, whose dismembered bodies had been found in a tributary of the River Annan near Moffat, Scotland. The forensic details, replete with horror, were offset by outbursts of laughter in court at the "Bombay Welsh" parlance of the little doctor, whose evidence was full of things like "That is absolute bunkum with a capital B, if I may say it", and "She said 'Toodle-oo, Pa' when she went"; and in a line which seemed to come from *Private Lives*, he said of his "marriage"—"We were the kind of people who could not live with each other and could not live without each other." All his little professional pedantries were wrong, like referring to Professor Glaister of Glasgow University ("Scotland's Spilsbury") as "my learned Senior"; and at one point he burst out: "This publicity is ruining my practice!" He was hanged at Strangeways Jail, Manchester, on May 21, 1936.

Child-murder was a rarity forty years ago; or if it was not, it seldom got into the papers. Ten-year-old Mona Tinsley, of Newark, Nottinghamshire, was strangled by Frederick Nodder, her parents' lodger, whom she knew as "Uncle Fred": her body was found in the River Idle near East Retford, having drifted downstream for six months, at a spot which had been accurately predicted several months before by a medium named Estelle Roberts, and hinted at by other clairvoyants, one of whom said she could taste mud in her mouth. The Mona Tinsley case was one of the first "nation-wide searches" which became staple headline material.

BABY DEAD. . . . In America, abductions for ransom were developing into an industry. BABY DEAD. . . . Bootlegging, vice, bank robbing, and now kidnapping. BABY DEAD. . . . The reason this headline was remembered with more horror than any other news item between the two World Wars was that the baby, Charles Lindbergh Jr., aged twenty months, had been killed *before* the $70,000 ransom had been paid; had been killed on the day of his capture because he was an encumbrance. The only son of a national hero—it was as if, in England, a Royal grandchild had been murdered.

On the night of March 1, 1932, someone had been able to approach an isolated house at Hopewell, New Jersey, in the desolate Sourland Hills, the national hero's retreat from excessive publicity after he had married his princess, Anne, daughter of the millionaire banker Dwight Morrow; a well-lighted house containing five adults and a dog; had been able to cross more than a hundred yards of open ground carrying a 40-lb. ladder, place the ladder against a second storey nursery sill, seize the baby and get away, all in fifteen minutes. The kidnapper left a ransom note, demanding $50,000, full of misspellings indicating that the writer was either German or pretending to be German: "The child is in gut care." The ladder, home-made and now broken, was dropped sixty feet from the house.

It is not too much to say that nothing since the assassination of President Lincoln had stirred the country so much. President Hoover said: "We will move heaven and earth to find out who is this criminal who had the audacity to commit a crime like this." At first it looked like an inside job, and suspicion fell on Betty Gow, the baby's nurse, and even on the servants of the Morrows, who lived at Englewood. Most kidnappings were professional gang jobs, and Colonel Lindbergh actually engaged two New York racketeers, Irving Bitz and Salvy Spitale, to consult the underworld. Al Capone indignantly denied any connection—what was $50,000 to him?—he would himself offer $10,000 for information leading to the recovery of the baby. Anne Lindbergh issued a diet sheet for the kidnappers to follow. Although the kidnapper's letters used the words "we" and "us", the police (advised by racketeers) now felt that a lone amateur was at work.

Now entered another amateur, in the person of Dr. J. F. ("Jafsie") Condon, seventy-four, sportsman and lecturer, a garrulous homespun philosopher who told his local newspaper, the *Bronx Home News*, that he would act as intermediary, and offered all his savings, $1,000, if it would help. Near Woodlawn Cemetery he met a man with a German accent who said he was "only a go-between". At a second meeting, with Lindbergh waiting in a car nearby, Condon handed over a prepared package of $50,000 in notes whose serial numbers had been taken down. Lindbergh was now told that the baby was on a boat called *Nelly* near Elisabeth Island. There was no such boat. A hoaxer then described another boat, the *Mary B. Moss*, said to be in Chesapeake Bay. . . . Then, on May 12, the baby's body was found, five miles from Hopewell.

Three police forces were now at work on the case, including the F.B.I., because kidnapping, by the new "Lindbergh Law", was now a Federal offence. Meanwhile the ransom money was appearing all over New York, especially at filling-stations, whose attendants noted the number of the customer's car. A detective named Arthur Koehler, a timber specialist, traced the source of the wood used to make the ladder. So, on September 18, 1934, five police cars converged on the Bronx home of Bruno Hauptmann, a German carpenter, an illegal immigrant with a police record in his own country. He had stopped working on April 2, 1932, and had begun to lead the life of a rich man. His trial was vitiated by publicity, sensation-mongers, press speculation about his guilt, and disorderly sightseers, some of whom bought miniature "kidnap ladders" which were on sale outside the court at Flemington, N.J, after a temporary reprieve for 'further inquiries'. And when Hauptmann was at last electrocuted there was an uncomfortable feeling of public revenge.

How far did this tragedy affect the rest of Lindbergh's life? He was a man of action and many men of action felt as he did about world affairs. His closest friend was probably Dr. Alexis Carrel, the French scientist who had won a Nobel Prize in 1912 for work on organ transplants, on whose behalf Lindbergh promoted a "mechanical heart", sometimes known as the "Lindbergh Perfusion Pump". He travelled restlessly; met Goering, seemed at one time to want to make his home in Berlin, inspected the Luftwaffe, toured German aircraft factories, accepted an honorary Service Cross of the Order of the German Eagle, and made speeches about Germany's invincible air strength. His isolationism caused Roosevelt to call him a "copperhead" (snake). In other speeches he was apt to use expressions like "alien breeds", and propounded some of Carrel's ideas on the supremacy of the white race and the possibility of breeding supermen. He had long considered America to be "disorderly" and "immoral", and wrote articles criticizing democracy "in which the voice of weakness is equal to the voice of strength."

Some weeks before Hauptmann's execution Charles and Anne Lindbergh, with their second son Jon, born in August 1932 (there were already threats to his life too), sought refuge in England, renting a house called Long Barn, in Kent, from Harold Nicolson, who had written a biography of Anne's father. They mingled in London society and were the guests of Edward VIII, with whom Lindbergh had sometimes compared himself as the over-adulated Prince Charming of his country. Nicolson, always making allowances for "what Charles and Anne have been through", described him variously as shrewd, intelligent, shy, charming, "quite uneducated", "as nice as can be". Nicolson had been present at Englewood when the Lindberghs heard the verdict of Hauptmann's guilt on the radio. The crowd outside the courthouse shrieked. "That's a lynching crowd," Lindbergh said. The family turned white and switched it off. They talked for a long time, easing their own minds, sitting in the pantry drinking ginger beer. "My one dread," Lindbergh said, "all these years has been that they would get hold of someone as a victim about whom I wasn't sure. I am about this—*quite* sure."

(*opposite*) George Bernard Shaw, 1939, by Feliks Topolski

# CHAPTER
## XVI

# BOOKS AND BOOKMEN

The Prince of Wales, not that he read many books himself, in 1934 made a speech in which he suggested that all published books should be sent, in van-loads, to Lambeth Palace for censorship. Possibly Cosmo Cantuar remembered it when he did his bit to secure his King's abdication two years later. The Prince was referring to an outburst of the Archbishop in which he had said that best-sellers ought to be burnt, presumably because they were immoral or because they kept people away from church. The best-sellers of 1934 in Britain were Robert Graves's *I, Claudius*, J. B. Priestley's *English Journey*, Jack Jones's *Rhondda Roundabout*, J. W. Dunne's *The Serial Universe*, James Hilton's *Goodbye, Mr. Chips*, Rose Macaulay's *Going Abroad*, and Hervey Allen's *Anthony Adverse*. The first was hailed at the time as, and remains forty years later, a prose epic of the first magnitude. The second was a conscience-rousing survey of four Englands, one that Shakespeare would have recognized, one industrial but tolerable, one shapeless and un-planned, and one on the dole, "our contemptible and short-sighted dole system", in which there was no such hope as the New Deal promised.

The third was a *comedy* about a "depressed area" written by an unemployed miner, very Welsh, making mild fun of Communists in the character of Mordecai Rees, who tries to start a Communist dance-hall where tunes of his own composition, one of them called 'Tremblin' in the Kremlin', shall be played for the edification of young people. The fourth set out a new theory of time by which one could perfect a technique for "expressing the future", and which would provide Mr. Priestley with ideas for several plays. The fifth was a sentimental tribute to an old schoolmaster, the sixth a mild skit on the Buchmanites, and the last heralded the new "jackpot age" of best-sellers with an enormously long picaresque costume piece of the Napoleonic era under a Smollett-ish title. All were wholesome books, which, on different levels, made the reader think, feel or laugh: any objection, Your Grace?

Long books were in: they ranged from Dr. Cronin's *Hatter's Castle* to Lloyd George's *War Memoirs*, in four volumes and 2,439 pages. The publishing theory that the formula for best-selling fiction is costumed history and/or a devotional theme, and for best-selling non-fiction "self-help and popularized religion" was both proved and violated. Proved by *Gone With The Wind* (1936), advertised as "a complete vacation's reading for 3 dollars," a 1,037-page narrative, well and toughly told, of the American Civil War and the post-war reconstruction as seen from the South, by a childless married lady of 36 with a sick mother, just under five feet tall, and crippled in one ankle, Margaret Mitchell. It was to have been called *Tomorrow Is Another Day*, from the last sentence of the book, when the auburn-haired, loved-hated Scarlett has just got her come-uppance; but Macmillans, her publishers, thought there had been too many Tomor-rows among recent titles, so once again Dawson's *Cynara* was plundered. Miss Mitchell had taken ten years to write *GWTW*, and she wrote no other novel. Cautiously hailed as a "successor to *Anthony Adverse*", the book sold a million copies in its first six months. Its message of endurance made Americans feel better about America.

Violated, that formula, by *The Grapes of Wrath* (1939), "the *Uncle Tom's Cabin* of the Depression," which followed the fortunes of a family of "Okies" migrating across the continent to California. Accused by some critics of sentimental leftism, Steinbeck told America something about itself. Ma, of course carries the family: they arrive at a camp near Bakersfield—"You got wash tubs, running water?"—"Sure".—"Oh, praise God!"—a central committee, elected by campers? Dances? No cops?

The Joads can't believe their luck. . . .

Perhaps, in publishing terms, *The Grapes of Wrath* was following another formula, the "acceptable" proletarian-radical novel of pity rather than indignation, that had made best-sellers of Erskine Caldwell's *Tobacco Road* and *God's Little Acre*. "In Detroit a person dies of starvation every $7\frac{1}{2}$ hours," wrote Louis Adamic in a letter to the *New York Sun*. "Young novelists are no longer thinking of writing smart, witty novels. They are working on labour novels." Those young novelists may have called themselves Communists, but few of them actually visualized "revolution" as barricades, street fighting, seizing factories, as William Z. Foster did in his *Toward Soviet America*, in which he advocated "liquidating" Republicans, Democrats, Progressives, Socialists, chambers of commerce, Rotarians, Masons, the YMCA—they were all, all manifestations of capitalism. The Dos Passos—Farrell—Steinbeck trend at least smoothed the path of the New Deal, because their readers were made to feel that the New Deal was better than revolution.

So you could, as thousands did, fashionably read eye-witness accounts of what was still called "the Russian experiment", such as Maurice Hindus's *Red Bread*, admitting that Five-Year-planning was probably a good thing, without actually conceding that violence was necessary to achieve it. Moscow itself was in two minds: was F.D.R. a capitalist lackey or a partner in the Popular Front?

The significant novelists, in fact, moved slowly to the right, helped by disappointment with Left behaviour in the Spanish Civil War. John Dos Passos, in his *U.S.A.* trilogy, attacked post-Depression America, using the symbol of a ragged man trying to thumb a ride along a highway; but his failure to save a friend from being shot by Spanish Loyalists did something to him. That the true literary artist does not accept the Marxist view of the author's function was suggested by James T. Farrell, whose *Studs Lonigan* trilogy traced the effect of decaying Chicago on the life of a lower middle class Catholic boy: in *A Note on Literary Criticism* (1936) he made his own position clear.

The best work of Sinclair Lewis had been done: had he ever really left Sauk Center? If he had, he returned to a central position; or rather, he seemed to be exchanging the Left-Right conflict for the Black-White conflict. His *It Can't Happen Here* (1935) was an attempt to wake America up to the Nazi danger; and in a forgettable novel, *The Prodigal Parents* (1938), he seemed to be confessing that he really loved Babbitt after all, at least he was better than revolution. Lewis nevertheless was ready to hand over to the young. In 1930, still only forty-five, he went to Stockholm to get his Nobel Prize and said: "There are young Americans today who are doing such passionate and authentic work that it makes me sick to see that I am a little too old to be one of them." He mentioned "a bitter youth" called Hemingway (then thirty-one) and "a child of thirty" named Thomas Wolfe.

Hemingway, resting on the laurels of *A Farewell To Arms*, was writing about bullfighting and big game hunting; lots of short stories, no major novel; waiting for a cause to fight for. He found it in Spain—result, in 1940: *For Whom The Bell Tolls*. Tom Wolfe—a genius, of course, all the critics say so; may I timidly add the word "flawed", and suggest that few British publishers would ever have had patience with him? Ask him to cut 25,000 words, and he'd add 50,000. *The Web and The Rock* (1939), published the year after his death at the age of thirty-eight, contains some 275,000 words—and we are told that this, like his other novels, was condensed and reorganized by his publishers: "Max Perkins and the assembly line at Scribners," sneered a hostile critic, Bernard de Voto. Wolfe said he had "an almost insane hunger to devour the entire body of human experience." Lacking discipline, invention and power of construction, he produced about a million words a year, all about himself, his family, his friends, hardly troubling to change their names. It's awfully *long*, New York publishers seemed often to think, it *may* turn out to be the Great American Novel. . . .

Wolfe turned down an invitation to go to Hollywood, just as he sometimes turned down weekend invitations to the country, because he daren't stop writing. William Faulkner accepted a movie contract. In writing *Sanctuary*, "the most horrific tale I could imagine", quickly in three weeks he had deliberately set out to earn money. *Light in August* (1932) and *Absalom! Absalom!* (1936) presented a violent and very different South from Margaret Mitchell's. It is somehow personified in the character of Joe Christmas, in *Light in August*, who does not know whether he is black or white and is lynched as a Negro. Yet it was a South that Faulkner could not wait to get back to; so that when he complained to

Darryl Zanuck "I can't work in my office. Would you mind if I worked at home?" and Zanuck, to whom home meant Beverley Hills, replied "Sure," the creator of Yoknapatawpha County went home—to Oxford, Mississippi.

In 1934, after nearly eight bookless years and numberless recastings, Scott Fitzgerald published *Tender Is The Night*. It was the year of Zelda's third breakdown: the hero, Dick Diver, was a psychiatrist heading, like Fitzgerald himself and the world he knew, for a crack-up—*The Crack-Up*, title-essay of his next book. His Jazz Age was over, he was out of fashion, he spoke of "my talent" in the past tense. For him the bottle, Hollywood, and death.

Another Irish name was in the ascendant: John O'Hara, in a coonskin coat, from Pottsville, Penna., the Gibbsville of his stories. Earthier, drunk in a different way, more openly ambitious for money ("I dream of going to Hollywood and making large sums there"), less of a poet but a shrewder observer, he was of the Thirties. In *Butterfield 8* he used the mysterious death of Starr Faithfull to record the pre- and post-Wall Street years, naming names like the reporter he had been (on the New York *Herald-Tribune*, and, briefly, on the *New Yorker*, where he had contributed short 200-word pieces to fill up the gaps in the advertising—editor Harold Ross praised his dialogue, "the beautiful precision of his ear," and sometimes let him cover football). Master of a plain style, nearly all nouns and verbs, he gradually made his books longer and longer because "fat books sell better than thin books." His masterpiece, *Appointment in Samarra* (1935), was short, unfashionably so. Here is the America Sinclair Lewis had left behind in *Babbitt*, transferred to the anthracite belt of Pennsylvania, the social stratification of Gibbsville, Lantenengo Street where it is almost worse to be a Jew than to be a Negro, and not very good to be a Catholic; the envy of wealth (different from Fitzgerald's), the Country Club where the "smoking-room crowd" either made you feel "socially secure" or they didn't.

O'Hara never really felt or became an "insider", which for him was largely a question of going to a university. It was Ernest Hemingway who suggested to his friends that they should all club together to send John to Harvard, because it seemed to mean so much to him. Even Hollywood was a disappointment: O'Hara was only used as a "dialogue polish man." Never mind: *Samarra*, the tragedy of Julian English and his own personal crack-up, lives, as it did on the day Dorothy Parker reviewed it: "This swift, savage story, set down as sharp and deep as if the author had used steel for paper . . . a document of American history." Many readers were shocked: not at the picture it gave of America, but because it opened with a couple making love on Christmas morning—a *married* couple, as if their legitimate happiness were a particular indecency.

There was a cosier America in Clarence Day's *Life With Father*, a funnier one in Thurber's *My Life and Hard Times* (funniest book since Mark Twain, some said), a wittier one in Alexander Woollcott's *While Rome Burns*, an anecdote-filled collection of short articles on people, crime, travel. In 1931 everybody read *The Good Earth*, about Chinese peasants; in 1932, Bernard Shaw's *The Adventures of the Black Girl in her Search for God*—blasphemous, of course, but John Farleigh's beautiful woodcuts made it a suitable gift. In 1938 there was Daphne du Maurier's *Rebecca*, in 1939 Richard Llewellyn's *How Green Was My Valley*, which made people feel guilty, and therefore a little easier, about South Wales. Escape, all escape—even other people's poverty was escape. And, for the self-help formula, there was *Life Begins at Forty, Live Alone and Like It, The Importance of Living* (Lin Yutang's gentle protest against western tension), and, if you could control your laughter, Dale Carnegie's *How To Win Friends and Influence People*, first of many "you-too" exhortations. For America only, there were helpful sex-books which tended to be bought as pornography, such as Calverton and Schmalhausen's *Sex in Civilization* and *Woman's Coming of Age*.

Britain had to wait until 1937 for the first unlimited edition of *Ulysses*; but America had one three years earlier, after Judge Woolsey's celebrated verdict that it was *not* pornographic, bearing in mind that Joyce's "locale was Celtic and his season Spring", and implying that one didn't have to associate with rather common people in Dublin if one preferred not to. When, in 1939 after sixteen years' labour, *Finnegans Wake* came along, even a Joyce-ite who held the key confessed that it left the reader "foundering in a welter of possible interpretations."

D. H. Lawrence had died in 1930: at once there was a burst of books about him, by his wife, by Mabel Luhan, by Anaïs Nin, by F. R. Leavis and by Stephen Potter. Had he lived, he would have been in dead trouble about Germany, for the new generation, in

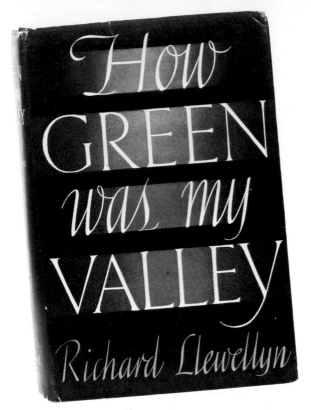

their black-and-white way, might have labelled him fascist. There were those, loud with the confidence of their bourgeois public-school-university old-boy net, who felt guilty; and those, genuinely proletarian, who respectfully pointed out how awful were their backgrounds, their valleys not so green.

The other Lawrence, T. E., now calling himself Shaw, crashed to his death on a motorcycle in May 1935, four months before the first trade edition of *The Seven Pillars of Wisdom*, all 300,000 words of it on fine deckle-edged paper with illustrations by Eric Kennington and other artists. After fifteen years of rewriting, losing the manuscript, mystification, rumour that certain homosexual implications had had to be cut, two limited editions and an abridgment, *Revolt In The Desert*, this highly personal history of the Arab Revolt suddenly became a best seller at the then enormous price of 35s.

George Orwell, Eton and Burma Police, found it necessary to live and suffer with the underdog. He worked in the kitchens of a Paris restaurant, was a patient in a hospital where the very poor went to die, lived with the family of an unemployed miner in the north of England. This was the stuff of *Down and Out in Paris and London* and *The Road to Wigan Pier*. The miner had been drawing 29s. a week dole for nine months, but the colliery wanted to put him on "partial compensation" of 14s. a week: to get it, he would have to spend 6d. on bus fares and queue for hours in a cold wind. Orwell thought it likely that "the movies, the radio, strong tea and the football pools have between them averted revolution." A reluctant Socialist, half in love with the dying England of his youth, he had, like so many writers of the time, turned against his background. He believed in the fundamental decency of the working man: but was it decency, or a spirit too crushed by poverty to express itself?

Christopher Isherwood, who, Somerset Maugham said, held the future of the English novel in his hands, produced a slender canon in these times. Incomparably readable, he made his name, not with the forgotten *The Memorial* ("the effect of the idea of War on my generation"), but with fictional reportage about Berlin in *Mr. Norris Changes Trains* (Mr. Norris in real life was Gerald Hamilton, a kind of Maundy Gregory without the active criminal streak) and *Goodbye to Berlin*, which, Heaven knows, has become *I Am A Camera* and *Cabaret*, and whose heroine, Sally

Bowles, was based on a rather county-looking English girl who afterwards went to the Spanish Civil War as a Communist and died in Scotland in 1973.

There was, in the mid-1930s, a small bunch of genuine British working-class writers few of whom managed to produce enduring stuff. Walter Greenwood's *Love On the Dole*, of course, written in Salford, Manchester, on an old trouser-press because the kitchen table had been sold under the means-test rules; and Edward O'Brien, hopeful editor of experimental short stories, identified a "Birmingham Group" which included Leslie Halward, a plasterer, and Walter Allen, a writer who had escaped by scholarships from manual labour, and who argued (in a great debate in the *London Mercury*) that only American writers so far had created a truly working-class literature. The limitations of Halward's "documentary realism" were seen by the young publisher, John Hadfield, who wrote: "There ought to be room for a proletarian Dostoievsky or Virginia Woolf as well as a proletarian Bennett."

A vogue for low life broke briefly out: indeed, *Low Life* was the title of an autobiography by a literate ex-convict, Mark Benney. A waiter wrote his autobiography, *Coming, Sir!* An attack on the prison system, *Walls Have Mouths* by another ex-convict, W. F. R. Macartney, had a sympathetic introduction by Compton Mackenzie. The word "spiv" (one who lives without working) entered contemporary slang. The London *Evening Standard* took a considerable risk by publishing the stories of Damon Runyon, about the New York gangster fringe, written in a lingo that quickly passed from incomprehensibility to a craze, so that the paper eventually ran a Runyonese Competition. Runyon, who, we are told, "wore a belted polo coat and a velour hat the size of a coal-scuttle", had somehow made gangsters *funny*, giving them names like Frankie Ferocious. For a few weeks those of us who were young called each other guys and dolls.

For serious students of the political mess, Victor Gollancz's Left Book Club started up in 1936, blessed (literally) by the Red Dean of Canterbury; its 50,000 membership bought books selected monthly by the publisher, Victor Gollancz, Professor Harold Laski and John Strachey: to re-read its earnest publications today is to feel old. In the same year Allen Lane published the first six Penguin Books and showed that sixpenny paperbacks (of books still in copyright) were

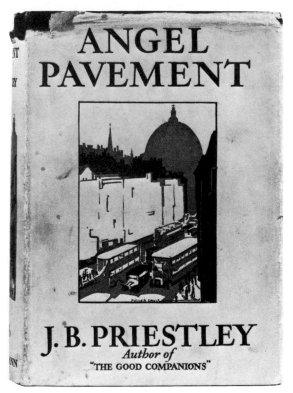

a commercial proposition as well as a cultural need.

A young sub-editor on *The Times*, Graham Greene, was persuaded by his publisher to leave his safe job and write fiction full-time. Beginning with what he self-consciously termed "entertainments", thrillers spiced with pity and religion, about people whose chief quality was (his own word) "seediness", he suddenly lifted the genre to a new height in *Brighton Rock* (1938) and reached complete maturity in 1940 with his Mexican whisky-priest in *The Power and the Glory*. Greene's fellow Catholic convert Evelyn Waugh gave one more backward look at the Twenties in *Vile Bodies* and then, with no let-up in his terrible infancy, travelled afar, in both life and fiction, creating, in *Black Mischief* and *Scoop*, the imaginary yet recognizable countries of Azania and Ishmaelia, both in Africa.

Arnold Bennett sipped the fatal typhoid-bearing glass of water and died one day in 1931: straw had been laid in the street outside to deaden the traffic noise, as he slept. Galsworthy had got the Nobel Prize and died in 1933. Kipling was carried off on a dark January day in 1936, two days before George V. Where were the new Men and Women of Letters, the really big professional writers? Maugham had produced *Cakes and Ale* in 1930: it was said to be about Thomas Hardy, and the character of Alroy Kear was a venomous portrait of poor Hugh Walpole, whose *Herries* books looked like going on for ever. Maugham produced his autobiography, *The Summing Up*, in 1938, as if he were going to stop writing; he did not, but no major novel appeared until during the War. J. B. Priestley had followed *The Good Companions* with his (for me) best novel, set in London, *Angel Pavement*, required reading for anyone who wants a warm picture of office life in the Depression, and then *Faraway*, then *Wonder Hero*—it seemed that he was drifting away from the novel, to the theatre's gain.

Aldous Huxley, fast becoming a padded Mandarin (in the Cyril Connolly sense), began to go against the young "join the workers" trend, to move towards the Swami instead of the Commissar: he would soon be taking Isherwood with him. Striving to keep up his output, he was (Connolly again) "overproducing". It may be that of all his books in the 1930's *Brave New World* will, surprisingly, stand the test of time. Being a better scientist than Wells, whose *The Shape of Things to Come* (1933) came out a year later, he was able to foresee the dangers of hypnopedia ("sleep teach-

ing"), state brainwashing from infancy, test-tube babies, and examinations in Elementary Class Consciousness. More than twenty years later Huxley confessed, in *Esquire*, that the future was more likely to resemble Orwell's 1984 than his own predictions.

*The Waves*, Virginia Woolf's best book, was published in 1931: she had (Connolly again) overcome her "cocoon-spinning" and "come nearest to stating the mystery of life" by studying, in cross-section, a group of friends as they grow up. The perceptive few noted a curious novel, *Men and Wives*, by someone called Ivy Compton-Burnett, and, in the same year (1931), a certain Anthony Powell published a rather Prousty book *Afternoon Men*, following it up with others. No doubt about Elizabeth Bowen, and if you want the atmosphere of the 1930's as it felt to a sensitive woman, read *To The North* and *The Death of the Heart*. I search vainly, in books of literary criticism, for serious mention of Rosamond Lehmann (after all, she *was* part of Bloomsbury, though it was now dying); and may I please pick out her little masterpiece, *Invitation to the Waltz* (1932), a study of adolescence, done with lightness and pathos and humour.

The muddle of the Thirties was in the changing mind of Beverley Nichols. *Cry Havoc* was an hysterical outburst against war: he would rather be shot than fight. His readers, who knew him best for chatty, friendly books about gardening and his country cottage, were probably more influenced by him than by the rational anti-war arguments of the Left. In *News of England*, "a study in national decadence", he hated all sorts of things he had previously admired: the League of Nations, Disarmament Conferences, Oxford undergraduates, mingling with them air raid precautions, football pools, drink, Communists and the Distressed Areas. He was looking for a hero: the only one on the horizon seemed to be Sir Oswald Mosley; and here he safeguarded himself: "I am not a Fascist. I don't want to wear any shirt, black, brown, green or red. But I do want to tell the truth as I see it." The quest for a father-figure took a new form in *The Fool Hath Said*, and if, for a few moments, the figure looked a little like Frank Buchman, the sermonizing was done with such showmanship that he was praised in pulpits throughout the land.

Something was happening to the thriller. With villainy and violence in Europe staring at one from newspaper front-pages every day, the old quiet murder by pearl-handled revolver in the library of The Grange would no longer do. "I was leaning against the bar in a speakeasy on 52nd Street, waiting for Nora to finish her Christmas shopping. . . ." Only in Dashiell Hammett could you find an opening sentence like that (it is from *The Thin Man*). Hammett, an ex-Pinkerton's detective himself, knew what he was writing about, drank even more than his hero, wasted not a word, and criticized society as he went along. His detective stories are *novels*: you don't forget his people. He was joined, in 1939, by Raymond Chandler, whose *The Big Sleep* introduced another private eye, Philip Marlowe; less tough, more literary, as interested in life as in death, a subtler social critic, he was at once hailed by J. B. Priestley as a crime-writer who had strayed into art.

A connoisseur of first sentences would also have been stopped in his tracks by this, from Francis Iles's *Malice Aforethought* (1931): "It was not until several weeks after he had decided to murder his wife that Dr. Bickleigh took any active steps in the matter."

Dorothy Sayers is now at her peak, and so is Margery Allingham, whose Mr. Campion has in him something of Lord Peter Wimsey; but we are now often in the world, not of who-done-it, but who's-going-to-do-it, of men who are hunted like animals in order to kill them. Suspense and espionage are about to replace simple murder and detection. In Geoffrey Household's *Rogue Male* (1939), a man, working for nobody but himself, sets out to improve the state of Europe by setting up a rifle with a telescopic sight trained on the private retreat of a dictator, who could not, in the timidity of the Thirties, be named, but who was obviously Hitler. He is caught, beaten up, escapes. . . . A new, anti-war, anti-capitalist attitude, personified in a friendly Soviet spy named Zaleshoff, informed the early novels of Eric Ambler, notably *Epitaph for a Spy* (1938), in which espionage was stripped of all glamour—for the epitaph was "He needed the money". Ambler's supreme achievement was *The Mask of Dimitrios*, in which he used the jig-saw method of A. J. A. Symon's *The Quest for Corvo* to track down a Balkan villain, conveying information about the white slave traffic and other rackets on the way. Zaleshoff is now incredible; but Dimitrios never dates.

Escape, escape—into fantasy, into realism, into terror, into—humour. Especially Crazy Humour, with private jokes for the initiated. Nat Gubbins in the *Sunday Express*, whose suburban characters and dialogues would later help Britain through the Blitz. "Timothy Shy" (D. B. Wyndham Lewis) in the *News Chronicle*, whose jokes and fantasies were almost interchangeable with those of "Beachcomber" (J. B. Morton) in the *Daily Express*. The contemporary Wellsian appetite for improving tomes like *The Outline of Modern Knowledge* and *Mathematics for the Million* were burlesqued by a Charterhouse house-master and an advertising copywriter, Sellars and Yeatman, first in *Punch* and then in books—*1066 And All That* (about English history) and *And Now All This* (about modern knowledge, including a chapter on knitting entitled Woology). A skit on the earthy novels of Mary Webb and Sheila Kaye-Smith became immortal: Stella Gibbon's *Cold Comfort Farm* is as fresh today as it was in 1932, and Aunt Ada's refrain, "something nasty in the woodshed", became a family joke even among people who had never read the book. Of them all, it is probably Beachcomber who left the greatest gallery of mad creations. Mr. Justice Cocklecarrot attempting to deal with the Seven Red-Bearded Dwarfs, the Filthistan Trio, Dr. Smart-Allick the Headmaster of Narkover, the List of Huntingdonshire Cabmen, Evans the Hearse, Big White Carstairs the Empire-builder, how to invent a spoon with a hole in it so that "the cook can look at whatever she is about to stir" . . . You don't think it's funny? God help you.

# CHAPTER
## XVII

# I SEE BY THE PAPERS

I am twenty-two. I have just been made Fiction Editor of a glossy magazine called *Nash's* after telling the Editor, a kind American named Dick Mealand who happens to like what he calls "crazy English college boys," what is wrong with the magazine. He looks at my grubby raincoat and my only suit, and asks: "How much money do you want?" "Would—three pounds a week be too much?" He stares: "Can you really live on that?" "Oh, yes, sir." There are $2\frac{1}{2}$ million unemployed, I have only enough money to last another week, if I don't get this job I shall have to go back to Birmingham, which is worse than death. Besides, the Editor has just bought an article of mine, an impudent attack on Beverley Nichols in which I predict Beverley's future as a Grand Old Man (to me he *is* old, he's all of thirty-eight), but I won't get the cheque till next month.

"Okay," shrugs Mealand. "I'll take you at your own valuation." *Nash's*, younger brother to *Good Housekeeping*, is a Hearst magazine: I am to be careful about all references to a film star called Marion Davies, who seems to belong to Mr. Hearst, and I am not to alter a word of Louella Parsons' Hollywood newsletter when it comes in, especially when she reports parties at which "Marion was looking lovelier than ever." I am to report fully on all short story scripts from literary agents, and in one sentence on everything else. Dick teaches me subbing—how to carve out paragraphs and whole chapters of novels for serialization without losing opportunities for Harold Forster's sexy illustrations. I carve paragraphs out of Maugham (difficult), Walpole (easy), Alec Waugh (child's play), Hemingway (almost impossible). Seven months later an accountant called Mr. Buttikofer comes over from New York and the magazine collapses.

By the autumn I have a new job editing encyclopedias and part-works under Sir John Ham-

1936

merton at Amalgamated Press. We—about a dozen hacks between the ages of sixty and nineteen—write most of the stuff ourselves, occasionally stiffening the mixture with articles by well-known writers. Then I am given the *Argosy*, a reprint-fiction magazine, to run single-handed (I have now risen to £8 a week). But my eyes are on a new development in Fleet Street: a young millionaire named Edward Hulton is about to start a British counterpart to *Life* Magazine. It comes out the week after Munich. I *must* get in on

The first cover of *Picture Post* launched October 1st, 1938

this. . . . It takes time, but I eventually join Hulton as Assistant Editor of a rather serious monthly called *World Review* where I stay until my call-up papers arrive. . . . I am now a Young Lion of Fleet Street who knows some of the Beaverbrook boys and girls by their first names. I earn £10 a week.

*Picture Post*, a left-wing *Life* with an almost identical cover, was the creation of a Hungarian-Jewish refugee from Hitler, Stefan Lorant, who had already edited *Weekly Illustrated* at Odhams Press. It was prepared to lose a million pounds in its first year, and Hulton's rivals regarded it as a crazy risk taken by a rich amateur. Two of *Picture Post*'s staff photographers were German refugees, bringing with them techniques of pictorial journalism then almost unknown in Britain. A pocket-size sister magazine, *Lilliput*, printing more sophisticated satire and humour than the long-established *Punch*, also used "picture comparisons" (e.g. Neville Chamberlain and a camel), a device which had been pioneered by *Querschnitt* in Germany, considered very "daring" in the London of 1938.

*Picture Post*'s circulation confounded the publishing trade by reaching 1,350,000 in four months. Readers

Stefan Lorant (left), the first editor of *Picture Post*, with the founder, Edward Hulton

were delighted by a magazine that openly attacked the Nazis, spoke up for persecuted Jewry, explained how a by-election worked, showed a girl on a round-about with her skirt blowing up, a queue at an employment exchange, interviewed Scottish nationalists, pinpointed Churchill ("the man the Tories don't trust") as Britain's leader "should some great emergency arise." Its impact on a magazine market which had hardly changed for twenty years, in a world which had no television, was tremendous. It was something with a hard edge, in a Fleet Street softened by what the public was supposed to want, such as Godfrey Winn's "Sincerity Page" in the *Daily Mirror* which was largely about his adorable little dog Mr. Sponge.

This was only two years after *Life*, taking its title from an old satirical magazine, had appeared in New York, to be followed quickly by *Look*. *Life*, more safely middle-of-the-road than *Picture Post*, was fathered by Time Inc., which also published *Fortune*, a weighty, lavish survey of business which used the team-research method of presenting a current problem. *Time*, the first "news magazine", had been founded in 1922 by Henry Luce and Briton Hadden, and 1933 saw the publication of a rival, *Newsweek*. In London, pale imitations, run on relative shoe-strings, appeared, *News Review* and *Cavalcade*, both infected with the "*Time*-style" about which one of *Time*'s editors, Noel Busch, had warned John O'Hara when he was on the staff—"Go easy on it, John." Inversions like "Quipped Ambassador Kennedy . . ." portmanteau-words and two-word captions were as habit-forming as Winchell's "slanguage". It is said that *Time*-style was invented by Briton Hadden, who "had picked up the classical epithet from Homer and the double-barrelled adjectives from Carlyle." It never quite recovered from Wolcott Gibbs's send-up in the *New Yorker*: "Backward run sentences, till reels the mind."

Some of it, and certainly a *Time* heading ("These Names Make News"), turned up in a London *Daily Express* column by "William Hickey" (Tom Driberg) who infuriated schoolmasters by spelling "through" *thru* and "night" *nite*, as *Variety*, the American show-business paper, did. These were great years for gossip. Nobody in Britain went as far for a scoop as Walter Winchell, read in the New York *Daily Mirror* and other papers every day by thirty million people: he too added words to the language—"middle-aisling

it" for getting married, "groom-shelving" for getting divorced, "cinemadorable" for almost any film-star; and he invented "making whoopee". Gossip had once revolved round Café Society: now anyone was fair game. In London the prince of gossip writers was Valentine, Lord Castlerosse, of the *Sunday Express*, a 250-pound Irish peer whom Beaverbrook occasionally had to rescue from his creditors. Even the social pages of the *Tatler* grew sharper, with innuendi (no names—if you were "in", you knew), as Barbara Cartland took over from Evelyn Bagg and created a new feature, "Panorama", to replace "Letters of Eve". The *Sunday Dispatch* offered the Marquis of Donegall, the *Evening Standard* had Minnie Hogg as "Corisande", and both Bruce Lockhart and Harold Nicolson on "The Londoner's Diary". "I never foresaw", Harold wept in his own diary, "that writing for the Press would be so degrading."

Britain, because the structure of her newspaper industry was different, had nothing like the American "syndicated columnists", commanding tens of millions of readers over the whole continent—the two Walters, Winchell and Lippmann, O. O. McIntyre's Broadway snippets, Dorothy Thompson on world politics, Drew Pearson, Westbrook Pegler, and of course Mrs. Roosevelt. Greatest of these was Lippmann, sometime editor of the old *New York World*, now read by the whole nation three times a week as, from the failure of the 1933 London Economic Conference onwards, he consistently warned that war was inevitable, Stalin was dangerous, Hitler and Mussolini had "manacled their hands to prevent them shaking."

As both Britain and America were forced to grow less insular, foreign correspondents were read with avid anxiety. They became quasi-heroes, racketing round Europe in search of trouble, drinking deep at the Sacher Hotel, the Ritz Bar, the Adlon. Many of them expanded their articles into books—Negley Farson's *The Way of a Transgressor*, John Gunther's *Inside Europe* (a marvellous, slap-dash gallimaufray of press-cuttings, gossip and anecdote) and *Inside Asia*, Sisley Huddlestone's *War, Unless—*, Walter Duranty on Russia. Britain, more soberly, boasted Norman Ebbutt of *The Times* and F. A. Voigt of the *Manchester Guardian*; and G. E. R. Gedye of the *Daily Telegraph*, based in Vienna, who, reporting Hitler's seizure of Austria, wrote this: "You will shrug your comfortable shoulders in England . . . when I tell you of Viennese women whose husbands were arrested without charge receiving a small parcel from the postman with the curt intimation—'to pay 150 marks for the cremation of your husband—ashes enclosed, from Dachau'." Gedye had loved the old, *gemütlich* Vienna to distraction. The *Daily Express* and the *Daily Mail* both glamorized their men in Europe, Sefton Delmer and Ward Price respectively, as men who had actually talked to Hitler. Madame Tabouis, believed to have been the mistress of at least one French minister, was thought to have *inside*-inside knowledge, and was quoted all over the world.

In London, there was an outbreak, just before the War, of privately mailed news-letters, paid for by subscription. Some, like the *King-Hall Newsletter*, run by a pinkish retired Naval Commander, were discreetly educational: all were subservient to *The Week*, edited and mostly written by Communist Claud Cockburn, a scruffily-duplicated sheet which got its scandalous facts right too often for comfort, identified the 'Cliveden Set' of alleged pro-Germans around Lady Astor, and gave the impression that it knew even more than it had printed, so that it was not uncommon for statesmen to telephone the editor asking for the facts behind the facts behind the facts. *The Week*, produced in a single room in Victoria Street and over the marble-topped tables of the Café Royal, was, Cockburn claimed, quoted all over the world, and subscribed to by Embassies, diplomatic correspondents, banks, stockbrokers, American Senators, M.P.s, trade union secretaries, "King Edward VIII, Charlie Chaplin and the Nizam of Hyderabad."

For lighter irreverence there were *Ballyhoo*, a short-lived American "send up" magazine with a flavour of undergraduate rudery, and its British counterpart *Razzle*. For armchair or railway reading, average American businessmen swore by the *Reader's Digest*, published from a town called Pleasantville, N.Y., of which nothing else was known: the magazine for the man who had no time to read magazines. *Reader's Digest* came to Britain in 1939, but not before an imitation, *English Digest*, had been produced by Amalgamated Press.

The autumn of 1933 was not the most auspicious time to launch a new luxury magazine for men, a magazine devoted to "the art of living and the new leisure"—the forty-hour week which, now that banks seemed to have stopped closing, the New Deal was promising. Planned as a quarterly, *Esquire* was forced to publish monthly, and the little pop-eyed man on the cover was named Esky. It published the world's best authors of fiction, from Pound to Molnar, from Hemingway to Pirandello; and provocative articles with titles like 'Latins Are Lousy Lovers' (this one brought in furious letters from Cuba), interleaved with appeals to baser and more basic man in the form of girls in swimsuits and girls in nothing, many of them drawn, in the stylized way that makes a pin-up, by Petty and Varga.

For nine years the *American Mercury*, edited by H. L. Mencken, had been poking fun at Rotarians, Babbitts and the Bible Belt; but the Twenties were over, and publisher Alfred A. Knopf, replacing Mencken with Henry Hazlitt, announced that in future the magazine's outlook would be international—"it will give more attention to stupidity and swinishness in high places." Hazlitt lasted only four months, another editor lasted nine months, and then Knopf sold the magazine: it had made money under Mencken, and the readers missed him: they wanted him—and the Twenties—back again.

The *London Mercury* too had a change of editor. Since 1919 it had been conducted on "establishment" lines by Sir John Squire, bibulous, cricket-mad poet and satirist in whose pages anything experimental was seldom found. He was succeeded in 1934 by Reginald Scott-James, who at least made it *look* livelier and broadened its scope to include reportage such as an eye-witness account of the bombing of Guernica. Desmond MacCarthy's *Life and Letters*, like the *Mercury*, was basically "establishment"—Gisele Freund, who specialized in photographing writers and editors, calls them both "complacent, whimsical and well-bred": she adds—"two jingling hearses". The word "new" no longer excited people as it had done in the Twenties; and yet it was to small magazines and anthologies with titles like *New Writing* and *New Signatures* that one had to go to find the names of the future. (Did I say small? *New Writing*, published by Penguin Books and edited by John Lehmann, reached a sale of 50,000.)

The new dynamic among "serious" reviews in Britain was the *New Statesman and Nation*, the product of a merger between two magazines to which was added a third, *The Week-End Review*. The "Staggers and Naggers", as its new editor, Kingsley Martin, called it, gathered round it some of the best brains of the age, and had a Diary column that took considerable risks and maintained a sort of joyous pessimism. It was smart to be seen reading it, no matter what politics you professed (my Uncle Ernest bought it because he enjoyed the apoplectic fury it stirred up in him). It was good on the stock market, too. And it had a new kind of snippets column called "This England" which relished items like Lady Montgomery-Massingberd's advice to total abstainers to drink up *all* the cocktail in the glass rather than leave any "to be drunk in the pantry by someone who . . . has not acquired the taste." Advertisers began to support the *New Statesman*, which soon showed a healthy profit.

In America, there was Edmund Wilson, author of one of the two really important books of literary criticism in these times—*Axel's Castle*; in Britain Cyril Connolly, who in 1938 published *Enemies of Promise*. Both stood apart from the scholarship of the day—the stern atmosphere of Dr. Leavis's *Scrutiny* (1932), the discipline of I. A. Richards—in being unashamed to be journalists and to communicate enthusiasm; also to warn. "My journalism," Connolly said, "is literature". Marxist Wilson recommended books to be read as a duty to mankind; hedonist Connolly almost *dared* you to read them.

T. S. Eliot's *The Criterion* had come to an end in January, 1939, and in his last editorial Eliot foresaw a dark age in which culture would be kept alive only by "obscure papers . . . hardly read by anyone but their own contributors." Not so. A few months later Connolly was editing the first issues of *Horizon*, which lasted for ten years and achieved a circulation of 7,500.

There were less newspapers, but more copies of those that survived. Eighty-five per cent of the American press seemed to be against Roosevelt, yet everyone knew of journalists who wrote against FDR but secretly supported the New Deal. (One of them, Kenneth Durante, who came from a wealthy family in Philadelphia, eventually joined the staff of Tass, the Soviet news agency.) The Hearst press weakened: radio was the new medium, and, although these were the "propaganda years", ideas were more powerful than words; and when, in 1936, Hearst supported Governor Landon against Roosevelt for President, and the Gallup poll predicted a huge swing to the "Kansas Coolidge", and the Roosevelt landslide happened, Harold Ickes, Secretary of the Interior, said: "To my view, the outstanding thing about the campaign was the lack of influence of the newspapers. . . . Never have the newspapers conducted a more mendacious and venomous campaign against a candidate for President."

Circulation wars went on, and in Britain they almost defeated themselves. Doorstep canvassing, free gifts, free insurance—even the *Daily Herald*, now half-owned by the trade unions, was at it. Both the *Herald* and the *Daily Express* reached circulations of two million, but advertisers were beginning to argue that their new readers, who had cost them about eight shillings a head in promotion, had very little spending power. One death, from low circulation, was that of the *Morning Post*, the Empire's senior daily, sixteen years older than *The Times*, in 1937: it had been accused of "fascism" because it was apt to publish anti-semitic stories, equating Jews with Communists, without bothering to check their authenticity, and was a rich field for quotations in the *New Statesman's* "This England" column.

When the news was too gloomy, there were the comics and cartoons to cheer one up. Comic books, like D. C. Thomson's *Dandy*, *Beano* and *Magic* for children; comic strips for the children inside grown-ups. Harold Gray's *Little Orphan Annie* had been going in America since 1924: now, in the Thirties, she and her guardian, Daddy Warbucks, told everyone that the power of big business would set the world to rights—"Leapin' Lizards! Who says business is bad?" Sometimes she advertised Ovaltine. Chester Gould's *Dick Tracy*, a sort of uninhibited J. Edgar Hoover, not only apprehended criminals—he shot them. Sometimes he advertised Quaker Oats. Alex Raymond's *Flash Gordon* operated in space, mainly on the planet Mongo. *Li'l Abner* (Andy Capp) used (and uses) a strange kind of hill-billy satire to mock American bigwigs (and other cartoonists). Milton Caniff's *Terry and the Pirates*, after Japan's attack on China in 1937, specialised in Japanese villains: the strip was reprinted without comment in Japan right up to Pearl Harbor. *Skippy*, *Popeye*, *Betty Boop*—some of these came to Britain, some didn't. One that did, never to leave us, was *Blondie*, by Chic Young, the saga of Mr. and Mrs. Dagwood Bumstead, Mr. Dithers, Dagwood's frenetic boss, the eternal dizziness of blondes, and the forever unsolved problem of who-wears-the-pants-around-here.

In 1932 the London *Daily Mirror* began printing a strip called 'Jane's Journal', the Diary of a Bright

*(above)* Crystal Palace after the fire, December 1st, 1936
*(left)* Before the fire

Young Thing. Jane, too, was a blonde, with a dachshund named Fritz who enjoyed the privilege of watching her dress and undress. Jane, with the approach of war, stripped more and more, until her nudity became the Eighth Army's principal morale-booster.

Even David Low, "greatest cartoonist since Daumier", occasionally used the comic strip for political comment: at a time when the British Government was terrified of upsetting the Dictators Low produced a strip called "Hit and Muss". His brush had an inimitable economy of line, as he created Colonel Blimp (diehard Britain), the Trades Union white horse that can't be budged, and a gallery of politicians that will tell posterity things about them that no camera could have captured. America's Herblock was often more savage, but never more deadly.

You could tell the history of the Thirties almost by cartoons alone; but if you look at the world news-stories of the decade, apart from war and fears of war, you get the strangest view of humankind's pre-occupations. We have seen the shock of the Lindbergh baby kidnap, the romanticized muddle of the

Abdication, the "black" comedy of "the night the Martians came". What else tore people's minds away from the endless crises? On December 1, 1936, the day of Bishop Blunt's remarks which started the Abdication crisis, the Crystal Palace, scene of brass-band contests, exhibitions, massed choirs singing the *Messiah*, cat shows and Thursday night firework displays, was burnt down, fun-fair and all, in a blaze whose glow in the night-sky was visible fifty miles away in Brighton. All the main thoroughfares of South London were choked with car-loads of sight-seers: they included the Prince of Wales and the Duke of Kent, and the morning after found Queen Mary, pointing at things with her brolly, walking through the reeking ruins, the ashes of the Victorian age. A year later, one Captain Potato Jones monopolized the headlines for two days by running Franco's blockade of Spain and bringing his cargo of potatoes to starving Bilbao.

A fire aboard the American liner *Morro Castle* suddenly attracted world attention in September 1934. It had made 173 successful voyages, and was on its way from Havana to New York, carrying 318 passengers and 231 crew. Captain Willmott, taken ill

(*above*) Chic Young's 'Blondie', February 17th, 1933

(*below*) 'Jane's Journal', *Daily Mirror*, February 1st, 1933

### JANE'S JOURNAL—Or the Diary of a Bright Young Thing - - - - - - - - - Rattled

at dinner, was dead, when fire was reported in the stokehold. The ship was off the New Jersey coast, nearly home. Why did it take eighteen minutes to order a radio call CQ for assistance? Panic, no orders, passengers jumping through portholes into a storm, 134 killed; one officer took a lifeboat all to himself, sixteen crew took another without bothering about the passengers, other lifeboats couldn't be lowered because the gear was rusty. Was the entire crew in the narcotics racket, of which Havana was the centre? America had hardly any merchant navy, and the little she had was now disgraced. At Asbury Park, New Jersey, people were charged twenty-five cents to look at the charred hulk; as bodies were washed up, reports said, looters cut off fingers to get rings, and an undertaker handed round business cards to distressed relatives. Had the captain been poisoned? Was it arson? Was it the Communists? The debate continues.

Blessedly free from politics was the Loch Ness Monster. Serpent? Hippopotamoid? (A footmark was found.) Twelve humps and a mane like a horse? An illusion of light? A faked photograph? A baby whale? (But if so, what could it live on?) Dead sheep were found, attacked by something nasty. Berlin and Tokyo papers, as well as credulous English-speaking countries, took it fairly seriously. Sir Edward Mountain organized a monster hunt, and twenty unemployed men were given jobs as "Watchers for the Monster". Tin Pan Alley wrote a song about it. A circus offered £30,000 for it. It was awfully good for the Scottish tourist trade.

To Eddie Bunyan, City Editor of the North Bay *Nugget*, Ontario, the story he sent on the Canadian Press wire on May 28, 1934, was good but not earth-shaking: "Mrs. Oliva Dionne, residing within a few miles of Callander, nine miles south of here, gave birth to five girls today. All are healthy, said Dr. A. R. Dafoe, Callander attending physician. Mrs. Dionne is 24 and had previously given birth to six children." For ever afterwards the babies would be known as Quints in Canada and Quins in Britain. To the contraceiving British, whose population was almost stationary, multiple births had a peculiar fascination: was it a Catholic-Latin phenomenon? No, indeed, for in the very next year, 1935, Mrs. Miles of St. Neots, Huntingdonshire, produced quadruplets who were immediately taken care of by the Cow and Gate baby-food company.

The reporters swarmed on the Callander, Ontario,

(*above*) 'The Man Who Caught the Loch Ness Monster', by H. M. Bateman, 1934

(*opposite above*) John Warde the moment his body struck the marquee of the Hotel Gotham
(*opposite below*) John Warde's body outside the Hotel

farmhouse. The first thing they had to learn was that Oliva was *Mr.* Dionne's christian name. Charlie Blake, of the *Chicago's American*, thoughtfully brought a hot-water incubator with him, for it was now known that the births were premature, that all five infants weighed only 11½ pounds between them, and that there was no electricity there. Keith Munro, of the *Toronto Daily Star*, brought twelve dozen diapers: he was to devote the next ten years of his life to the Dionnes, seven of them as manager and press officer. Eventually tubby Dr. Dafoe, whose pipe never seemed to leave his mouth even when examining patients, forbade reporters: in future they could only look through the window while the babies were being bathed in oil. Marie, the weakest of the babies, had drops of rum in her milk; they were all constipated, two, Marie and Emilie, so badly that Dafoe had to make a tiny enema out of a hypodermic syringe and a

rubber tube. "I don't see how they can live," he said cheerfully, "but they're living."

Mr. Dionne and the local priest, who needed money for his church, entered into negotiations with promoters of the Chicago World's Fair, but were attacked by the press for commercialism. Dr. Dafoe was attacked by the Toronto Medical Association for courting publicity. Poor man: in after years the Quins rejected him. Still, he hadn't done badly out of the syndicated "family doctor" articles he had written, with Keith Munro's help. The Quins were featured by Darryl Zanuck in three films: his biggest asset at the time was Shirley Temple, and one of the greatest crises of his life was when, aged six, she lost her first teeth; that was when he began to look around for a substitute.

Jumping out of high windows is a very American way of ending it all, and the threat to jump tends to be taken seriously. (People as icy as Orson Welles's mother, who, when her self-dramatizing son threatened to jump out of the London Ritz, said "Go right ahead, dear," are rare.) So that when, on Thursday July 26, 1938, John William Warde, twenty-six, a manic-depressive with a history of attempted self-destruction, stood on a seventeenth-floor ledge of the 202-feet high Gotham Hotel, New York, and did not seem to be either a window-cleaner or a stockbroker, a huge traffic jam was immediately caused at the intersection of 5th Avenue and 55th Street below, at a peak shopping time (11.40 a.m.). On that eighteen-inch ledge he stood, just looking down at the fire-ladders which were too short to reach him, the police cars, the useless ambulances, the newsreel camera-men with telephoto lenses shooting upwards from the sidewalk. Was he clowning? Patrolman Charles Glasco was supposed to be directing traffic, but obviously no one was going to move on until Warde either jumped or didn't. Ledge-walking was a fairly regular phenomenon, and Glasco knew of policemen who specialized in handling it. The official theory was: "If they don't jump the first hour, they never jump."

In hotel room 1714, behind Warde, were his friends Mr. and Mrs. Valentine and his sister Katherine, who were trying verbal persuasion to get him to come in: "Come in and have a drink—you have so much to live for. . . . We have a nice lunch here . . . then you and I will go to the ball game."

"I want to be left alone . . . I've got problems to think about," muttered Warde. Then Glasco took over: he had taken off his police uniform and was now dressed as a hotel bell boy. He talked softly to Warde, told him about his wife and children, how they'd all been on relief. If Warde jumped, it would be bad for the hotel, and he, Glasco, would be fired and he'd be on relief again.

Warde asked for a glass of water—placed on the ledge so he couldn't be grabbed; and another glass—surely he'd want to go to the lavatory soon, and then—? Every time he swayed, the crowd shrieked. "Look at those morons!" Warde said. They talked about baseball and other sports, for an hour and a half. By now sight-seers were streaming in from the suburbs; doctors arrived, clergymen arrived, all in vain. Warde had been on the ledge for eleven hours. They tried tempting him with a blonde girl, tried to hand him a doped drink; darkness was falling; Glasco was hoarse with talking. No good. "I wish you could convince me that life's worth living," Warde said seriously; and just as the last hope arrived, a school friend who might be able to take him back to his true condition of childhood—Warde fell. It takes quite a time for a body to fall 160 feet, and it looked like slow motion on the newsreels as John Warde opted out of the age of fear.

# STRANGERS

"How long have you been a homosexual—How many Aryan girls have you raped?" A few blows with an S.S. rifle butt. "You're bleeding. Nobody beat you, did they? You were drunk and fell downstairs, didn't you?" Berlin, November, 1938; or it could have been Vienna. A pogrom, a word one only just knew, is in progress. Jewish shops smashed, looted; deportations; Jews forced to scrub Vienna streets; is it true, or just propaganda, that they are made to do it with acid?

All this, carefully prepared, has happened because, two days ago, a seventeen-year-old Jewish boy, Herschel Grynsban, whose parents have disappeared in Poland, has shot and killed the Counsellor at the German embassy in Paris, vom Rath.

Since 1933 those Jews who could afford it had been quietly emigrating from Germany, Austria, Hungary, Czechoslovakia. Mostly artists; one met them at parties in London; but there were others who brought new industries with them; and yet others who had no means and had entered the country illegally. They didn't necessarily want to go to Palestine, then a "mandated territory" administered by Britain where, according to a muddled half-promise by Balfour, they were ultimately to have a "national home". In the Thirties, as a young Englishman of sensibility, you either went to fight in Spain or you tried to help refugees. I was a refugee-helper.

In Hampstead and Golders Green (London), and Didsbury (which had always been nicknamed Yidsbury) Manchester, Jewish communities awaited the influx, all was ready. In other districts refugees were less fortunate. For Orthodox Jews intermarriage with the British *goyim* was out of the question. For others, how different. Among those of us who were in our twenties at the time, marrying foreigners was fashionable, almost a form of protest. Our elders warned us that these might turn out to be only

"passport marriages," and indeed some of them were. German, Austrian and Czech girls, less inhibited, less narrowly educated than the young middle-class Englishmen they found, taking love lightly, had a deep effect on a whole generation of them. "Continental" restaurants and delicatessen stores opened up, and Lyons, with their sure touch for a new trend, quickly redecorated their Corner Houses with an underground *Bierkeller*, complete with Munich beers, and a Vienna Café, all in red plush and *kaiserlich* trimmings, for the Austrians to feel homesick in.

Britain, being mother of the free, saw herself as stretching out her gracious hands to the oppressed—well, the better-off oppressed, anyway—and expected gratitude. What she got was something much better than gratitude: criticism and information. *Bei uns* everything used to be much better than here. This silly cricket-game you play, those filthy puddings you eat, why are you always saying things are so expensive, if you want it, *buy* it, spend your money before someone takes it away from you, if you want *me*, don't ask me, just *take* me.

America, brought up on Miss Lazarus's noble lines at the base of the Statue of Liberty, saw refugees differently. They could be quota immigrants on Ellis Island terms, risking deportation, their worldly goods tied up in a handkerchief; or they could be distinguished intellectuals who would bring fresh cultural riches to the New World. America had her own internal refugees, the Okies fleeing the Dust Bowl ("Negroes and Okies upstairs," said a notice in a Bakersfield, California, cinema). The door may have been a little less than golden, and when you have escaped the "teeming shore" you do not wish to regard yourself as "wretched refuse"; "homeless", yes, "tempest-tossed", yes, and the "huddled masses" might have to stay huddled for a while. America was a vast country one third of whose population had immigrated recently, and only one quarter was of British stock: in insular British terms, they had more *room*, they were *used* to foreigners whose English would take at least a generation to lose its European accent, with the help of an established system—the American Night Preparatory School for Adults immortalized by Leonard Q. Ross in *The Education of Hyman Kaplan*.

The refugees found some Americans who were willing to blame them or their like for at least part of the Depression. There was Father Coughlin on the radio ranting about "Jewish bankers" and "Jewish atheists". The *Saturday Evening Post*, under George Horace Lorimer's editorship, was apt to talk about "aliens", "unassimilable blood strains" and "saving America for *real* Americans" (who were not defined). During the Depression nearly twice as many Americans, real or unreal, left America as entered it, and it was possible to regard Ellis Island as a deportation centre as much as an immigration centre. Colonel Daniel W. MacCormack, Commissioner of Immigration, had a plan for deporting "criminal aliens" (gangsters) and admitting "hardship cases". A lawyer named John B. Trevor started an "American Coalition" to coordinate the work of all organizations that wanted to "keep America American", and they included the American Legion, a women's club in Chicago, and a number of local societies with splendid names like the Old Glory Club of Flatbush Inc. The Spanish War Veterans (the 1898 war, of course) thought that the best way to end the Depression was to deport all foreigners.

From this it is no distance at all to the proposition that "Reds and Communists are all aliens", although a moment's reflection would have shown that Earl Browder, Communist candidate for the Presidency in 1936, voted Republican and came from corny old Kansas; his predecessor William Z. Foster came from Taunton, Mass.; and if you were looking for Jews and aliens among Marxist literary critics, you would find that most of them came from good middle-class homes in New England. John L. Lewis, who was not a Marxist at all and spoke of "haves" and "have-nots" rather than the class-struggle, was pure Welsh on both sides.

New arrivals on Ellis Island

Luise Rainer in *The Good Earth*

Woodrow Wilson had called America a "melting pot". Shouldn't it rather be a symphony orchestra, asked Louis Adamic? There were attempts to integrate new minorities while helping them to preserve their cultural heritage. In Cleveland, Ohio, a city sixty per cent of whose inhabitants were immigrants, the press, led by the *Plain-Dealer*, took the initiative, sponsored a Theatre of Nations, folk-dancing clubs and, under the leadership of a young Romanian, Theodore Anderica, started a two-way news service between European countries and their Cleveland communities. Did it produce "real Americans", or did it just make the Slovak Women's Society of Cleveland homesick?

To Britain, immediately after the *Anschluss* of Austria within Germany, came Sigmund Freud, given naturalization on arrival without the usual waiting period of five years and made a member of

Sigmund Freud

the Royal Society overnight. To Glyndebourne, Sussex, came Ebert and Busch and Bing, not as refugees but as artists with no particular country, willing to go on to America or (in Ebert's case) Turkey; yet Glyndebourne was very German—a Vienna paper called it "the English Nuremberg"—and what we used to know as *The Magic Flute* and *Il Seraglio* became *Die Zauberflöte* and *Die Entführung aus dem Serail*, and the lavatories were marked *Damen* and *Herren*. To Britain came Kurt Hahn from Salem, Germany, to start a school of less than thirty boys and no playing fields: he had been released from a German jail in 1933 by the intervention of Ramsay Macdonald, and a few weeks later he was assembling an all-British Board of Governors which included the Archbishop of York, the Headmaster of Eton, Professor G. M. Trevelyan and John Buchan, so that, in Basil Boothroyd's words, he might "impart Athenian theories to the Greek, if now increasingly English, Philip," who would one day become Consort to his cousin Elizabeth.

To America went, as boys, Henry Kissinger and André Previn. To America went Max Reinhardt, father of the Salzburg Festival, likewise Bruno Walter; to Hollywood Luise Rainer, star of *The Good Earth*; to London Elizabeth Bergner, of *Escape Me Never*; to London, and eventually to Brazil and suicide, went Stefan Zweig the Viennese author. To America went the greatest physicist since Newton, Albert Einstein; and so the Nazi horror was turned, indirectly, upon itself. For Hitler had driven his greatest scientists out of Europe. Some of them, led by Edward Teller, happened to be Hungarian, and they knew something about uranium, and that having seized Czechoslovakia Germany was in control of its principal European source. They told Einstein: Einstein told Roosevelt—about nuclear fission. How many people in the world, outside science fiction, had imagined an atomic bomb? Not Wells. Not Aldous Huxley. But a very unscientific mind, that of Harold Nicolson, had both imagined it and named it, in a satirical novel *Public Faces* (1932): it was based on an "unstable element", found only on an island in the Persian Gulf, which "could by the discharge of its electrons destroy New York". New York, you notice; not Berlin.

Mr. and Mrs. Albert Einstein

# CHAPTER
## XIX

# BEHOLD!

In Hampstead, north-west London, an Artists' Refugee Committee was at work, providing shelter for a stream of anti-Nazi painters, sculptors and architects from Europe. Some stayed; some went on to New York. Walter Gropius, Piet Mondrian, Kokoschka, Moholy-Nagy, Marcel Breuer, Mies van der Rohe, Erich Mendelsohn, Max Beckmann, John Heartfield, mingled in what their helper and defender Herbert Read, the art critic, called "the nest of gentle artists", and got to know the young Henry Moore and Barbara Hepworth, who with her second husband Ben Nicholson travelled round Europe making contact with other leading artists, from Picasso and Miró to Giacometti and Lipchitz. Art, in these turbulent times, became international, as if only artists could preserve something of the humankind that seemed about to die.

Yet there were, as there always are, "movements". In 1933 Paul Nash started "Unit One", which stood for "the expression of a truly contemporary spirit." Like the "20th Century Group" and "MARS" (Modern Architectural Research Association) it took all design, including architecture and furniture, for its province; for this was the era in which we first began to hear the term "industrial design" and names such as Raymond Loewy, too often in connection with the fad of "streamlining". Joan Miró designed fabrics, Graham Sutherland designed tea sets, Norman Bel Geddes designed radios, gas cookers, stage décor, everything. Designing for utility ("fitness for purpose", in the Bauhaus phrase) was respectable: for a young artist it helped him over the period of "creating mainly for other artists" in a world which is always lagging behind, for whom, said Paul Nash, "Everything new is ugly and everything old is beautiful."

Augustus John, Sickert ("I have always been a *literary* painter, thank goodness") and Stanley Spencer were now almost Old Guard. Edward Burra was turning his satirical eye to religion and death in Mexico and Spain, and to the political impotence of the Thirties in paintings like *The Prisoner of Fate* (1938). Edward Wadsworth, who despised English art as "provincial, ineffectual and determined at all costs to glorify prettiness", had come through all the -isms and was serenely executing his precise engineer's sea-pictures. He too was recruited for decoration: the large panels of the Smoke Room of the *Queen Mary* were his. He would no doubt have disliked the most popular picture in the 1934 Royal Academy, Gerald Brockhurst's *Jeunesse Dorée*, which was reproduced in every glossy magazine.

As if to reassert a British tradition, William Coldstream, Rodrigo Moynihan, Victor Pasmore and the "Euston Road" painters turned back to portraits, landscapes and still lifes. John Piper, starting as an abstractionist, was beginning to develop a romantic feeling for old buildings: he would find his Englishness later, through being commissioned to paint the war damage of London.

"Her favourite art had been photography, and her favourite painter Georgia O'Keeffe," we are told of progressive Norine (Vassar, 1933) in Mary McCarthy's *The Group*. "On the walls were ... framed Stieglitz photographs of New York City slum scenes." Miss O'Keeffe was now Mrs. Stieglitz: she painted phallic flowers, was associated by some critics with Imagism and Symbolism, by others with Kandinsky's influence. Many American painters of the time revolved round the "291 Gallery" of Alfred Stieglitz, a dealer as well as a photographer: Sherwood Anderson wrote that he was "father to so many puzzled, wistful children of the arts in the big, noisy, growing and groping America." John Marin, in his sixties, working often in watercolour, took sea and city for his material in paintings like *Region of Brooklyn Bridge Fantasy* (1932). Charles Demuth, only

(*above*) Reclining Figure, 1930, by Henry Moore
(*right*) Three Forms, 1935, by Barbara Hepworth
(*below*) white relief, 1935, by Ben Nicholson

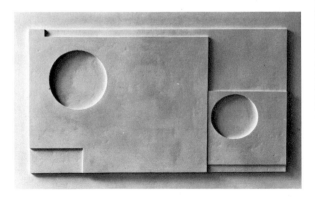

(*above left*) Calla lilies, *c*. 1930, by Georgia O'Keeffe
(*above right*) 'American Gothic', 1930, by Grant Wood
(*below*) 'Visibility Moderate', 1934, by Edward Wadsworth

'Women's Christian Temperance Union Parade', *c.* 1933, by Ben Shahn

fifty-two when he died in 1935, was something of a Cubist: "John Marin and I drew our inspiration from the same source, French modernism. He brought his up in buckets and spilled much along the way. I dipped mine out with a teaspoon, but I never spilled a drop." Cubist, too, was Marsden Hartley, "America's Cézanne", fond of heraldic devices and symmetry. Arthur Dove, once a successful magazine illustrator, now went native with a kind of abstract lyricism.

Influences, influences: where was native American art going? Perhaps this was not the time to ask, for under the Depression social realism and its propaganda value was the order of the day. (It is difficult to protest in abstract art). There was something to be learnt from the Mexicans Diego Rivera and José Orozco (their pictures were on Norine's wall, too!) who painted war and revolution. Protest received official encouragement in the Works Progress Administration's Federal Art Project, described as "a national experience in self-discovery." Hence the Soyer brothers, Isaac, Raphael and Moses, with their weary shop-girls and office workers, and pictures with titles such as *Employment Agency* (Isaac Soyer, 1937), Reginald Marsh's studies of slum life, especially in the Bowery, Edward Hopper's near-photographic street-scenes. Grant Wood got out of the city into Middle West landscapes, and John Steuart Curry painted prairie farms: "homespun regionalism", "American Gothic", it may have been, but it counteracted the claustrophobia of cities in the Depression. Ben Shahn was frankly radical-propagandist, protesting drably about social injustice; so was William Gropper, with his inflated politicians and hard-faced businessmen.

Back to the land, too, so long as it wasn't Dustbowl country, with Thomas Hart Benton, perhaps the most popular American artist of the century, "the Pa Kettle of American art", not ashamed of being compared with magazine covers, regretting his Cubist past, "my aesthetic drivellings and morbid self-concern," as he strove to be, and succeeded in being, above all intelligible to the people. Sculpture, following the "realistic" trend, was mainly representational, though Alexander Calder was experimenting with free-standing "stabiles", using steel and wire, and David Smith ("I do not recognize the limits where painting ends and sculpture begins") was working in welded metals.

The visual world of the Thirties was profoundly

'Drummer', 1937, by David Smith

affected by certain key exhibitions. American abstract artists formed themselves into a group in 1936, and Alfred H. Barr Jr. was not slow to organize a Cubism and Abstract Art exhibition at the Museum of Modern Art. (Mr. Barr, a great showman, had four years before borrowed "Whistler's Mother" from the Louvre, sent it on the road, brought it back to New York and charged a dollar a head for a one-picture exhibition of it, unveiled by President Roosevelt's mother—whose middle name, Delano, was the maiden surname of Mrs. Whistler. It sounds too good to be true, but the Post Office featured the picture in a special issue of stamps for Mother's Day.)

Surrealism was a long time coming to America: when at last it arrived, it had much to do with Peggy Guggenheim. It didn't really reach Britain until the

(below) 'The Whale', 1937, by Alexander Calder

great Surrealist Exhibition at Burlington House organized by Roland Penrose in 1936. Most visitors were baffled by what seemed to them a mixture of Communism, Freud, nonsense and unhealthy fantasy; among them J. B. Priestley, who found the pictures full of "violence and neurotic unreason. They are truly decadent." A girl with handcuffed wrists and face covered with flowers wandered through the rooms calling herself the Surrealist Phantom. Salvador Dali gave a lecture dressed in a diving suit. For one reason or another, the exhibition was seen by twenty thousand people. A bigger Surrealist Exhibition was held in New York, and a still bigger one in Paris in 1938.

Some of the Surrealists were represented in the "Twentieth Century German Art" Exhibition at the New Burlington in 1938. The idea was to give London a chance to see pictures, especially by German Expressionists, which had been condemned as "degenerate" by the Nazis in Germany, presumably to support the painters against persecution. But London, while reserving judgment on Paul Klee and one or two others, frankly disliked what seemed to be an aggressive brutality visible in the work of, for example, Beckmann, who by now was in America. A "Nordic Picasso"? Never. One critic told Fred Uhlman, who had helped to organize the exhibition: "I paid 2s. 6d. for seeing it: I would willingly pay 5s. for not having seen it." Another said: "I hate Nazis but I can't deny that Hitler was right to call this stuff degenerate." The *London Mercury* was content to say that the exhibition "had caused very general disappointment", adding that many of these pictures "effectively express the Nazi mentality", with the exception of Kokoschka, "the only true painter of them all."

There had been a Swedish Exhibition in 1930: its effect was to be seen chiefly on furniture design. A Soviet Graphic Art Exhibition in 1934 caused Herbert Read to say that there was nothing in it that could not have been produced in a bourgeois, capitalist country, and in its provinces at that. It was a Bloomsbury exhibition, and a Bloomsbury judgment. More promising was the Art in Industry Exhibition of 1935, which sought equally to unite the fine and applied arts and to boost British exports; but there was still too much of the idea that design is something you graft on to a product after you have made it.

There were two brave national gestures on the eve of world war. The Paris Exposition of 1937, shot through with political propaganda (such as the Spanish Loyalist Pavilion which featured paintings by anti-Franco artists such as Miró, and where Picasso's *Guernica* was first shown), left behind it the Palais de Chaillot, hailed by the *New Yorker's* Janet Flanner as "the handsomest modern building in Western Europe", but no such influence on *style moderne* as its 1925 predecessor had done. And in 1939, to celebrate the 150th anniversary of George Washington's inauguration as President, Grover Whalen presented the New York World's Fair. It did not, as the Chicago Century of Progress had done in 1933, make six per cent profit for its bondholders; but what the hell, the Depression was nearly over. Influence on design? Well, there were geometrical shapes called the Trylon and the Perisphere, and an abundance of fountains and waterfalls, which all turned up again in the Festival of Britain in London in 1951; but it was the glorious Coney Island vulgarity that got everybody.

Declared open in the "Court of Peace", it was meant to portray "The World of Tomorrow" in vast exhibits such as General Motors' Futurama, in which Norman Bel Geddes imagined the world of 1960. After queueing for an hour to get in, you sat in a chair on a moving belt which took you through the American landscape of 1960—1,500-feet high residential blocks, fourteen-lane highways on which you can drive at 100 m.p.h., subject always to a radio control tower. Everyone is a graduate, everyone gets two months' vacation a year. You remembered this, of course, as you remembered the Time Capsule, buried so as to inform the world of five thousand years hence what a can-opener and a silver dollar were for, who Roosevelt was and what he said; with messages from twentieth-century savants, and an alphabet to decode them with; microfilm photographs of industry; the Lord's Prayer in three hundred languages; a copy of *Gone With The Wind*; and a picture of Jesse Owens winning the hundred-metre sprint. And even if you forgot all these, you would remember Billy Rose's Aquafemmes and Oscar the Obscene Octopus, just as visitors to Chicago six years before never forgot Sally Rand's nude fan dance (seven times a day for $90 a week).

Until 1930 the world's tallest skyscraper was the Woolworth Building. But now the old Waldorf-

The Empire State Building featured on *The Queen* for April 5th, 1939

(*above*) Senate House, London University
(*below*) Battersea Power Station, London

Astoria had been knocked down and in its place the Empire State, with airship mooring atop, was nearly complete. So was the "frozen fountain" of the Chrysler Building. The Empire State was rumoured to make groaning noises in a high wind, and to sway as much as 4.7 inches in a 60 m.p.h. north-easter. But new skyscrapers were standing empty or only partly filled in Depression times, and the next few years were notable for less high, and often better designed, buildings. Radio City, which John D. Rockefeller Jr. hoped would include an opera house, was going up as part of Rockefeller Center, one of the few new developments that allowed for pedestrian movement instead of merely filling the air with concrete. Harold Petersen, spokesman of progressiveness in *The Group*, called it civic planning by enlightened capitalism, like the Modern Museum and even Macy's store.

No skyscrapers yet in London, although the new London University tower reached high; a graceful new power station at Battersea; plenty of Odeon cinemas and forbidding blocks of flats and some quite forwarding-thinking designs for schools, suggesting that children might even enjoy learning. The word "functional" was much used, and perhaps abused: it all depends whether you like curves and pillars and

Falling Water, Pennsylvania, designed by Frank Lloyd Wright

railings, as in the De La Warr Pavilion at Bexhill, or the brutal contempt for its neighbours of the new *Daily Express* building in Fleet Street.

Frank Lloyd Wright, believing no longer in skyscrapers, turned to lower-cost houses. His pupils said that he could design a house in ten minutes, leaving the rest to his draughtsmen. At Falling Water, Pennsylvania, in 1936 he built the famous week-end house for Edward J. Kaufmann Sr., temporarily abandoning his love of timber for cantilevered slabs of reinforced concrete. Was it functional or arrogant? Why such low ceilings, so that anyone over 5ft. 6in. bumped his head? And poor Mr. Kaufmann spent the rest of his life being kept awake by the roar of the waterfall. Three years later Wright designed his own house and school of architecture at Taliesin West, Arizona, returning to timber and using glass and canvas roofs to get strange internal light effects.

The term Art Déco was used to describe the effects on design of the 1925 Paris Exposition, but it was now somewhat confused with Modernism (less decoration, more function). Sometimes they were blended , as in the work of Oswald Milne (Claridge's Hotel), Oliver Hill and Basil Ionides (the new Savoy Theatre, all in gold and silver). Both now mingled with several other passing fashions, so that there was an "anything goes" atmosphere for a few years. Because young couples were hard up, and often had to start married life in an old house converted into flats, much furniture was extremely simple. Built-in cupboards, space-saving, walnut-and-chromium, tubular steel, Swedish-style woods, the omnipresent cocktail cabinet because

drinks were cheaper than dinner parties. Further up the social scale, Lady Mendl went baroque, Lady Colefax liked chintz and homeliness, Syrie Maugham was starkly white with perhaps a striped wallpaper. The Twenties had jeered, with Lytton Strachey, at the Victorians, but now, through the Sitwells and younger sponsors such as John Betjeman (whose *Ghastly Good Taste* appeared in 1934, followed by Osbert Lancaster's anti-functional *Progress at Pelvis Bay*, 1936), Victoriana were in again, and Rex Whistler was designing the décor for the New York Production of Laurence Housman's *Victoria Regina*.

Looking around at these times, a character in Nancy Mitford's *The Pursuit of Love* thinks that a future generation will be interested in them "for all the wrong reasons, and collect Lalique dressing-table sets and shagreen boxes and cocktail cabinets lined with looking-glass and find them very amusing." When George VI and Queen Elizabeth visited Paris in 1938, they were presented with Lalique glass. Mirrors (I cannot bring myself to use the Mitford refinement) were now used as complete walls for

Syrie Maugham (left) with Marion V. Dorn at an exhibition at White and Syrie Ltd, Mrs. Maugham's shop, 1932

bathrooms. Lalique panels, with lights shining through them, decorated the main dining room on the *Normandie*, which had murals by all leading French artists, tapestries and (an unhomely touch) metal walls and furniture in state rooms. There were not many takers for the furniture designs of Salvador Dali—a telephone like a lobster, tables like hands and a sofa in the shape of Mae West's lips, and there must have been many who would have settled for Lord Louis Mountbatten's tiny bedroom in Brook House—a replica of a ship's cabin with portholes looking out on a lighted backcloth of Monte Carlo harbour.

Streamlining for buildings, indeed for anything that doesn't move, is now realized to be ridiculous, since the object of it is to solve an aerodynamic problem. So that there was some excuse for streamlining cars, which now (to quote A. P. Herbert's 'Faster, Faster!' again) resembled "a bird or a bomb or a bloater," though in England they never went to the American extremes of "styling", with radiators like grinning mouth-organs and an outline, not justified by any aerodynamic theory, categorized as "the obese look".

The favourite art of Mary McCarthy's Norine, photography, was developing in a new direction, helped by the new miniature camera with high-speed film and powerful lenses, which could capture events of a split second's duration and was a natural weapon in the new pictorial journalism. It could also capture people who had had no opportunity to pose or rearrange their expressions, and this was known as "candid camera". *Life* and *Picture Post* were full of it, and the division between art- and news-photography became very narrow. Three names out of many leap to the memory: Henri Cartier-Bresson from France, Bill Brandt from Switzerland (stark contrasts of middle- and working-class life), and Brassai from Hungary. Brassai, who had been both painter and journalist, had taken superb photographs of Picasso. Henry Miller, who knew him in Paris, called him "the Eye of Paris", able to "read into the humblest object, person or incident things which no-one else would have noticed."

Advertising claims a place among the visual arts, and certainly added to the escapism of the age. We have seen, in the case of Mr. Blennerhassett, how to sell yo-yos by wit and laughter. Now layouts grew more generous, type-faces more skilfully chosen,

more sophisticated artists enrolled, in both posters and press advertisements. Fashion artists were still much in demand, and specialized in things like stockings and furs, and the most memorable advertisements of the time used drawings rather than photographs. . . . Fougasse of *Punch* drew gambolling Pyramid handkerchiefs; "What should 'A' do?—Light an Abdulla"; Gilroy's "My Goodness, My Guinness" series about animals at the Zoo ("just see what Toucan do!"); Lyons' teashop campaign—"Where's George?" "Gone to Lyonch"; and the famous Shell series, planned by Jack Beddington, based on the absurder names of English villages—"Mucking and Messing in Essex, but Shell on the Road", followed by the two-headed yokel watching a passing car—"That's Shell, That Was!"

Sponsorship still drew upon titles: the socialist Countess of Warwick in 1935 was persuaded to publicize a Paris hotel, and the Countess Howe was quoted as saying that "the heart of a good cocktail is Gordon's Gin." Horlick's pointed out the dangers of "night starvation" in cartoon strips by Harold Forster and others, and Eno's Fruit Salts offended prudes by dramatizing constipation in two characters, one sad, one joyful, Mr. Can't and Mr. Can. Tobacco advertisements, led by the pipe-smoking Vicar of "Three Nuns", in the absence of medical research, were free to say things like "Du Maurier . . . the filter tips will keep you fit!" and "You needn't cut down smoking if you smoke Cooltipt, 10 for 6d. . . . the cotton-wool filter absorbs half the nicotine and oils."

Design-consciousness and skilled typography were entering both advertising and the press, led by the *Daily Worker* and *Daily Express*, whose front page had been revolutionized by the use of Ultra Bodoni in the hands of St. John Cooper. The great influences on book design were Francis Meynell (Nonesuch Press), the Curwen Press, and the *London Mercury*, which had the typographer Bernard Newdigate writing regularly on book production.

The *Radio Times*, under Maurice Gorham's editorship, was good at discovering new illustrators: one of them was Edward Ardizzone, who never took kindly to the ways of advertising agencies but had by 1935 published the first of a famous series of books for children, *Little Tim and the Brave Sea Captain*, which would soon be known all over the world.

Epstein completed two major sculptures, *Genesis* (1931), considered by all the press and some critics as

"gross and obscene", and *Consummatum Est*. He had studied Negro art, anticipating a Thirties trend towards the primitive and the African. "The next great civilization", Bernard Shaw had said in his *Black Girl*, "will be a black one"; there were artists who believed this, agitating for African liberation and imitating native styles in their own work; and all this was emotionally stimulated by the seemingly endless trial of the Scottsboro' Negroes, accused by police of rape of two white prostitutes.

Next to *Genesis*, Britain's most acridly discussed sculpture was probably A. F. Hardiman's equestrian statue of Earl Haig, unveiled on Armistice Day 1937. Horsy people said the horse was wrong, Army people said the accoutrements were wrong, and Lady Haig said everything was wrong. Some old soldiers who remembered the mud of Passchendaele into which Haig had sent them twenty years before didn't see why there should be a statue at all.

The situation would have appealed to Pont, a young cartoonist named Graham Laidler who had just been discovered by *Punch*. He specialized in gentle, deadpan drawings of middle-class people in a series called "The British Character", little essays in ink line which all expressed the idea that the British, about to be sharply awakened, will do anything rather than think. He died too young.

It is well known that most artists have to be dead to rise in value and public appreciation. The prints most commonly seen on progressive middle class walls were likely to be French Impressionists, with perhaps a Dufy or a Nash to represent the living. Restful, peeling Montmartre walls, wonderfully conventional perspective—Maurice Utrillo was also fashionable; but, of course, he was dead too, wasn't he? There were rumours of forgeries, some painted by his mother. The Tate Gallery catalogue in 1937 said of him: "Utrillo became a confirmed dipsomaniac. . . . He died in 1934." But he didn't: the man who died was a Spanish art critic, Miguel Utrillo, and it was unfortunate that in Spanish "utrillo" means "little wineskin". A writ was issued against the Tate Gallery. The defendants did not appear to know that Utrillo had married a Sunday painter named Lucie Pauwels who had cured him of alcoholism. Utrillo asked only for a public apology, which made it plain to all the world "that Monsieur Utrillo is alive and active in his old profession."

Woodcut plate by John Farleigh from
*The Adventures of the Black Girl in her Search for God*,
1932, by Bernard Shaw

*(opposite)* 'Harlem', 1934, by Edward Burra

# SPIRIT AND MATTER

It was a bad time for bishops. They might be innocent, like His Grace of Bath and Wells, whose recipe for relaxation was to re-read the Barsetshire novels: "There's nothing I like better than to lie on my bed for an hour with my favourite Trollope," he told a meeting in his diocese. They might be jolly, like the Bishop of Chester, who played a barrel organ for charity. They might even be mildly heretical, like the scientifically-minded Bishop Barnes of Birmingham who doubted the Incarnation. They might be outspoken, like His Grace of Bradford, whose sermon on the private life of the Monarch brought about the first abdication in England for 537 years. But nobody liked bishops much.

In the middle of the Abdication crisis, the Archbishop of Canterbury launched a "Back to God" campaign. He meant, of course, "back to church", which was attended by about half as many people in 1935 as in 1901, if we go by the only statistic we have, that of Seebohm Rowntree's poll in York, which produced a figure of 17.7 per cent of the city's population. The Church, torn between the duty of turning the other cheek and the duty of resisting Godless aggression and persecution, fearing revolution above all, thought even Nazi Germany preferable to Soviet Russia. Life in Canterbury Cathedral must have been particularly difficult, for the Dean, the Very Rev. (and very Red) Hewlett Johnson, thought that Christianity had been more completely realized in Soviet Russia than anywhere else. Another Dean (retired), W. R. Inge, was practically a Fascist, seeking authority from the Right, often quoting Count Keyserling, the German philosopher of quasi-military "spiritual regeneration". Seeking authority took another form among intellectuals—conversion to Rome, especially in Oxford, where in 1931 Evelyn Waugh was received by Father d'Arcy, to be followed in 1939 by Frank Pakenham, the future Lord Longford. Roman Catholics were also powerful in the trade unions, especially among Irish members who were resolutely anti-Communist.

Only the Buchmanites seemed to know exactly where they were going. I had them on my staircase at Oxford. Did I realize that I had unsuspected qualities of leadership in me? Had I experienced Impurity at school? Well, never mind, it was all right as long as I Shared. Why not drop everything and come out to South Africa? Or at least come to a House Party in Switzerland—God, who was a millionaire, would provide the fare; if I had a Quiet Time and Got Guidance, He would show me the way. Last vac. they had made new converts among the top Nazis—old Heinrich (Himmler) wasn't a bad fellow really, he had to be tough with some people, he'd settle down soon. Our class had to take advantage of its privileges and work together; we couldn't tackle the workers yet. . . . They were so *nice*, these Groupers who would one day rename themselves Moral Rearmament; they had clear skins and shining eyes. Bunny Austin, the tennis player, was one of them; so was Peter Howard the rugger Blue, who wrote articles in the *Daily Express* about it, approved in principle by Lord Beaverbrook, who however found himself unattracted by it: "I was brought up in the Presbyterian faith. And that faith still seems to me the creed making the strongest appeal to logical minds."

More leadership came from pacifists and scientists than from the Church. In America Dr. Harry Emerson Fosdick, a liberal Baptist, was praised by *Vanity Fair* for having "reconciled science and religion in the minds of countless thousands", while undergraduates marched with strikers under Christian banners and formed societies with names like "Veterans of Future Wars". Pacifism became almost a religion in itself. In Britain, there were religious overtones to membership of the League of Nations Union, which wanted disarmament by international agreement, and in 1935 organized a Peace Ballot which brought in $11\frac{1}{2}$ million votes. Did people want economic sanctions against a country which started a war, and were they willing to take military measures if economic sanctions failed? It was clear that the answer was "yes" to both parts.

Canon Dick Sheppard in October 1934 had written to all national newspapers inviting all men who were willing to reject violence as a solution to any dispute to send him a post-card swearing to a declaration: "We renounce war and never again, directly or indirectly, will we support or sanction another." This, if the words "directly or indirectly" were taken literally, meant a position of absolute pacifism, refusing even to serve in an ambulance unit. Sheppard received a hundred thousand replies from men who were presumably willing to stand with him unarmed between two opposing armies (in Flanders—of course it would be in Flanders, and there would be trenches). This led to the formation of the Peace Pledge Union, which included many people who were not "religious" in the church-going sense, and ranged from artists like Eric Gill to old George Lansbury, recently retired Labour leader, from Aldous Huxley, already turning towards eastern philosophy, to the Methodist leader Donald Soper. Aldous Huxley even edited *An Encyclopedia of Pacifism* (1937), covering 55 subjects in 128 pages.

Middleton Murry, editing the *New Adelphi*, was preaching Christian Communism. Others took up Christian Science: "I had *such* a headache," says a woman in a Rodney Ackland comedy, "but I Christian Scienced it away." Others, seeking inner peace, practised Yoga, among them Gerald Heard, the journalist of science and its fringe studies. Professor C. E. M. Joad, soon to project his extraordinary, squeaky, guttural voice over the radio in a popular, sometimes hilarious question-and-answer programme, *The Brains Trust*, parrying almost every question with "It depends what you mean by . . .", followed (at least for a time) the teaching of Radhakrishnan: somehow the practical energy of the West must combine with the inactive inner peace of the East.

The acquisition by the British Museum of the Codex Sinaiticus in 1933 (from the Russian Government for £100,000) enjoyed a kind of mini-Tutankhamun publicity. This Greek manuscript of the Bible was nearly 1,600 years old. People queued to see it, wondering whether it was a forgery; forty-three pages of it had been brought to Paris nearly eighty years before by a scholar named Lobegott von Tischendorf, who had refused to reveal where he had found it, until at last he had persuaded the monks of Sinai to present it to the Tsar. What was so wonderful about it, apart from its age? It contributed nothing to the "back to God" campaign.

If science was to show the way, one had better find out about it. H. G. Wells, his son Gyp and Professor Julian Huxley edited an enormous tome, *The Science of Life*, Sir James Jeans wrote *The Stars in Their Courses*, Lancelot Hogben wrote *Mathematics for the Million*, and Victor Gollancz published *The Outline of Modern Knowledge*: we were given them as prizes at school. Even Oxford University built a grim new science block, opened in 1934 by the Princess Royal, who was given an honorary degree. There was a tendency to assume that a scientist knew everything about all sciences, and so it was not considered strange that a biologist, J. B. S. Haldane, should be consulted about the defence of civilians against air raids. Haldane, indeed (a Communist, as several scientists were), was credited with the weird forecast, based apparently on a *non sequitur*, that because both the birth rate and the death rate of Britain were going down, the country would in about thirty years' time have only about two-thirds its 1932 population, which would consist of more old people than young, so that the young would spend most of their time looking after the old.

New thought was concentrated on the structure of the atom and on cosmic rays. One day in 1932 Sir Ernest Rutherford and his assistants Cockcroft and Walton stared into an improvised apparatus made largely from biscuit tins and plasticine. Cockcroft reported: "We saw very bright scintillations, showing that the lithium nucleus was being split up into two helium nuclei by the impact of these hydrogen projectiles." Out of this "transmutation" (he still used the old alchemist's word) the team were getting "something like eighty times as much energy as we put in." The energy came from the "disappearance of matter", which proved Einstein's law that mass and energy were the same. The atom had at long last been "split".

The cyclotron, a particle accelerator for similar experiments, had been invented by Lawrence and

Livingstone at the University of California, Berkeley, in 1930. Developments now moved fast. Carl Anderson of California discovered the positron in cosmic rays, James Chadwick in Cambridge discovered the neutron, both in 1932; in the following year Irène Curie and Frédéric Joliot produced radioactive isotopes of nitrogen, phosphorus and aluminium; in 1937 Anderson and others found mesons in solar radiation; and in 1938, in Berlin, Otto Hahn and Fritz Strassmann bombarded uranium with neutrons, breaking it down into radioactive isotopes of barium with a release of energy. This was called nuclear fission; it remained for Enrico Fermi of the University of Chicago to establish the principle of chain-reaction, and the way was clear for Hiroshima. It was noted that the Jachymov district of Czechoslovakia, invaded by Germany in March 1939, was rich in uranium.

So this was the Atom in the Thirties: a different picture every five years. "Modern matter is ... a hump in space-time, a 'mush' of electricity, a wave of probability undulating into nothingness" (C. E. M. Joad—a philosopher). The atom is a miniature solar system. Is the electron out of date? No, but it isn't what we thought it was in the 1920's. We can't observe it without interfering with it, or precisely determine both its position and its velocity. Therefore some kind of free will is involved in the universe. So what is matter? It has become, Bertrand Russell said in a lighter moment, "a convenient formula for describing what happens where it isn't." Or, in the words of Joad, the great popular educator of the time, "Modern matter is like the grin on the face of the Cheshire cat.... If the atom is a system of waves, they are waves which are not waves in or of anything."

How old was the Universe? The stars could have been shining for about five million million years, give or take a few hundred million. But already a new theory of heat, which depended on the amount of hydrogen in stars, was beginning to suggest that the sun and the stars were only three thousand million years old. . . .

The idea of space-travel still belonged to science fiction: yet America had the Hayden Planetarium, and Britain had (in 1933) the British Interplanetary Society.

At Birkbeck College, London, Professor P. M. S. Blackett, nicknamed "the Archbishop of Science", was using his Cambridge researches into the atom to develop study of cosmic rays. In America in 1931 Karl Jansky, a Bell Telephone engineer, discovered radio waves emanating from the Milky Way, and seven years later Grote Reber, another Bell man, used a primitive dish-shaped radio telescope to record them. This was the beginning of radio-astronomy.

You could now telephone from London to Moscow and Sydney if you could afford it. More accessible to the general public was the British Post Office's inauguration of the "Dial TIM" Speaking Clock, in which the voice of Miss Jane Cain fastidiously articulated such words as: "At the third stroke it will be six forty-four ... precisely"; and in America, Western Union opened the world's first telephoned birthday greetings service, with Rudy Vallee's voice singing "Happy Birthday to you." The first lucky recipient was a Pekinese dog.

A word born in California in 1919 became extremely fashionable: Technocracy. In future the world would have to be run by engineers and scientists because politicians could not grasp the complexity of modern economics (hence Roosevelt's "Brains Trust"). Money was now meaningless as a measure of value: everyone should be paid in energy-certificates, denominated not in pounds or dollars but in ergs and joules. These ideas had been current in American thought for some years, but it took the Hoover Depression and a Mr. Howard Scott, author of Science versus Chaos, to make it all the rage for a few years until it was realized that the New Deal was aiming at the same targets but using different arrows. Was it Fascist or Communist or just Fabian? "We Technocrats," Scott said, "like to think of an optimist as a man who believes that everything is for the best in the best of all possible worlds, and of a pessimist as a man who agrees with him." A useful "Energy Survey of North America" was started at Columbia University in 1932, comparable, perhaps, to the 1970's study of Futurology. In Britain the spokesman of Technocracy was Professor Frederick Soddy, the man who had predicted isotopes, and the Daily Mail took it up for a short while. The "energy" principle was also found in Major Douglas's Social Credit, which tended to blame the banking system for economic ills: instead of charging interest they should distribute "national dividends" to everyone, so that the masses should have more purchasing power and thus contribute more to the nation's prosperity. Social

Credit people wore green shirts, as Communists wore red and Fascists black.

Technology, as distinct from technocracy, went ahead in its commercial way. Much of Southern Iowa had no electricity until the end of World War II, and on both sides of the Atlantic millions of country people had no running water. In Britain in 1939 only fourteen per cent of farms had electricity. In America, "One of the greatest contributions of the Works Progress Administration," said a teacher in a country district, "was the standardized outdoor toilet." Elmer, as readers of *The Specialist* will recognize, had at last got "a mighty pretty privy." Technology did not prevent 260 miners from dying in a colliery disaster at Gresford, Wales, or 99 submariners in H.M.S. *Thetis* from being suffocated in Liverpool Bay; but it saw that Germany was developing *ersatz* substitutes for raw materials, and research was finding new man-made fibres (still generally known as "plastics") such as polythene and nylon (1938), which Du Pont were weaving into the first experimental stockings, and which would soon be used for parachutes.

New metal alloys; Diesel locomotives competing with electrification on railways; ballpoint pens; neon signs (strip lighting); Mr. Schick invents the electric shaver; Frank Whittle, at Power Jets Ltd., experiments with gas turbines for jet propulsion, but it is the German Heinkel company that builds the first jet aircraft in 1939. But these are all male things: Mary McCarthy is on record as saying that the greatest technological advance of the twentieth century was the invention of Tampax, which may have taken the liberation of women to the point where it needed only the Pill to complete it.

In November 1934 Anaïs Nin visits New York from Paris, is shown round the city by her analyst Dr. Rank—"in the evening he took me to see the magic doors at Pennsylvania Station, which opened as one approached them, as if they could read our thoughts": the photo-electric cell had arrived. So had radio pulse-echo aircraft detection, one day to be known as radar, planned by Sir Robert Watson-Watt in 1935 after frightening intelligence reports about the growth of the German Air Force: five radar stations built around the coast of Britain, followed by a further eleven, the general public having no idea what they were. Watson-Watt, of the National Physical Laboratory, had been asked by the Director of Scientific Research to experiment with a death-ray: he replied that it was more important to *detect* enemy aircraft. That such a device as radar was possible had been suggested by complaints from Post Office engineers at Hatfield that aircraft were interfering with radio reception.

The best-known scientist in the English-speaking world was Sir Julian Huxley, who had a great gift for popularizing knowledge. He was for seven years Secretary of the London Zoo, which had opened in 1931 a country reserve for wild animals at Whipsnade, Bedfordshire, and did much to popularize it, nothing more so than the introduction of Britain's first giant panda soon after the Munich Conference.

Animal- and bird-watching, long among the more peaceful hobbies of the island race, were now joined by people-watching, not to say eavesdropping. It began, scientifically, in America, with market research and Dr. Gallup's Institute of Public Opinion, which got the answer right about whether Roosevelt or Landon would win the 1936 election when most of the press got it wrong. In Britain Tom Harrisson, anthropologist, and Charles Madge, poet, set up Mass Observation, which to many people seemed at first unscientific—scruffy young men sitting about in pubs listening to trivial bits of conversation; Communists, too, I shouldn't wonder. However, Julian Huxley and Professor Malinowski, leading authority on Melanesian tribes, said it was a good thing, so that was all right. One of the things Mass Observation claimed to have found out was that the working classes were not in the least perturbed by the Abdication: "If he doesn't want the bloody job, let him marry her and good luck to him." Of more permanent interest was a social survey of one small town, called *Middletown*, in the Middle West of America by R. S. and H. M. Lynd, which covered everything from politics to teenage morals.

Medicine still did more for cure than prevention of disease, and with one-third of the nation ill-housed and on the subsistence line, it could hardly do otherwise. But nutrition was making progress: health foods were not only the cranky preoccupation of Welwyn Garden City and Letchworth, but were now known to be based on vitamins as well as calories; and the bugbear of constipation, necessitating dreadful little "daily doses", was found to be due as much to wrong feeding as to insufficient exercise. There was a National Fitness Campaign, mocked by cartoonists.

Keeping fit was objectionably hearty, but losing weight was OK. It all depended on vitamins, which were good, and carbohydrates, which were bad. Messrs. King and Waugh having isolated vitamin C (ascorbic acid), fruit importers leapt on the bandwagon with publicity campaigns. In 1933 riboflavin was recognized as a vitamin and labelled $B_2$: it turned out that there were as many as six kinds of vitamin B, probably more. People were ill because they didn't have all these vitamins: therefore, in advertising tonics, you had to stress how many vitamins they contained, and if they didn't, you put them into the foul brew.

The leading propagandist for better nutrition was Sir John Boyd Orr, who realized that malnutrition was due partly to ignorance but mostly to sheer poverty. Ignorance, or head-burying, existed at top level in the Government. "Mr. Kingsley Wood, the Minister of Health, asked me to come and see him," Orr wrote in his autobiography. "He wanted to know why I was making such a fuss about poverty when, with old age pensions and unemployment insurance, there was no poverty in the country. . . . He knew nothing about the research on vitamins and protein requirements, and had never visited the slums to see things for himself." One of Orr's recommendations was school milk: by 1933 nearly a million children were taking advantage of it, and in 1934 the newly-established Milk Marketing Board took over responsibility for the scheme. The chief worry was that not all milk in Britain was yet safe: there was still a school of thought that believed that pasteurization "took the goodness out of" milk. In 1939 an M.P. said: "If God had meant milk to be pasteurized, He would have made cows which worked at boiling point."

We learnt that we all belonged to blood groups, and this was important because blood could now be transfused from one person to another: also paternity could now be disproved but not proved. There were new treatments for V.D., varicose veins, pneumonia, peritonitis, pernicious anaemia. The iron lung now existed. So did benzedrine, used by students to sustain themselves through examinations (the old method had been "caffeine mixture"). Barbiturates were known, but were used for short-term anaesthesia. W. R. Park, an American bacteriologist, discovered a vaccine for polio. Mumps, about which nobody had known much except that it hurt, was isolated. Few

new diseases were discovered, but one that made headlines was psittacosis, about which a researcher named Meyer in America and another named Bedson in Britain were teeming with a lot of news. Apparently you could catch it from parrots, and this led not only to a great many jokes but to a debate in the House of Lords, conducted mainly by Lord Marley, whose conclusion was that "where there are no parrots in a house, the people in that house appear to be safe."

The great leaps forward, which the general public were not to benefit from until the war, were sulpha drugs and antibiotics. Sulphonamides (beginning with sulphapyridine, May and Baker 693, popularly known as "M & B", unless you lived in Birmingham, where these initials meant Mitchells and Butlers' beer) were developed in 1938, synthesized by Ewins and Phillips. In Oxford Sir Howard Florey's team purified and concentrated penicillin: they would take it to America for mass production. The world before sulphonamides and antibiotics is not easy to remember, and their timing opens up endless "ifs". For example, they arrived too late to save two Hollywood lives: producer Irving Thalberg, carried off by pneumonia at thirty-seven, and platinum-blonde Jean Harlow at twenty-six. Miss Harlow's kidney disorder required an operation which was forbidden by her Christian Scientist mother, but it has been argued that new drugs might have made it unnecessary. When she died MGM took full-page advertisements showing a lion in evening dress weeping, and placed a list of her screen credits on her tomb at Forest Lawns. A $5,000 casket, and a special crypt costing $25,000 were both paid for by William Powell. The funeral service began with Jeanette MacDonald singing 'The Indian Love Call' and ended with Nelson Eddy singing 'Ah, Sweet Mystery of Life'.

The mystery of both life and death was being investigated by Harry Price, head of the National Laboratory for Psychical Research. Two days after the airship R.101 crashed, he was with a medium named Mrs. Garrett who brought him a "spirit message" from Lieutenant Irwin, its commander, who listed the defects which had caused the crash; these were confirmed by the inquiry afterwards. Among many hundreds of phenomena investigated by Price was Gef, the Talking Mongoose of Cashen's Gap in the Isle of Man, which suddenly, in November 1936, became the subject of a libel action brought by R. S. Lambert, editor of *The Listener*, the review of broadcasting published by the BBC, against Sir Cecil Levita. Sir Cecil and Mr. Lambert were both Governors of the British Film Institute, and the libel was coloured by Sir Cecil's contempt for psychical research, in which Lambert was keenly interested. The court found against Sir Cecil, who had to pay £7,500 damages.

The point was that ghosts were now being treated sceptically and, it seemed, scientifically by a man who, being also a member of the Magic Circle, could detect skilful illusion; so that when Borley Rectory, in Essex, where two rectors had been driven out by more manifestations than had ever before been recorded for a single place, was rented by Price for a year in 1937/8, the world watched with no mere sensational interest. Price recruited a team of observers from several countries, people of all classes, sceptics and believers, and asked them to spend nights and days in the house with notebooks. They recorded sixty different kinds of phenomenon, ranging from poltergeists to odours, face-slapping in bed to broken windows, besides the famous local legends of a nun and a coach and horses. In November 1938 the Rectory was bought by a Captain Gregson, who was to enjoy it, if that is the word, for only three months; for on February 27, 1939, it was burnt to the ground, thus fulfilling the prediction of a spirit calling himself Sunex Amures nearly a year before: he had appeared at a planchette séance held by a Mr. S. H. Glanville, and announced that he was going to set fire to it himself.

The search for miracles and predictions was always on. People went to clairvoyants, and admitted as much: since science didn't seem able to put the world right, perhaps fringe-science could. For more than ten years "Dr. Abram's Box", said to record a person's electrical vibrations and so to cure his ailment, had been recommended by patients to each other. After all, there were many things which science could not explain: did scientists think they were God? There was this mad New Yorker Charles Fort, who had spent a lifetime collecting 40,000 examples of inexplicable phenomena when he died in 1932. "Knowledge", he wrote in *The Book of the Damned*, "is ignorance surrounded by laughter." Why was there a shower of periwinkles near Worcester, England, on June 4, 1881? Why, every Good Friday since 1926, had a girl named Theresa Neumann, of Konnersreuth, Bavaria, shown bleeding wounds on hands, feet and eyes, the traditional stigmata of the Crucifixion? Thousands of pilgrims had witnessed them. . . .

At Lowell Observatory, Flagstaff, Arizona, on February 18, 1930, Clyde William Tombaugh had discovered a new planet, Pluto, beyond Neptune. Others had said it was there, but astronomers had expected something bigger. It turned out that Pluto's diameter was only about half that of the Earth. At once the world of astrology was thrown into confusion, for the existing system of horoscopy was based on Sun, Moon and seven planets, one of which, Uranus, was still called Herschel. Pluto was the god of the underworld, so it was easy to rationalize its significance as eruption, violent change, war, revolution, the coming disclosure of the true depths of evil in man.

Astrology had been languishing since the turn of the twentieth century, except for *Old Moore's Almanack*, though there were a number of well-known practitioners in America, among them Evangeline Adams, who was said to have advised J. Pierpont Morgan on the stock market. By the end of the Thirties almost every popular national newspaper in Britain would have a "Stars" feature, sometimes concocted in the office, sometimes seriously worked out by the "solar horoscope" system. There was also a monthly magazine, *Prediction*, which covered all occult matters, even phrenology. Newspaper astrology began in the *Sunday Express* on August 24, 1930, when R. H. Naylor became resident seer: he already had a private practice, charging £10 for a consultation. The first horoscope published was that of Princess Margaret, who had been born three days before, at 8.17 p.m. (British Summer Time). Among its predictions was that "events of tremendous importance to the Royal Family and the nation will come about near her seventh year." In 1937, by a chain of events which nobody could have foreseen (except perhaps by reference to the Prince of Wales's horoscope) Margaret's father was crowned George VI.

# YOUNG IN THE THIRTIES

"The hope and supposition of young people in the 1930s was that men and women would meet and mate in gallant, graceful, stylish love, as expressed in the dancing of Ginger Rogers and Fred Astaire." Thus Finis Farr, in his biography of John O'Hara. Dinner at eight, two gardenias by your plate, cocktails for two, two cigarettes in the dark—Kenneth Tynan, speaking to the Russian dancer, Valery Panov, who regarded Astaire-Rogers as high art, once called it the last flower of bourgeois decadence, but the song lyrics reflect the precise feeling of middle-class society about love. The Thirties, though not less "immoral" than the Twenties, were more romantic and didn't talk about it so earnestly and so much. The Twenties had wanted to be "sophisticated": the Thirties *were*. The Twenties had said wildly "Let's do it." The Thirties seemed to be saying "We've done it, and we're bored—it needs refining and decorating."

"Heavy necking," reported the Lynds from Middletown, was "a taken-for-granted part of a date." How far it went depended on how far the young feared or trusted a particular method of contraception—novels of the day generally left this bit out, and it was often safer to invent substitutes for the real thing until you were engaged. Many were the *demi-vièrges* of the Thirties. Contraceptives of various kinds, but mostly rubber sheaths (it was gentlemanly to carry one in your wallet), sold in vast quantities (Trojans in America, Durex in Britain). Asked to define his code of sexual morality, a well-brought up youth would probably have said something like: "One doesn't sleep with chaps' sisters"; adding, perhaps, a few years later—"or with the daughters of Brother Masons." In 1936 *Fortune* attempted a survey of American college life and came up with the answer: "The campus takes it more casually than it did ten years ago. . . . Sex is no longer news."

Yet undergraduates in both Britain and America continued to get engaged. At college it was the only way of acquiring the privilege of being alone together. It was likely to be either a very long or a broken engagement because nobody without considerable private means could afford to marry young. Both marriage- and birth-rate were falling. There was a surface attitude against marriage: "We can't bring children into an appalling world like this." Depression kept many marriages childless: "No more money in the bank," said the song; "No cute baby we can spank./What's to do about it? Let's put out the light and go to sleep."

The divorce-rate, strangely, was also falling—in America because it was too expensive, in Britain because it was too difficult: A. P. Herbert, lawyer, witty librettist of Cochran shows and resident *Punch* humorist, got himself taken seriously as Member of Parliament for Oxford University by producing a Divorce Bill whose watered-down final version allowed divorce for desertion or for insanity after three years. Otherwise one had to go through the dreary farce of staying in a Brighton hotel with a professional co-respondent to "prove" infidelity. Some of one's friends were the children of marriages, made in the Twenties, which had now broken up; those children also seemed to be making bad marriages, and some (especially in America) were going to psychiatrists; and so (particularly in Britain) there was a distrust of divorce because it seemed to bequeath its unhappiness to future generations.

"Gallant, graceful, stylish love" was hindered by the sheer messiness of contraception. Mary McCarthy explores this with dreadful thoroughness in *The Group*—*coitus interruptus*, fountain syringes, pessaries, Dutch caps, jelly, and where do you keep your douche-bag so your mother won't find it? There were two main jokes in Britain about contraception. One was a riddle, based on the Wall's Ice Cream tricycles: "What is the difference between Marie Stopes and the ice-cream man?"—"One says Stop Me and Buy One, the other says Buy Me and Stop One." The second used a current silly game, "She was only an Admiral's daughter, but yo-ho for the whirling spray." About two million sheaths a year were manufactured in Britain: the rest, it was whispered, were imported from Germany.

"This is a generation," said the *Fortune* survey, "that won't stick its neck out." What did *Fortune* mean? That the young preached revolution and pacifism while, in Depression days, nervously seeking security? Like every other younger generation in every age, it horrified its elders. It smoked even more than its elders had done in the Twenties (eight out of ten men, four out of ten women). Those elders who had pioneered the Charleston now threw up their hands to see the athletic ugliness of jiving and jitterbugging. The new generation, however, drank less: the repeal of Prohibition in 1933 made drinking less of a defiant duty, more of a pleasure. Many Americans were saddened to see the old speakeasies go. "A pretty girl in a speakeasy," sighed Alex Wilder the song writer, "was the most beautiful girl in the world." Happiness, thought James Thurber, was "sitting in a speakeasy on a rainy evening with someone else's wife." You could now go into an hotel and order a cocktail openly, thus losing the thrill of having it served in a dainty tea-cup. The new, legitimate liquor was taxed, expensive, and in short supply; moreover, eight States were still "dry"; and so "bath-tub gin" parties still went on for a few years. Bootleggers, hard hit by Repeal, organized cruises outside the twelve-mile limit of the customs authorities on which, it was said, you could be blind drunk all day. Illicit stills, producing spirits that were sometimes sold in Government liquor shops, went on risking prosecution and still made a great deal of money. Someone found a statistic that fifteen per cent of men and thirty per cent of women, even in "wet" States, wanted Prohibition back. Cocktail lounges, often in Art Déco style, were a compromise: as long as you sat at a table, it was better than standing at a bar with one foot on a brass-rail, spitting in the saw-dust: this was the dreaded saloon where women were excluded, and where men seemed so reprehensibly happy.

In Britain the young drank mainly beer and sherry: in May 1933 the Chancellor of the Exchequer

Drinking cocktails in a Mayfair restaurant, 1939

actually increased the gravity of beer while reducing the tax on it by a penny a pint. Beer was regarded as a clean, manly drink, and was advertised cooperatively by the Brewers Society with a special kind of rolling prose: "Good it is to relax at a wayside inn and pass the time of day with country folk. . . ." But in America something unnervingly odd was happening. Youth seemed bored with alcohol; tidal waves of Coca-Cola were breaking in from the South, and would soon be on tap in American warships. Milk! The young were drinking *milk*, plain or in shakes, at bars into which you walked straight off the street, to the delight both of Boyd Orr and the Milk Marketing Board. London's first milk bar was opened by an Australian on August 1, 1935, in—of all places—Fleet Street,

'The Soda Fountain', 1935, by William Glackens

the Hour Glass, the Montparnasse and Armando's, medium-sized supper clubs, and Giovanni's, which is still there. The Casino in the Park had Eddie Duchin at the piano, with sometimes Paul Whiteman at the Biltmore, and blonde Hildegarde from Milwaukee at the Plaza, wearing long gloves and throwing red roses to men sitting at ringside tables.

In London the bottle party was catching up on the night club and passing it. This was a way of getting round the drink laws by having the proprietor style himself "host", thus making it private entertainment in his own home. Many of them were frankly clip-joints where you ordered your drink in advance, not quite knowing what you were going to have to pay for it. A random selection from the year 1937, reported in *Night and Day* by Maurice Richardson, yields Frisco's and The Nest, "both shaped like railway carriages", the first "melancholico-nostalgic" and run by a West Indian, the second "tougher and noisier", multiracial and run by a night-club queen called Mrs. Cohen. The Shim-Sham was "rather like the Nest, only larger." There was the Nut-House, and Smokey Joe's, where about a third of the clientèle were homosexual. In Kingly Street was the high-class Four Hundred, where you had to wear evening dress or uniform, run by the dignified Mr. Rossi and featuring

serving 150 different soft drinks and ice-cream too. Another, in Regent Street, was managed by a Mr. Charles Forte, destined one day to become the Napoleon of the catering industry.

What happened to the old speakeasies in America? Some went "big and brassy", like the Stork Club under Sherman Billingsley, until 1933 general manager of a speakeasy syndicate, who gave little bottles of scent to girl customers, and always put John O'Hara at a table near the door so that he could be ejected if he got nasty-drunk. In sunny places like Hollywood the fashion for dim lighting began in bars such as the Cock 'n' Bull on Sunset Strip. Jack and Charlie's became the Twenty-One: Jack Kriendler and Charlie Burns were now also wine merchants, and had David Niven briefly as their salesman. At the Paradise Club you might have seen Sally Rand, the fan dancer. If you were a boy or girl about New York, you probably went to El Morocco (where you might have to slip the head-waiter up to $200 to get a good table: Café Society flocked there to be photographed by Jerome Zerbe for the glossies); the Rainbow Room at the top of Rockefeller Center;

Mr. Edmond Anderson and Miss Toni Johnson at the opening of El Morocco, October 2nd 1935

Jitterbugging in Harlem in the mid-1930s

the 1950's. Of several new dances, such as 'Flat Foot Floogee with the Floy Floy', which had to be sung as well, only the Big Apple really swept the dance halls on both sides of the Atlantic. You danced it in a circle, with somebody shouting out instructions to change the steps, which could be old ones like Charleston or Black Bottom, or new ones like truckin', Suzi-Q and shag. It was horrible.

At the Eton and Harrow Cricket match, where toppers and long dresses were obligatory, one pretended that it was cricket that mattered, not strawberries and cream and other chaps' sisters. That long chiffon could also be worn for luncheon at Hurlingham, the Chelsea Flower Show and garden parties, Royal or otherwise.

At teenage parties supervised by elders the Twenties game of Murders was still played: it allowed you to hide in a cupboard with a girl and mildly neck until the murderer was discovered. You were probably given wine-cup to drink (in Britain) or (in America) grape-fruit juice with a minute quantity of gin. We had yo-yos, which in skilled hands could be made to do things like "walking the dog". One received and passed on chain letters which were never heard of again, presumably bringing bad luck to everyone. People gave backgammon parties; but the great new

Tim Clayton's band: during the war it became the emotional centre of the entire Brigade of Guards. Of the older night clubs, the Embassy, still patronized by the Prince of Wales, went on imperturbably, and so did Ciro's and the Florida (of which a friend of mine, now a judge, claims to have been a member at the age of fourteen when he was at one of the more loosely-supervised public schools).

Around London, along the new by-pass roads, "roadhouses" were springing up. These were precursors of motels—hotel-pubs with restaurants, dance-floors, swimming pools, tennis courts, bars, music and (it was rumoured) pleasure-girls: the two best-known were the Ace of Spades (on Kingston By-pass) and the Spider's Web (on the North Circular). Dancing was for some an easy stage in establishing physical intimacy with the opposite sex. This was ballroom or roadhouse cheek-to-cheek dancing ("Heaven," sang Astaire, "I'm in heaven. . . . When we're out together dancing cheek to cheek"); but there was also jitterbugging, a subdivision of the "jive" cult, which had its own vocabulary, some of which ("hepcat" and "in the groove") survived into

Visitors to the first day of Royal Ascot, 1932

Marathon-dancing

think-game, replacing the Twenties' mah-jong, was Monopoly, destined to survive much longer. Invented by an unemployed heating engineer, Charles Darrow of Philadelphia, it seems to have entered Britain through the London Stock Exchange, who got it from Wall Street: the fantasy of owning all the real estate in the City was apparently consoling for business men in a slump. It was less enterprising than the crazes for flagpole-squatting and tree-sitting which broke out in America, or the man who attempted to push a peanut with his nose across the State of Kentucky (or it may have been Indiana, which is narrower). Grimmest of all was marathon-dancing, undertaken by people who needed the money, and watched by ghouls who hoped to see someone fall down dead.

At the stickier sort of deb party there were joke-gambits for opening a conversation: "Which end of the bath do you sit at?" and "Do you chew string?"

There were jokes about "Little Audrey, who laughed and laughed, because she knew . . . etc.", and a question-and-answer game which went: "Knock-knock!"—"Who's there?"—"Max."—"Max Who?"—"Max no difference!" About 1932 children went mad on keeping silkworms, which had to be fed on mulberry leaves and crawled all over the house. Cole Porter still went on calling things "divine" as in the Twenties, but hardly anyone else did. It seems that young men in New York wrote letters to girls ending with CYK (consider yourself kissed), girls indicated surprise by saying "who'd have thunk it?", good things were "spiffy", smart things "snazzy". "Spiffy" never reached Britain because we already had the Edwardian "spiffing". We were borrowing service slang in phrases such as "good show" and "wizard" and "I'm in a flat spin". "Super", revived in the 1950's, was considered schoolgirlish, "The party last night was absolutely *king!*" was localized to Oxford, and in particular to Somerville College. From about 1934 on, one heard the adverb "actually" (pronounced *ekshly*) being added to almost any statement: "You're the cat's pyjamas, you actually *are!*"—"How old are you?"—"I'm twenty-two, actually." As the War approached, German words entered youth-talk—"Here, I say, give us a bit more *lebensraum!*" and "Those sausage rolls look a bit *ersatz!*" So did Marxism—"that's a very *petit-bourgeois* tie you're wearing!" And of course the terrible Mitford sisters had for years been addressing their father as Feudal Remnant.

Youth couldn't be completely decadent, some parents thought: look at that young chap Peter Fleming, only twenty-five, seemed to *like* danger, wrote for *The Times* too; organized an expedition to look for Colonel Fawcett in Brazil, roughed it in China, nice gift of understatement ("I have never been in what is known as a tight corner"), handy shot with a Rigby-Mauser—well, no denying it, there's still something to be said for Eton, Oxford and the Grenadier Guards.

Slowly we progressed towards a five-day week: roads out of London and New York were now thick with cars on Friday evenings instead of Saturday afternoons as people went away for longer weekends. This was noted in Berlin and Rome, whose aggressions tended to happen while the democracies were at play. As a young sub-editor, I worked Saturday mornings but was allowed to come to the office in a tweed jacket. More golf, some of it miniature; more swimming. New ice-rinks with bands for dancing on skates. Robert Moses was covering New York with parkways and playgrounds. At Jones Beach, newly established on Long Island, more than a hundred thousand people could swim and sunbathe, hire beach chairs and umbrellas in a state of propinquity which only Gluyas Williams could capture in a drawing, leave their cars in eighty acres of parking space and rely on lifeguards, a doctor and eight nurses to come to the aid of 1,800 nearly-drowning swimmers a year.

Indoors, people played more bridge than ever before, read Ely Culbertson's books, followed, card by card, the international bridge contests organized at Selfridge's department store. In bars, "one-armed bandits" made their first appearance, with mechanized pin-tables, though in Britain traditional shove-ha'penny still went on, but now in the saloon as well as the public bar. Britain had football pools, the only legal form of gambling other than betting on horse races, which gave the unemployed the only hope they had. Illegal, but charitable and well-organized, was the Irish Sweepstake, in aid of Irish hospitals. You knew someone who knew someone who had a supply of ten-shilling tickets which came by post from Dublin, everyone trusted everyone else, and somehow it worked. You drew a horse picked out of a huge drum at the Plaza Cinema, Dublin, if you were lucky; the scheme was linked to the Grand National, the Derby, the Cesarewitch and the Manchester Handicap, and the Irish Government took a percentage of the profits. You had to listen to Irish Radio to hear the results. In 1931 an ice-cream seller named Emilio Scala, of Battersea, London, who had drawn Grakle, that year's Grand National winner, won £354,544. Everything went wrong for him. His mother died of shock when she heard the news. He lost his children, friends, hobbies. He bought a twenty-two room house which his family didn't want to live in. Interviewed a year later, he answered, as so many lottery winners have answered, "£50,000 is enough for anyone."

Coney Island, 1938

'Hiking', exhibited 1936, by James Walker Tucker

In Nevada a boom-town called Las Vegas was profiting from the illegality of gambling in California. Tourists, after 1935, were going to see the new Boulder Dam, only thirty-two miles away, and driving over to Las Vegas for a flutter, there to meet construction workers from Boulder City, who had brought their pay cheques there for the same purpose.

One of the inexpensive things the unemployed and slump-impoverished could do was walk in the country. It was now called, not rambling, but hiking, and there was a cheerful song about it. You could get cheap rail tickets from London to country places thirty miles away if you were an accredited Rambler. The Youth Hostels Association had nearly three hundred hostels, where breakfast cost a shilling and supper one-and-six. Hikers generally wore berets and shorts. The country was fashionable, and you were

one up if you had actually seen the smithy at Pyecombe, Sussex, that still made crooks for shepherds. Seeing that the countryside was being ruined by cars and speculative building, London County Council and other councils in the Home Counties began planning the Green Belt. The suburbanization of cities meant that millions of people had gardens for the first time, and in Britain a Mr. C. H. Middleton gave earthy radio talks on diseases of the potato and when to prune roses.

In 1936 Billy Butlin, noting the dismal holidays in seaside lodgings endured by so many people, adapted an idea he had seen in Canada and set up the first holiday camp in Britain. "It took me fifteen years to save enough to buy a 60-acre field at Skegness and build chalets for 1,500 people." He offered a week's trouble-free holiday for £4. Skegness Camp, Lincolnshire, was opened by Amy Johnson and Jim Mollison. Next year there was another Butlin Camp at Clacton, Essex, and trains called "Butlin Specials" brought happy campers there. You were expected to sing a lot at Butlins, who had their own song, 'Hi-ya, fellas, we are the Butlin Buddies!', and signalled lights-out by singing 'Goodnight Campers', to the tune of 'Goodnight, Sweetheart'. All this was given a boost by the Holidays with Pay Act of 1938.

The annual influx of American tourists to Britain tailed off during the Depression, and shipping companies looked elsewhere for business. They offered cruises, with all entertainments provided, to the Mediterranean, Scandinavia, North Africa and as far away as Bali. Shipboard romance, the subject of so many magazine stories, was the lure, and the stock joke was that cruises were "all bunk".

Two leisure trends were noted by Alfred A. Knopf, the New York publisher: keeping tropical fish, and nudism; books about both appeared in his Spring list for 1934. *Adventures in Nakedness*, by Julian Strange, was an account of the author's adventures in "twenty European nudist centres", with "74 exceptionally fine photographs". Its British counterpart was *Nudism in Modern Life*, by Dr. Maurice Parmelee (John Lane, 1933), which eliminated all excitement, claiming that by taking off their clothes "men and women will not so often be precipitated into sex relations through curiosity, mystery and sham modesty." Perhaps after all it was safer and healthier to join Mrs. Bagot Stack and her daughter Prunella's Women's League of Health and Beauty, wear sleeveless blouses and black shorts, and do exercises to music in Hyde Park and the Royal Albert Hall.

Butlin's Holiday Camp, Skegness, 1939

A holiday chalet at Butlin's

Health and Beauty demonstration at the Ministry of Health, 1938

Our study of Leisure in the Thirties has to recognize that there were still many people at the top who had nothing *but* leisure. We are back in the world of Chapter III, with Elsa Maxwell presiding over other people's parties (costing between $16,000 and $60,000 each), it might be for Brenda Frazier, various Russian Princes, Cobina Wright, Mimi Baker and her half-brother Alfred Vanderbilt, the sad, much-married Barbara Hutton, and sulky Doris Duke, the richest girl in the world; and the American hostesses to counterbalance Lady Cunard and Lady Londonderry were probably Mrs. Cornelius Vanderbilt, Mrs. John Hay Whitney and Mrs. E. T. Stotesbury. In their defence, it must be allowed that many of their parties raised money for charity. The only girl who saw through it all was Brenda Frazier, the American Margaret Whigham, who wrote a poem about herself called *Glamor Girl Serenade* which ended: "I sit at the Stork Club and talk to nonentities."

Over to the "Train Ball" at London's Covent Garden, organized by Barbara Cartland, where guests were asked to dress up as the Golden Arrow, the Southern Belle, the Blue Train, the *Engadine Express*, the Royal Highlander (this last was impersonated by Rosita Forbes the explorer, who wore "fifty

Leslie Hutchinson, a familiar entertainer at Quaglino's in the 1930s

yards of red velvet"); or to the Jewel Ball at the Park Lane Hotel where the ticket-holders wore between them £1,500,000 worth of jewellery—the kind of risk that makes underwriters overwrought. Lady Plunket sometimes danced for charity, partnered by Walter Crisham.

"In the Depression everyone closed down their houses; no-one had anywhere to live, so we all lived in restaurants—fell in love in restaurants—got divorced in restaurants," says Barbara Cartland, writing of London's café society. The Depression, it seems, made them hungry for different reasons from those of the unemployed on the dole.

Let us end with a quiet meal under soft lights in the West End of London. Shall it be Pinoli's in Wardour Street, where we can get a four-course dinner for 2s. 6d.? Or the Chantecler in Frith Street? Or Béguinot's in Old Compton Street, with the old, fat French waiter who was the model for so many George Belcher drawings in *Punch*, where there are five courses for 3s. 6d., more than I can eat, to the grief of the fat waiter, who pleads: "But Monsieur, it is so good"—and he puts first finger and thumb together by his lips and makes that Levantine kissing noise. No, tonight is a special occasion, and we economized by having an Express Dairy lunch (sausage and mash, college pudding, cup of tea, 11½d. including tip). We could go to the Ivy, where Abel will pretend to recognize us even if we aren't in show business. I don't think we can quite afford the Savoy. Papa Leoni at the Quo Vadis, perhaps; or his friendly rival on the other side of Dean Street, Mr. Weiss, at the Hungarian Csarda? Schmidt's, in Charlotte Street? Too many Nazis. The White Tower? Too many lesbians. No, I have it: we will dine at Quaglino's. It is September 1st, 1936. We begin with *oeufs pochés Piemontaise* at 2/6 (the price of the whole *table d'hôte* at the Chantecler or Bertorelli's). Then *darne de saumon grillé* (4/-), before getting down to the *carré d'agneau boulangère* (3/6) with some horribly expensive vegetables together costing 5/-, ending with chocolate *profiterolles* (2/-). A bottle of champagne of a "great" vintage sets us back £1, and the 1925 claret (Château Lafite, actually—sorry, *ekshly*) is 17/-. With *couvert* and tip, the whole meal will come to a cool £3 or so, and at the Chantecler we could have eaten two dozen more modest meals for the same money. Come to think of it, it costs less at the Savoy!

*(opposite)* Cover of *La Vie Parisienne*, January 31st, 1931

# La Vie Parisienne

Samedi 31 Janvier 1931
69e ANNÉE N° 5 — PRIX : 3 fr. 00

P. 2000/298.

La Grande Nouba!

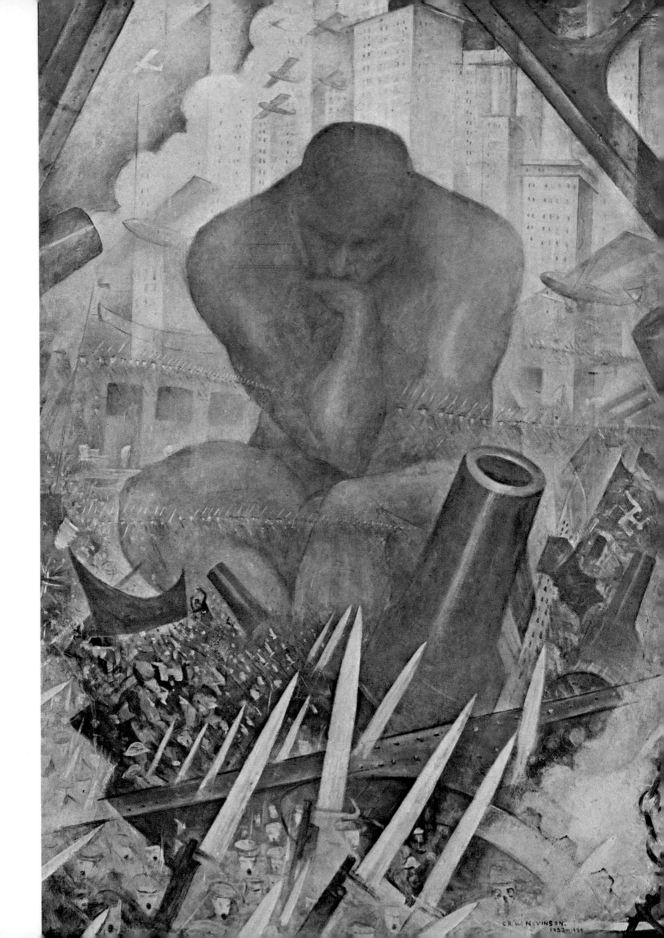

# CHAPTER
## XXII

# FEAR

July, 1935. I am just down from Oxford, staying in a house set upon the second highest point in mid-Sussex, from which you can see the whole of the South Downs, from the Long Man at Wilmington to Chanctonbury Ring in the west. Like all hot English summers it is filled with the threat of disaster. The girl who is with me is not afraid; yet the portable gramophone we have brought with us happens to be playing 'The Party's Over Now', sung by Noël Coward in his amateur warble that makes sad things sadder. I am worrying about the future: I know, although the results have not yet come through, that I have not done well enough in Schools, and if that is so, it is useless trying for the Administrative Civil Service, and that leaves teaching in a prep. school or—if only someone would publish my songs, if only. . . . I am also worrying about Abyssinia. For the first time in my life I know sickening fear: not the fear of waiting outside the headmaster's study, but the fear, the certainty, that everything that I have, this girl, that view, the small world I live in, is going to be taken away from me. I am naïve, and do not yet know evil. Abyssinia is a member of the League of Nations, in which we have all been brought up to believe. If Italy attacks Abyssinia at Wal Wal—ridiculous name, all mud and cattle-watering holes—then we must do something about it, otherwise the League is meaningless.

Anthony Eden has been to Rome to see if he can do a deal with Mussolini: a bit of British Somaliland desert to console Abyssinia for the loss of the fertile plains which Italy wants. Eden is the Tories' white hope: so handsome, so well-dressed, a multilinguist too. There is much talk of "collective security", "non-intervention" and "all sanctions short of war. . . ."

Oh, but Italy and France and Britain were partners in the "Stresa front" against breaches of the peace, so how could we contemplate war with Italy?

People like Lady Cunard thought Italy should have Abyssinia as a "protectorate", as Britain had Egypt. We would show goodwill by not helping Abyssinia with arms. The war began, the sanctions didn't work. Sir Samuel Hoare and Pierre Laval, of France, worked out a scheme rather like the Eden one; leaked to the Paris press, it was violently attacked. Hoare, who had gone skating in Switzerland after the negotiations, came back with a broken nose and had to resign. A bewildered Emperor took refuge in England.

The years 1933 to 1938 were a crescendo of fear for the democracies, reaching a climax of demoralization at Munich in 1938, after which all was drift and fatalism until the first bombs fell. (A German scholar, Joachim Fest, thinks that even Hitler's original motivation was fear, leading to a lust for power.) Peace conferences were used by the dictatorships to screen their plans for aggression (the old word *Realpolitik* was revived). Yet, looking out at the world of 1930, Britain and America had felt that their problems were domestic rather than foreign. War? Not really. Suspicious of each other as Atlantic naval powers, they came to some sort of understanding at the London Naval Conference, 1930, which achieved little else except perhaps the assassination of the Japanese Prime Minister Hamaguchi Osachi, who had lost face over the limitation of cruisers. The last Allied troops left Germany after the occupation; Rhineland, too, trusting the Germans not to re-militarize it. War debts and reparations were fizzling out.

In 1931 Japan, regaining face, invaded Manchuria; but that was far away: well, rather near Singapore and Hong Kong, actually, as the chiefs of the armed services were not slow to point out. Perhaps, since Manchuria was a lawless place, Japan had acted only to safeguard her own interests; no

doubt a compromise would be arranged, if it wasn't too late. . . . More comprehensible was the New Party, founded by Oswald Mosley, a rich Socialist who had offered the Government a blueprint for a planned economy which "went too far", and had eventually been expelled from the Labour Party. He founded a fascist-type paper called *Action*, which improbably had Harold Nicolson for its editor.

The New Party became the British Union of Fascists; some of its earlier members dropped out and were replaced by thugs and extreme reactionaries who included a number of Army and Navy officers and one or two peers; there were unspeakable scenes of violence in London's East End with voices chanting "Yids! Yids! We gotta get rid of the Yids!" What convinced everyone that it *could* happen here was a mass meeting of the B.U.F. at Olympia on June 7, 1934. While Mosley spoke about free speech, interrupters were sadistically beaten and kicked by strong-arm men, known to the B.U.F. as the "I" Squad and to the general public as Biff Boys. As it was a "private" meeting, the police (more than seven hundred of them waiting outside) could not enter. Fortunately there were M.P.s of all parties present who reported what they saw. The man of whom

*(left)* Oswald Mosley giving the Fascist salute at a rally in south-east London, 1937
*(below)* Fascist Meeting, July 29th, 1939

Hannen Swaffer of the *Daily Herald* once said that, since it would be un-British to organize opposition to him, all one needed to do was shout "Mickey Mouse!" derisively whenever his Blackshirts marched, the man to whose magnetic leadership the country might have turned in desperation, revealed himself as a fallen angel who seemed to be saying, with Milton's Satan, "Evil, be thou my Good!"

Maynard Keynes, whose *Economic Consequences of the Peace* has been blamed for Britain's bad conscience about Germany, and thus for the policy of appeasement, and who by the time his *General Theory* was published in 1936 was defeatist, had foreseen a general economic breakdown of the world. "America" (it is Harold Nicolson reporting him in 1931) "will revert to a Texas type of civilisation. France and Germany will go to war. Russia will starve. And we, though impoverished, may just survive." Yet food will be cheap, machines will produce boots at 1d a pair, and wireless-sets at 3d., and "everybody will be rich on £100 a year," in "the Organized State." Keynes, too, had been interested in the New Party.

Fear was the common denominator between disarmament, rearmament, pacifism and bellicosity. We now know that in these years there was no general, admiral or air-marshal in any European country who, whatever he said in public, and especially if he had been in the 1914–18 war, really believed that any country could really *win* a war.

Socialists believed that if you stockpile weapons, they will eventually be used; therefore it was safer to be without them, and we must go on having disarmament conferences even if they failed. The case for rearmament contained the unhappy truth that it would create employment, and indeed that is how the Depression was eventually solved. Did European nations really *want* disarmament conferences to succeed? Suppose, for example, the 1932 Disarmament Conference at Geneva had succeeded: would Hitler have become Chancellor of Germany? President Hoover wanted cuts all round in armies and navies and air forces: no tanks, no bombers, no big guns; ideally no battleships or military aeroplanes at all. The French wanted an international army controlled by the League of Nations. They wanted security: Germany wanted equality. Could the weight of tanks be limited? Could armament factories in all countries be subject to inspection? Probably the Hoover plan was the most practical, but the British Cabinet was divided

and the Service chiefs were against it. The coming to power of the Nazis the following year made it all academic, for Germany left both the Conference and the League. Yet the Conference went on and on until 1934.

Many Army officers still thought that cavalry was more effective than tanks, and it was generally held that bombers, not fighters, were what mattered in the air. Stanley Baldwin, then Deputy Prime Minister, saw fit, in the climate of disarmament, to frighten people by saying: "I think it is well for the man in the street to realize that there is no power on earth that can prevent him from being bombed. Whatever people may tell you, the bomber will always get through. The only defence is offence, which means that you have to kill more women and children more quickly than the enemy if you are to save yourselves."

Hitler at one point promised total disarmament if Germany were treated as an equal. Winston Churchill, deploring Britain's weakness, thanked God for the French army, which was still thought by many to be the finest army in the world with the best guns, the 75's. Beverley Nichols, in *Cry Havoc*, expressed the feelings of many young men by saying: "I would fight in an international army, in an international cause,

Winston Churchill

under some commander appointed by the League of Nations." That year (1933) Sir Norman Angell, author of *The Great Illusion* (1910), shared the Nobel Peace Prize with Foreign Secretary Arthur Henderson. Most American Correspondents in Europe thought the League was no good, the British press was burying its head in the sand, and that the whole Continent was certain to blow up soon.

People feared for their currencies, too. The World Economic Conference of 1933 began disintegrating after a month because, although it was supposed to be "stabilizing currency levels" and "removing trade barriers", America, whose new President Roosevelt had been in office for only three months, suddenly went off the Gold Standard and stabbed her own delegates in the back: Roosevelt's radio-ed "bombshell message" said that all this was not really in America's interests, implying that financiers everywhere were even bigger rogues than industrialists, and claiming that "old fetishes of so-called international bankers are being replaced by efforts to plan national currencies with the objective of giving to those currencies a continuing purchasing power." This was interpreted in Britain as cold-feet isolationism all over again.

Diplomatic relations between Russia and America were reopened after sixteen years. Unfortunate that this should coincide with the Metropolitan-Vickers Trial of British engineers in Moscow accused of sabotage, our first experience of a propaganda trial with "confessions". Admirers of the Soviet régime began to praise Stalin's ruthless realism: the time for disillusionment was not yet. The Reichstag burst into flames: who did it—cretin Van der Lubbe, Communist Dmitrov, bully-boy Goering? Another trial, equally propagandist, and the cretin's head was chopped off. Maybe Nazism and Bolshevism were really the same thing, some people thought, one Teutonic, the other Slav. We knew about camps in Siberia; now something like it was happening at Dachau near Munich, with its 18th century castle, once the summer seat of the Wittelsbach family of Bavarian princes. Before 1914 it had been a pretty little spa with an artists' colony. Now it was a cage full of trade unionists, Social Democrats, Communists, and leaders of a Catholic youth movement.

In April 1934 there were air exercises over London, and Baldwin made another of his "appallingly frank" speeches: "Since the days of the air, the old frontiers are gone. When you think of the defence of England, you no longer think of the chalk cliffs of Dover, you think of the Rhine." (At Oxford we were helping Maurice Dobbs, a Cambridge don, to organize an Anti-War Exhibition consisting chiefly of horrible photographs of soldiers so disfigured by gas warfare that they were considered unpublishable. To us, Baldwin's speech was sheer provocation.)

In June, Hitler's Night of the Long Knives; ninety people shot, including Captain Roehm, hero-into-villain, and General Schleicher, proving that the Dictator can murder army officers and the army will not resist. Germany now had conscription, and the League did not complain much: if it did something for Germany's inferiority complex, well and good. In July, tiny Engelbert Dollfüss, Chancellor of Austria, was murdered by German Nazis, showing that assassination in the Capone manner had become an instrument of state policy.

In November Winston Churchill, unheeded, still in the wilderness, waving his fists at the microphone because he was not used to an unseen audience, broadcast a talk on the causes of war: "We are no longer safe in our island home. . . . Only a few hours away by air there dwells a nation of nearly seventy millions of the most educated, industrious, scientific, disciplined people in the world, who are being taught from childhood to think of . . . death in battle as the noblest fate for man. . . . The only choice open is the old grim choice our forebears had to face, whether we shall submit or whether we shall prepare."

Next year he was returned to Parliament as M.P. for Woodford, Essex. 1935, year of the Peace Ballot, the Saar Plebiscite, Abyssinia. In Germany, Goering was making his "guns before butter" speech. Neville Chamberlain, Chancellor of the Exchequer, introduced his Budget with: "It has become urgently necessary to enter upon the largest defence programme ever undertaken by this country in peacetime." A fascist organization called the Croix de Feu appeared in France; another, called the Rexists, in Belgium. Statesmen of all parties in democratic countries made apologetic speeches: what fools we all are, but we have to rearm, because we are afraid.

Hitler, not bothering even to issue his troops with ammunition, reoccupied the Rhineland. Another treaty torn up. From Chautauqua, New York, a carefully angry Roosevelt speech (August, 1936) against "broken international agreements. . . . We

Neville Chamberlain speaking at a public dinner in 1938

shun political commitments which might entangle us in foreign wars." He also attacked industries which might profit from other countries' wars. Was he saying that not only would Britain have to go it alone in a future war, but that America wouldn't sell us supplies? Then the great peroration: "I have seen war . . . I have seen men coughing out their gassed lungs . . . *I hate war.*"

Japan had left the League of Nations: the Dictators began to talk of the "Rome-Berlin Axis", an "anti-Communist" pact, to the delight of cartoonists, and then of the "Rome-Berlin-Tokyo Axis", so it was quite clear how the alliances would fall. "War is to the man what maternity is to the woman," trumpeted Mussolini, who had just invented a Latin goose-step for his army called the *Passo Romano*. Italy left the League. In Britain the Air Raid Precautions Act made local authorities responsible for public safety in bombing, and a Defence Loans Act aimed at raising £400 million for rearmament. A boom was on, the R.A.F. was to be doubled; skilled men who had been

unemployed for five years suddenly had work again. Gas-mask drill, fire-drill, trial blackouts. (The standard joke about fire-drill was how to join the hose to the pump: "The male element," instructors unsmilingly intoned, "will be inserted into the female element.")

Even Lloyd George now favoured rearmament: why? not to overthrow Hitler, because that would mean a Communist Germany, which would be worse; besides, he had met Hitler—"He is a born leader of men. . . . The young idolise him, the old trust him. . . . The Germans have definitely made up their minds never to quarrel with us again." A new Anglo-German Association was holding dinners at the Savoy Hotel: present was Kim Philby, whose friend Guy Burgess had just told an unbelieving Goronwy Rees "I am a Comintern agent and have been ever since I came down from Cambridge."

In Russia more "confessions", farcical "trials" and executions of old-guard men like Kamenev, Zinoviev, Tukhachevsky. John Gunther reported back to America that in ten years' time, if she could stay out of the coming war, Russia would be the most powerful country in the world. Japan again attacked China: surely she would be too busy to enter a general war?

1938. In peaceful Cambridge, F. L. Lucas began a diary called *Journal Under the Terror*. In Italy Mussolini was now fashionably persecuting his Jews. In America Fritz Kuhn's German-American Bund were telling people that George Washington was the first Fascist, and establishing Nazi-type youth camps. In Britain the word "appeasement" began to be used to justify a policy which some called cowardice, but which had the useful effect of allowing rearmament to proceed uninterrupted. When Hitler annexed Austria in March, it was generally thought that nothing could be done "because we had only eleven anti-aircraft guns to defend London." Mrs. Ronald Greville, Society hostess, came back from Nuremberg full of praise for "my dear little Brownshirts". The Duchess of Roxburghe wondered whether things would improve "if we asked Goering over for the grouse-shooting." In Russia Stalin made a speech saying that war was now inevitable and that Russia must win the support of the working class everywhere. His Commissar for War, Voroshilov, said that Russia was prepared to use poison gas *and bacteria* (the first time this weapon had been mentioned in public) if her enemies used them.

'Toddlers' in gas masks, October 1937
*(right)* Digging trenches in Hyde Park, February 1939
*(below)* Air raid warning, September 3rd, 1939

The year of fear contained the Month of Fear. Never had international nerves been subjected to anything like what happened between September 12 and September 30, 1938. Hitler's "last territorial demand in Europe" was the Sudetenland, an area of Czechoslovakia containing three million Germans led by Konrad Henlein. Each of the following sentences represents a day's headlines, beginning with the thirteenth.

Czech Government imposes martial law on Sudetenland. Czech Government sends troops to Sudetenland. Chamberlain flies to Berchtesgaden to meet Hitler. Chamberlain flies home again. Czech Government extends martial law to whole of Czechoslovakia. Daladier and Bonnet fly from Paris to London. Britain and France accept Hitler's demands. Czechoslovakia rejects them as "partition". Czechoslovakia then agrees to let Germany have Sudetenland. Chamberlain meets Hitler in Bad Godesberg. Hitler threatens invasion: Benes orders mobilization: France calls up army. Chamberlain flies home: Mussolini will support Hitler: panic trench-digging in London parks: Royal Family fitted with gas-masks. New German demands: Czechs refuse: Roosevelt appeals to Hitler: Britain pledges support of France and Czechs. Chamberlain's final plea to Hitler, supported by Roosevelt: British fleet mobilized. Hitler calls Chamberlain, Daladier, and Mussolini to Munich. A day's talk. Agreement to let Germany occupy Sudetenland: Czechs collapse.

Chamberlain waving his piece of paper at the airport. Animal relief. "Neville has saved the world . . . the reincarnation of St. George . . . A saint" (Chips Channon). "Many of us burst into tears, and then laughed hilariously . . . the Mall and Whitehall . . . held millions of joy-mad people, swarming up the lamp-posts and railings, singing and crying with relief and belief that it was peace and never another war" (Diana Duff Cooper). Duff Cooper and Eden, called "war-mongers", resigned from the Government. The Coopers had made a suicide pact if invasion should come: so had Harold and Vita Nicolson.

No more fear for about three months. Now it was the Zoo's first Giant Panda that made the headlines. Where would Hitler strike next in Europe? or Mussolini in the Mediterranean? Czechoslovakia and Memel were occupied in March 1939, Albania on Good Friday: what did the new Pope think of that? No comment. A menacing voice, named by the

*Daily Express* Lord Haw-Haw, was broadcasting from Hamburg. Now Hitler wanted all the pre-1914 Germans colonies back: was it bluff? Britain hastily gave guarantees to Poland, Greece, Romania, the most vulnerable directions. Was anyone impressed, after Munich? At one point Roosevelt offered to mediate, and was cold-shouldered by Chamberlain.

In August the great shock, a Russo-German Pact, the beginning of disillusion for many Communists, political leader-writers in stunned confusion. Danzig, whose President, Herr Greiser, had cocked a snook at the League of Nations; and the Polish Corridor (where exactly *was* it?), something about a plebiscite. . . . Too late. Germany claims Poland has rejected demands she has never seen. German soldiers in Polish uniforms fake an attack on Gleiwitz Radio. The German army is in Poland. Thousands of children evacuated from London to the countryside with labels on them. Chamberlain's ultimatum: no reply. "The Prime Minister will broadcast at 11 o'clock." Interval for light music (unusual on a Sunday morning) ending with a selection from Sullivan. Silence. Then Chamberlain's voice, the best speech of his life: we are at war: "Everything that I have believed in during my public life has crashed in ruins. . . . It is evil things that we shall be fighting against, brute force, bad faith, injustice, oppression and persecution."

The false air-raid warning. Only two possible things to do: rush to the new Anderson shelter in the garden, or have a drink. Winston Churchill, like everyone else, expected an immediate, annihilating air-raid, probably with an unknown poison-gas against which Government gas-masks were useless: "My imagination drew pictures of ruin and carnage and vast explosions. . . ." Bombs, but not gas, would come; but not for eleven months. In Hollywood, Darryl Zanuck hears the news and decides that this is the end of the European market for pictures. James Agate, the *Sunday Times* drama critic, switches off his radio and goes to his local pub, finds a man outside looking at his watch: "They're open!" he says, at midday precisely. At the Dorchester Hotel, the band plays songs of World War I, 'Keep The Home Fires Burning', 'If You Were the Only Girl in the World'. Well, it *is* the same war really, isn't it?

Nothing much happens. The Bore War, the Sitzkrieg, a small war for Brave Little Finland. Radio comedians are at last allowed to make jokes about the

even if the years it contains seem to have a special character. Do we count from 0 to 9, or from 1 to 10? If 1 to 10, we should end this story at December 31, 1940; and that would enable us to say that the Thirties began with a whimper and ended with a bang. For America, perhaps, they began with Wall Street in 1929 and ended with Pearl Harbor. Or perhaps you could mark off the New Deal, or the Day the Banks Closed as turning points. For Britain the 1931 financial crisis mattered more than the repercussions of Wall Street.

At the time, the Thirties seemed the worst age America and Britain had ever known. Spengler was right, we were crumbling into a new, barbaric history-less Middle Ages. "It's a privilege," a friend of mine said ecstatically, "to be alive in such absolutely bloody times!" Was it, as glib Auden said, "a low, dishonest decade?" It gave the world, in the New Deal, the *idea* of social security, condemned by the Left as conservative, by the Right as radical dictatorship. It brought Government closer to the people: FDR's "me and you" style, talking to farmers at the White House, the Fireside Chats—showmanship? Never mind—it worked. There is no true parallel with the 1970's, because there was no runaway inflation, and trade unions were weak. In all the blunders of statecraft, the complacency, the muddle, you can, if you look, see basic ideas about mankind and government being worked out, at fearful cost. There is always something worse than the worst you can imagine—genocide, brain-washing, Hiroshima.

In the Thirties innocence was lost; or rather, the only innocence left was in our fantasies. We had the most efficient escape-mechanisms ever known. In *No Mean City* (1936), a novel of the Glasgow slums, boy and girl seek to escape poverty by becoming professional ballroom dancers. You dance your way out of misery. And so, the final symbol of The Thirties is not Patrolman Glasco pleading with John Warde on the seventeenth floor of the Gotham Hotel, not the little pigs singing (as if to Hitler) 'Who's Afraid of the Big Bad Wolf?', not the American schoolgirls on the night of the Martians crying "We're too young to die", not Chamberlain's bit of paper, not the yo-yo of hope and despair, but Fred Astaire and Ginger Rogers dancing on an Art Déco bandstand in the park singing 'Isn't It a Lovely Day to be Caught in the Rain?'

Dictators: Arthur Askey calls Hitler 'Old Nasty'. Foolish bragging songs: 'We're Gonna Hang Out The Washing on the Siegfried line', 'Run, Rabbit, Run', and, to the fury of the Scots, 'There'll Always Be An England'. Jokes about waterlogged, unused air raid shelters, sandbagging equestrian statues. Sir John Squire writes an 'Ode to a Barrage Balloon'.

Must The Thirties end like this? Come to think of it, what *were* The Thirties? A decade is an absurdity,

Art Gallery, Aberdeen 197 (*below*)
Art Gallery and Museum, Glasgow 171
Art Institute, Chicago 197 (*above right*)
Barber Institute of Fine Arts, Birmingham 70 (*above*)
BBC Copyright Photograph 132
City of Bradford Art Galleries and Museums 136, 172
Courtesy Bell, Book and Radmall, London 175 (*above*), 175
  (*below*), 176 (*below*), 178 (*below*).
Bettmann Archive Inc., New York 11, 16 (*centre*), 16 (*bottom*), 21
  (*above*), 71 (*below*), 74, 75 (*above*), 96, 127 (*above*), 128, 129
  (*above left*), 139 (*above*), 139 (*below left*), 165, 166 (*below*), 167
  (*below*), 192, 194, 203 (*above left*), 217 (*above left*)
Catspa Antiques, London 66
Columbia/Warner 38, 50 (*above*), 50 (*below*), 51
Connoisseur Films Ltd 58 (*above*)
Photo Ronald Grant Collection 135
Courtesy Guinness 205
Collection of Mr John Hadfield 223
Reproduced by courtesy of the Cecil Higgins Art Gallery,
  Bedford 206
Iconography Collection, Humanities Research Center, the
  University of Texas at Austin 83
Courtesy *Isis* 62, 63
Collection Mr. Alan Jenkins 181, 201
Collection Mrs. Alan Jenkins 34
The Raymond Mander and Joe Mitchenson Theatre Collection,
  London title page 8, 9, 12 (*above left*), 12 (*below*). 13 (*top*), 14,
  30 (*below right*), 33 (*below*), 41, 47 (*below left*), 55 (*below left*), 56
  (*below left*), 70 (*below*), 71 (*above*), 76, 77 (*centre left*), 78, 81
  (*top*), 81 (*centre*), 99 (*above*) 99 (*below*), 100, 110, 111 (*above
  right*), 111 (*below*), 113 (*below*), 114 (*above*), 114 (*centre left*), 114
  (*below*), 115, 116 (*above left*), 116 (*below right*), 117, 118, 119
  (*below*), 120 (*above*), 120 (*below left*), 121 (*above left*), 121 (*above
  right*), 122 (*above left*), 122 (*below right*), 123 (*above*), 123 (*below*),
  124, 126, 232 (*above*), 232 (*below*)
Photograph Angus McBean, Courtesy Harvard Theatre
  Collection 113 (*above*), 119 (*above*), 121 (*below*).
M.G.M. Release 30 (*above right*), 52, 53 (*above*), 193 (*above*)
Anthony Morris Associates 31 (*below*), 57
Museum of Art, Baltimore 199 (*left*)
Museum of Modern Art, New York 91 (c) S.P.A.D.E.M., 199
  (*right*)
Museum of the City of New York, New York 198
National Film Archive, London 13 (*below*), 26 (*below*), 27 (*above
  left*), 27 (*above right*), 27 (*below left*), 28, 29 (*above*), 29 (*below*),
  30 (*above left*), 30 (*above right*), 30 (*below left*), 31 (*below*), 32
  (*below left*), 38, 39, 43, 47 (*above*), 48 (*above*) 48 (*below*), 50
  (*above*), 50 (*below*), 51, 52, 53 (*above*), 53 (*below*), 54, 55 (*below
  right*), 56 (*above right*), 57, 58 (*above*), 58 (*below left*), 193 (*above*)
National Gallery of Canada, Ottawa 196 (*above*)
National Motor Museum, Beaulieu, Brockenhurst,

Hampshire 103 (*above*), 103 (*below left*), 103 (*below right*), 104
  (*above*), 104 (*below*), 105 (*top*), 105 (*centre*), 105 (*bottom*)
National Postal Museum, London 153
Collection Mrs. Norbury 64
George Orwell Archive, University College, London 89 (*above*),
  89 (*below left*)
Pennsylvania Academy of Fine Arts, Philadelphia 216 (*above
  left*)
Popperfoto, London 26 (*above*), 60, 186 (*below left*), 222
Private Collection 23
Private Collection (By courtesy of Parke-Bernet Galleries Inc.,
  New York) 197 (*above left*)
Radio Times Hulton Picture Library, London frontispiece, 10
  (*above left*), 10 (*below left*), 10 (*below right*), 17, 24, 31 (*above
  right*), 35 (*above right*), 35 (*below left*), 36 (*above*), 36 (*below*), 37
  (*above*), 37 (*below*), 40, 42, 44 (*above*), 44 (*below*), 45, 82, 86
  (*above*), 86 (*below*), 87, 90, 95, 96 (*above right*), 97, 98 (*above*),
  101 (*above right*), 101 (*below*), 106 (*above left*), 106 (*below*), 107
  (*above left*), 107 (*above right*), 107 (*below*), 137 (*above*), 137
  (*below*), 138, 141, 142 (*above*), 142 (*below*), 143 (*above*), 143
  (*below*), 144, 147, 148, 150 (*above left*), 150, 151, 152, 156, 160,
  161, 163, 182 (*below*), 186, 193 (*below left*), 202 (*above*), 202 (*below
  left*), 203 (*below right*), 215, 217 (*below right*), 221 (*above*), 221
  (*centre*), 221 (*below*), 226 (*above left*), 226 (*below*), 227, 229, 230
  (*above left*), 230 (*above right*), 230 (*below*)
The Rank Organisation Ltd 32 (*below left*), 39, 53 (*below*), 55
  (*below right*)
Collection Mr. and Mrs. A. G. Sanders 176 (*above*), 178 (*above*),
  179 (*above*), 179 (*below*), 207
Sport and General Press Agency, London 145 (*above left*), 145
  (*above right*), 145 (*below right*)
Syndication International, London 187 (*below*)
Tate Gallery, London 65, 84, 88 (on loan from the Edward
  James Foundation), 92, 154, 196 (*below left*), 196 (*below right*)
The Theatre Museum of the Victoria and Albert Museum,
  London 125
Tyne and Wear County Museums and Art Galleries Service
  (Laing Art gallery, Newcastle-upon-Tyne) 80, 220, 224
Copyright owners unknown 182 (*above*), 187 (*centre*), 188
United Artists 13 (*below*), 29 (*above*), 30 (*above right*), 48 (*above*),
  48 (*below*), 54
United Press International Photo, New York 15, 16 (*above*), 19,
  20, 21 (*below*), 22, 27 (*centre*), 33 (*above right*), 69, 72, 75
  (*below*), 77 (*below right*), 81 (*below*), 93 (*centre right*), 93 (*below*),
  96 (*top right*), 98 (*below*), 127 (*below*), 129 (*above right*), 129
  (*below*), 130, 140 (*above right*), 140 (*below left*), 157, 158, 162,
  166 (*above*), 167 (*above*), 189 (*above*), 189 (*below*), 216 (*below
  right*), 218, 219
Courtesy of Universal Pictures 56 (*above left*)
Victoria and Albert Museum, London 32 (*right*)
Photo Derrick Witty 65, 84, 154

Page numbers in *italic* type indicate illustrations.